THE COMPLETE IDIOT'S GUIDE TO

Private Investigating

Second Edition

Private Investigating

Second Edition

by Steven Kerry Brown

ALPHA

A member of Penguin Group (USA)

ALPHA BOOKS

Published by the Penguin Group

Penguin Group (USA) Inc., 375 Hudson Street, New York, New York 10014, USA

Penguin Group (Canada), 90 Eglinton Avenue East, Suite 700, Toronto, Ontario M4P 2Y3, Canada (a division of Pearson Penguin Canada Inc.)

Penguin Books Ltd., 80 Strand, London WC2R 0RL, England

Penguin Ireland, 25 St. Stephen's Green, Dublin 2, Ireland (a division of Penguin Books Ltd.)

Penguin Group (Australia), 250 Camberwell Road, Camberwell, Victoria 3124, Australia (a division of Pearson Australia Group Pty. Ltd.)

Penguin Books India Pvt. Ltd., 11 Community Centre, Panchsheel Park, New Delhi—110 017, India

Penguin Group (NZ), 67 Apollo Drive, Rosedale, North Shore, Auckland 1311, New Zealand (a division of Pearson New Zealand Ltd.)

Penguin Books (South Africa) (Pty.) Ltd., 24 Sturdee Avenue, Rosebank, Johannesburg 2196, South Africa

Penguin Books Ltd., Registered Offices: 80 Strand, London WC2R 0RL, England

International Standard Book Number: 978-1-59257-652-4
Library of Congress Catalog Card Number: 2006938606

13 12 11   9 8 7

Interpretation of the printing code: The rightmost number of the first series of numbers is the year of the book's printing; the rightmost number of the second series of numbers is the number of the book's printing. For example, a printing code of 07-1 shows that the first printing occurred in 2007.

Printed in the United States of America

Note: This publication contains the opinions and ideas of its author. It is intended to provide helpful and informative material on the subject matter covered. It is sold with the understanding that the author and publisher are not engaged in rendering professional services in the book. If the reader requires personal assistance or advice, a competent professional should be consulted.

The author and publisher specifically disclaim any responsibility for any liability, loss, or risk, personal or otherwise, which is incurred as a consequence, directly or indirectly, of the use and application of any of the contents of this book.

Most Alpha books are available at special quantity discounts for bulk purchases for sales promotions, premiums, fund-raising, or educational use. Special books, or book excerpts, can also be created to fit specific needs.

For details, write: Special Markets, Alpha Books, 375 Hudson Street, New York, NY 10014.

Publisher: *Marie Butler-Knight*
Editorial Director: *Mike Sanders*
Managing Editor: *Billy Fields*
Executive Editor: *Randy Ladenheim-Gil*
Development Editor: *Megan Douglass*
Senior Production Editor: *Janette Lynn*
Copy Editor: *Jennifer Connolly*

Cartoonist: *Shannon Wheeler*
Cover Designer: *Kurt Owens*
Book Designer: *Trina Wurst*
Indexer: *Heather McNeill*
Layout: *Brian Massey*
Proofreader: *Donna Martin, Mary Hunt*

Contents at a Glance

Contents

Introduction

Welcome to the second edition of *The Complete Idiot's Guide to Private Investigating*. In this edition you'll find a ton of new material and some of your old favorites. Even though I wrote this book, I still pull it off the shelf every couple of weeks to double check something. For the professional, it's a valuable guide on how to do your work. For the student in a PI course, this book may well be your text. It's used in public and private schools across the nation. If you're a do-it-yourselfer, you cannot find a better resource for the price than this book.

I spent a day a few weeks ago with a criminal defense attorney working a criminal rape case where his client was the defendant. This attorney asked me if I'd read Earl Stanley Gardner's *Perry Mason* books.

I'd never read any but had certainly seen lots of Perry Mason on television. This attorney said the criminal law in the Mason books and on TV was basically accurate, except even the best trial lawyer will never get the guilty person to confess on the stand. So did I know why Perry Mason won all of his cases? What was his secret to success?

"Paul Drake," he said. "Perry Mason's private investigator." A really good attorney will understand how an excellent investigator can help him win cases. If an attorney doesn't understand that principle, then he's not a good trial attorney for sure.

So what do private investigators really do to help attorneys win cases? To explain that, let me tell you about my college friend whose father was president of a company that made cans for vegetables and other food items. The company felt business was stagnating and wanted to expand. It hired a consultant to originate ideas on increasing business. The board of directors met with the consultant after he'd done his research. When they were all seated, he said to the board, "Okay, what kind of business do you think this company is in?"

"That's simple, we're in the can business," the board told him.

"No, you aren't," the consultant said. "Your company is not in the can business; it's in the packaging business."

With that concept in mind, the company went on to greatly expand into all areas of packaging.

Likewise, the private investigator is not in the surveillance business, or the electronic countermeasure business, or the background investigative business. Well, if it's not any of those businesses, what kind of business is it?

The private investigative agency is in the information business. The PI's client needs to know something. The PI gets the information. The unusual techniques that a PI uses are the fun part of the business and are what separates it from other information businesses, but nonetheless, information is what a PI sells.

How to get the information using tricks of the trade is what I'm teaching you in this book. Whether you're a professional PI or doing it for yourself, the techniques are the same and they're all here.

You have two choices: do it yourself, or hire it out. I've tried to put everything in this book, all the basics, to help you do it yourself or find the right PI for the job.

If you're already a professional PI, I think you'll find some "tricks and treats" in each chapter that'll help you build your business, be more professional, get more clients, and make more money.

Every chapter is woven through with real stories from the case files of my PI practice. The names and locations have been changed to protect my clients' identities, but the pertinent facts are there and the situations are real. The solutions are real, too. Real people, real facts, real life.

Now look through the table of contents to find your specific problem, and I'll show you how to get the information you need.

How This Book Is Organized

This book is presented in five sections:

Part 1, "Private Investigation, Business or Fun?" teaches a little history of the PI industry, how to find a professional PI, the legal requirements to obtaining your own PI license, the skills and equipment you'll need, and how to get hired by a PI agency.

Part 2, "Getting the Scoop," offers both the basic and advanced techniques for skip tracing. These chapters will teach you where to find information, how to dig up the dirt at the courthouse, where to access the public record databases, and how to log on to the secret "pay sites" that professional PIs use. And also, I give you a few tips on extracting information from the phone company.

Part 3, "On-the-Job Training," is a crash course in investigative techniques. You're taught how to do interrogations, how to run stationary and moving surveillances. Plus you'll get my favorite part, Tricks and Treats, basic and advanced.

Part 4, "In the Field," offers step-by-step instructional information on a variety of different types of cases. You're taught in detail how to sift through the evidence of marital infidelity, how to catch the runaway teenager, and how to set up surveillance in your home. You're also taught the basics of how to check phones for illegal wiretaps.

Part 5, "Advanced Techniques," teaches you how to perform in-depth background investigations and includes tips on setting up your own background-screening company. Also there's a new chapter for the professional PI on how to triple your hourly billing rate performing Diligent Adoption and Estate Searches. This section also shows how a professional should gather all the evidence, report it, and present it in court.

Things to Help You Out Along the Way

Some of the great features of *The Complete Idiot's Guides* are the boxes placed throughout the chapters with additional information. In these boxes I've tried to explain some extra facets of investigation. There are also tips and warnings about using investigative techniques mentioned in the chapter. At the end of each chapter, "The Least You Need to Know" sections are handy references.

Alternate Light Source

In crime scene processing, many items of evidence are not apparent to the human eye under daylight or incandescent lighting. Blood, semen, narcotics, fingerprints, and bite marks all become visible under Alternate Light Sources. Look here for new methods to see a subject that you might not have thought of otherwise.

The Division of Licensing

The state division of licensing governs and licenses private investigators in the various states. So when the Division of Licensing speaks, listen up. You'll hear warnings and they'll point out legal traps that can snare you.

def·i·ni·tion

PIs speak their own language. Here are definitions of the terms, slang, and jargon of the industry that you might not know.

Elementary, My Dear Watson

Watson is full of interesting facts, sidelights, and procedures relating to private investigation. He'll share all he knows with you.

Acknowledgments

I'd like to thank Melanie Brown for keeping me straight. And Frank Green and James N. Frey for their efforts at making me a better writer. Also my agent Jessica Faust at BookEnds literary agency. Next, thanks to Randy Ladenheim-Gil, my editor at Alpha/Penguin, and to Megan Douglass, my developmental editor at Alpha/Penguin for putting up with my quirks, and to Jennifer Connolly, the copy editor, for catching all of my mistakes, which of course I attribute to typing errors, but were actually mostly made out of ignorance.

Trademarks

All terms mentioned in this book that are known to be or are suspected of being trademarks or service marks have been appropriately capitalized. Alpha Books and Penguin Group (USA) Inc. cannot attest to the accuracy of this information. Use of a term in this book should not be regarded as affecting the validity of any trademark or service mark.

Part 1

Private Investigation, Business or Fun?

Looking to change your career and become a PI? Need some information? Trying to solve a crime? Looking for an old boyfriend or girlfriend? Do you want to check out a potential tenant or a new employee?

In this part, you learn the ins and outs of doing PI work. You'll discover how to find the information yourself, just like the pro PIs do it. If you want to become a professional PI, this section will hold your hand, show you the vision, and help you pursue that dream.

The Making of a PI

In This Chapter

- Taking lessons from the original PI
- No PI license necessary: related fields
- Solving crimes with intuitive leaps
- The making of a good private investigator
- Having your day in court
- Do not go to jail
- Avoiding the fight-and-flight scenario

The private investigative business is the search for truth. A PI must be impartial in this pursuit. The irony is that, many times, a private investigator's clients don't want the truth. They only want to win. It's the job of the PI to dig up the facts and help them win.

It's a dual-edged sword, because the investigator can't withhold facts that might injure his client's chances. The PI's client needs to know the "bad" stuff that is out there as well as the "good" stuff. There is nothing worse for an attorney than to go into court and be blindsided by some derogatory or hurtful piece of information that he didn't know about and should have. He needs to be aware of all the facts beforehand, and that's the private investigator's side of the business. Win, lose, or draw, we as PIs get the information, and then let the chips fall where they may.

If the other side of a lawsuit prevails, it doesn't mean the PI didn't do his job. If the PI has completed his work to the highest standards of his profession and to the best of his abilities, that is all anybody can ask.

In this book, you'll see we use the male and female pronouns, *he* and *she*, interchangeably. There are many, many good female private investigators. Also, every work-related story used as an example in this book is true and originates from the author's case files. The names and sometimes the locations or other facts that would identify the person have been changed, but the story's principle and its major accompanying facts are true.

Later in this book, you'll see why PI work is even more of a challenge than are police or FBI investigations. First, though, let's see how the private investigative business originated, and why we're called *"private eyes."*

The First U.S. Private Investigative Agency

Allan Pinkerton, who was born in Glasgow, Scotland, in 1819, is the father of private investigation in the United States. He began his career in law enforcement as a deputy sheriff for Kane County, Illinois, in 1846. Four years later, he opened his detective agency in Chicago.

Elementary, My Dear Watson
Some claim that Pinkerton's private detective agency with its "all-seeing eye" is the origin of the term *private eye* that we use today.

Pinkerton played a significant role in the history of nineteenth-century America. Documented facts are hard to come by, but it is alleged that Pinkerton became aware of a plot to assassinate President Lincoln while Lincoln was en route to his inauguration in Washington, D.C. Pinkerton overtook Lincoln's entourage and persuaded him to change his itinerary, thereby thwarting the attempted assassination.

In 1866, Pinkerton was hired by the railroads to put an end to the great train-robbery gangs, including the Jesse James gang (also called the James-Younger gang). Early on, Pinkerton's agency didn't fair so well with the James-Younger gang. At least two Pinkerton operatives were killed in their attempts to arrest the Younger brothers. John Younger was also killed in one of those gunfights, a fierce shootout in St. Clair County, Missouri, in March 1874.

By the early 1900s, the railroad robbery gangs were out of business, thanks primarily to Pinkerton's aggressive pursuit. It is alleged that a number of innocent men were sent to jail in this gang cleanup, and hence the term came into use whenever an innocent person was "railroaded" to prison.

Pinkerton's agency has now merged with Burns Security, a conglomerate listed on the Swiss stock exchange and a member of the Securitas family.

Pick a Niche

Entry into the PI field is usually gained through one of two doors: either by gaining on-the-job experience as an intern for an established private investigative agency, or else by leaving an investigative position with law enforcement or the military.

Chapter 2 will take you through the twists and turns of beginning a career in this exciting field. It's not an easy line of work to enter, but once in it, you'll find it's a lot more fun than a real job.

Notice that even Mr. Pinkerton did his turn as a deputy sheriff before starting his agency. Does this mean you must have previous law enforcement experience? No, there are lots of niches in the PI field that most people never think about and in which previous law enforcement training has no bearing on the work at all. Besides, in some states that require previous "investigative" experience, 25 years as a street cop will not meet the "investigative" requirement.

Public Record Retrieval

In Chapters 6 and 7, you'll learn what records are available at your local county and federal courthouses. An entire career can be made retrieving courthouse documents. There is a national association of document retrievers, and they earn very good incomes by circulating through the local courthouses, pulling documents requested by clients, and searching civil and criminal histories.

We'll go into detail and show you how, even pulling records for $4 or $5 a record, you can make several thousand dollars a month, with no overhead. This is especially good if you live in a very rural area because there you can earn twice that amount. In most states a private investigator's license won't be required, either.

In-House Investigators

If you're only interested in conducting background investigations for yourself, maybe on your new boyfriend, then you'll find tips throughout the book, but especially in Chapters 8 and 21. Learn how to do it yourself, no license needed. Or, if you are an in-house investigator for a business, most states allow you to do the background investigations and internal-theft investigations without a license. If you're good at investigations and have picked up a little experience along the way, then consider becoming an in-house investigator. It's a good way to get the additional experience you need to qualify for your PI license. Chapter 2 clues you in to which states require a PI license and which ones don't.

Serving Subpoenas for a Living

Subpoena service is another niche that does not require a PI license, although many of the skills needed by PIs are also needed to serve subpoenas. States have varying license requirements for subpoena services. You'll need to check with your own state to see what is required. Usually, the local sheriff's office or the courts regulate the authorized servers and can educate you as to what is required.

Can you make a good living serving subpoenas? Absolutely. The keys to making money by serving subpoenas are high volume and high efficiency. In many ways, the financial aspect of a subpoena service business is very similar to a PI agency. If you want a six-figure income you'll need to have your own subpoena service company or your own PI agency. Normally, the server gets paid by the number of "papers" he serves. Sometimes, it's as low as $5 per service. You might be serving large corporations and registered agents for corporations where the subpoenas are easy to serve, and you might have half a dozen to serve at one time. So even though the rate is low, it is possible to make money with sufficient volume.

The second key to making money in the subpoena business is to be more efficient than the local sheriff's office. They will charge $20–$30 for a service, and frequently, they're very slow. You might charge $50 or $60 for the service, but provide a much quicker turnaround time and better reporting to the client when the process has been served. It doesn't do anybody any good if the subpoena is served after the trial is over.

By utilizing today's wireless communications to serve subpoenas, you can increase the level of service you provide to your client. Anyone not on the front of the technology envelope is going to be left behind. Get comfortable with wireless technology and let the competition eat your dust. We'll talk more about this in Chapter 8.

Alternate Light Source

Wireless PDAs and wireless laptops are used by many process servers to e-mail their clients as soon as they complete a service. Others have set up websites where a client can enter a secure area via password and see what subpoenas have been served and when, and which are still outstanding. Prompt and efficient client service is the key to building a business in the investigative field or any of its related service areas.

Skip Tracing, Locates, and Deadbeat Parents

There are investigative agencies that only do skip tracing, perform locates, and hunt down deadbeat parents. These agencies would normally have a private investigator license if required by their state. I'm familiar with one agency that only works deadbeat parent cases. It has the client sign a contract where the agency collects a percentage of the child support or alimony payments after it finds the parent. It is quite successful in its locating efforts and in collecting the money owed to the custodial parents.

Other agencies specialize in finding the birth parents of adopted children. This is a difficult area, and has as many rewarding moments as it does disappointments.

Mary Beth, a 30-year-old woman who lived in Maryland, contacted us and asked us to find her birth mother. The mother who'd adopted her told her she was born in Florida. When her adoptive mother died, Mary Beth began sorting out her papers and came across some notes her mother had made that included the name of her birth mother. Of course, 30 years later her birth mother had probably been married at least once, and therefore, certainly had a different name. Mary Beth had no idea if she was still alive or living in another state.

By searching state marriage records and other databases, we ascertained that her birth mother actually now resided in a very posh, gated community in the Jacksonville, Florida, area. We discreetly made contact with the birth mother, who denied ever having a daughter and certainly ever giving her up for adoption.

We contacted her again, and this time she told us that she didn't want anything to do with her daughter, that the child had been from a different part of her life, and asked us to please leave her alone. Sad, but true.

On principle, we do not reunite adopted children with their birth parents unless both parties agree. Mary Beth's natural mother had her reasons, which obviously were important to her. We had to respect her desire for privacy, as much as we didn't want to. Maybe one day in the future she'll rethink the situation and change her mind.

Hiring the Hired Gun

If you're interested in pursuing the executive protection line of PI work, you'll first need to have some professional firearms training and defensive-tactics training. There is a lot more to being a professional bodyguard than standing 6 feet, 4 inches tall and carrying a big gun, although that's a good start. Unfortunately, in our lawsuit-happy society, if a confrontation is not handled properly, then you, as bodyguard, will probably end up being sued by both your client and the person who started the confrontation.

There is a fine line between providing personal protective services and security-guard services. Most states require different licenses for each service, a PI license for straight personal protection and a guard-company license for the other. In addition, most security-guard services also provide some investigative services and frequently carry both licenses.

Another lucrative aspect of PI work that falls between personal protection and the security business is concert security and nightclub security. Each is a specialization and constitutes its own little niche in the PI market.

Thinking Sideways and Out of the Box

Successful private investigators must learn to think outside the box. I prefer the term "thinking sideways," but both phrases encompass the meaning of the needed talent.

An attorney who represented the Jacksonville Shipyards came to my firm with a problem. The Shipyards had an employee, Richard, who was not working due to an alleged knee injury he'd received while overhauling a ship in the yard. Some Shipyards employees, co-workers of Richard, told the Shipyards manager that Richard was malingering. According to his co-workers, he was able to repair automobiles in his backyard, do household maintenance, and replace part of his roof. If he could do that, then he certainly could find useful work at the shipyard.

It irked the other employees that he seemed perfectly healthy and was collecting a full paycheck while not working, and they had to work for their paychecks.

The Shipyards hired a PI firm to put Richard under surveillance. Richard had an 8-foot privacy fence surrounding the side- and backyards of his home. The firm had set surveillance vans in Richard's neighborhood, but never could catch him performing strenuous tasks. They heard metal banging on metal in the backyard, but couldn't see through the privacy fence. They even hired a helicopter to fly over, but Richard stayed in the house that day.

The Shipyards, more frustrated than ever, instructed their attorney to find another PI firm that might have better luck. This attorney recommended us because he'd previously represented a client who had an insurance claim. We had his claimant under surveillance, caught him working, and nailed him as much as anybody has ever been nailed before. His client had worked very hard laying a concrete driveway and we videotaped him for six hours straight as he worked without a break. As soon as the attorney saw our surveillance tapes, he dropped the client. For that reason, the attorney knew we could produce excellent results.

The Shipyards didn't care what it cost. They wanted Richard either back to work or fired. They needed proof that he could work. I assigned the case to one of my senior investigators. After a couple of days, the investigator told me it was impossible. Richard never came out of the house, and if he was doing anything strenuous, it had to be in the backyard. He, too, heard noises coming from the back of the house, but couldn't testify as to what was taking place back there or who was doing it.

When presented with a problem like we had with Richard, a good investigator steps back and takes a look at the big problem. Creativity and innovation are required. You have to think outside the box. Think sideways. Think laterally or upside down if you have to. Attack the problem from a new angle. Let your mind roam and make that intuitive leap.

I went out to Richard's neighborhood and drove around the area up to several blocks away. Behind Richard's house was a two-story apartment complex. I approached the manager and indicated my desire to rent one of the apartments. She showed me one of the vacant second-floor units. From its back window, it had a clear view over Richard's privacy fence, and I could see the entire rear yard and one side of his house.

The problem? They had a one-year minimum lease. I didn't think the Shipyards would pay the rent on an empty apartment for an entire year. They might have. They wanted this situation resolved. But there had to be a better solution. I confided in the apartment manager the basics of my situation, but I didn't tell her who the subject was that we wanted to put under surveillance. I assured her there would be no wear and tear on the apartment. We were only going to use the apartment a few hours a day.

We struck a deal where I would pay the apartment manager $25 cash for each day that we entered the apartment. She agreed not to rent the apartment until she had no other vacancies, and then she'd give us first right of refusal on the unit.

You can guess the rest. We shot hours and hours of videotape of Richard repairing cars and working around the back of his house. We even had several days of tape of him roofing the back portion of his house. He carried stacks of shingles up a ladder and placed them around the roof so they were available when he needed them.

One of Richard's injuries was to his knee. We showed the videotape to one of his doctors, hoping she would say he was fit enough to go back to work. At one point, the doctor said that if we could show him climbing a ladder with a heavy burden, she would send him right back to work. Bingo. I pulled out the right tape and there he was on the television screen, carrying a 50-pound stack of shingles up the ladder.

From that day on, the Jacksonville Shipyards used us as their primary investigative resource until the day they closed. They spent hundreds of thousands of dollars a year with my firm. I did an analysis of all the cases we worked for them. The analysis showed we saved them several million dollars each year in wages that would have been lost and in frivolous medical bills they no longer had to pay.

> **The Division of Licensing** _____
>
> You have to know the rules of *right to privacy*. There's a difference between videotaping from an upstairs window of an adjacent building and climbing a tree to see into another person's bedroom. You can push right up to that line, but don't go over it or your evidence will not be allowed in court. Or worse, you'll be arrested as a Peeping Tom.

Cop Wannabes

How many antennae are on your car? That's a crazy question, huh? This may hurt some feelings, but read it carefully and see if it applies to you. If not, then skip over it. If it does apply to you, then before you jump into the PI life, consider the years you're likely to waste trying to be a success in the PI business, because you'll surely fail. The more antennae, the higher the likelihood of failing in the PI business.

Tow truck drivers, ham radio devotees, and police-beat reporters excluded, if you drive around town with a police scanner blasting on your dash, then you're not the right personality for being a successful private investigator. In addition to the police scanner, are you also driving a used police car? You know the ones—solid white, with black-wall tires and a spotlight just forward of the driver's-side window. Do you already have a concealed-weapons permit? Do you keep the gun in a little case under the front seat or hooked under the dash, where you can reach it easily? Or do you prefer the shoulder holster, like James Bond and the TV cops?

If you find yourself nodding along with any of those, then I'd suggest you try out at the police academy first. Cop wannabes don't make good private investigators. They're more in love with the idea of "being like a PI" than actually doing the work that a PI has to do.

Robert Bailey, a former PI and now author of PI novels, begins his novel *Private Heat* with PI Art Hardin this way:

> Everybody wants to be a detective, carry a big shiny gun, and be all the rage at cocktail parties. Nobody wants to get up at o-dark-thirty and drive ninety-three miles to see if Joe Insurance Claimant—who has been collecting a total disability check for the last three years—is also working for wages on the sly, but that's the kind of work that usually pays the bills, not the flashy stuff you see on the tube.
>
> —From *Private Heat*, by Robert Bailey. Used by permission of the publisher, M. Evans and Company, New York.

If you're looking for a career that is interesting and exciting, private investigation fits that bill. I can't think of anything more interesting than being a private investigator. But it also has hour after hour of sheer tedium. The job requires a mountain of paperwork and documentation. If small details are your thing, then the private investigative field may be for you. If you're not up for the paperwork, dotting the *i* and crossing every *t*, then you'd better think again.

Admissibility—The Key to Good Investigations

There are times when it would be better to hire a professional PI. Make no mistake about this. For instance, if you reside in a state where adultery will be considered in your divorce, keep in mind what's at stake. Less alimony will be awarded to a spouse who has been proven unfaithful than to one who has not been so proven.

A husband decides to save on the expense of a PI and follows his wife to her rendezvous with the lover. Later, he testifies about the tryst he observed. To his horror, his wife denies that she has a lover, and it boils down to his word against hers.

Unfortunately, people lie in court. Judges know that. Many husbands and wives have testified that they've seen, with their own eyes, their spouses being unfaithful to them. There's nothing the judge can do without corroborating evidence or testimony. In this case, the husband should have hired a PI. Then he would have had the videotapes, photographs, and the testimony from a licensed private investigator as to the spouse's actions. In those states where it matters, it matters big time.

If you've decided to do the work of a PI yourself, make absolutely sure that it is done in such a manner as to be admissible in court if it's even remotely possible that courtroom testimony will be needed. If you are going to be a party to the case, such as in your own divorce matter, then your testimony would be considered prejudiced. In fact, it might not even be allowed, or if it is, it would certainly be severely discounted. If the matter will never go to court and you just need the information for your own satisfaction, then read Chapter 13 on moving surveillance and Chapter 16 on clues to infidelity.

Keeping It Legal

When conducting your own investigation, be careful about violating any local, state, or federal statutes. If you're about to take an action and are not sure if it's legal, find out before you leap into it. If you don't have the time to research the applicable statute, then just don't do it.

The places where you could get into legal trouble are spelled out in the applicable chapters, but obviously, this book can't cover every potential situation. It's up to you to use good judgment and be conservative in the tactics you employ.

It's good to know the law in your particular state. Trespassing, for instance, is usually against the law. However, in most states, before you can be prosecuted for trespassing, you must be warned against it the first time. Once you've been warned, you've used up your "gimme" and the next time you're caught, you'll be arrested and charged. That's not true in all states, though, so learn your state law. Most libraries have a set of the state statutes. You can look up the applicable laws there.

I was investigating a double homicide committed by a police officer at his residence. He had been living with a woman who was married to another man at the time. The woman's husband and a co-worker of the husband came over to the officer's home. An argument ensued and the two visitors ended up dead, shot by the officer, who claimed he was in fear of his life. Both of the dead men were unarmed.

My firm was hired by the relatives of the deceased men. Many of the facts of the homicide were unclear because the only living witness to the events was the officer. A question arose as to how many shots had actually been fired by the policeman. Both dead men had been shot multiple times.

In conducting this investigation, I took a metal detector out to the officer's home to search for bullet casings. The officer's weapon, a semiautomatic pistol, ejects the shells as they are fired. We thought perhaps more shots had been fired than he'd admitted to. I had two of my other investigators with me, both also former FBI agents.

The officer in question apparently had been called by a neighbor, telling him we were on his lawn with a metal detector. He dispatched some other officers and they stopped us before we'd had much of a chance to search. They gave us written warnings of trespass on that property. If we'd gone back later and stepped onto his grass, I and my investigators who'd been with me could then have been arrested.

The Division of Licensing

In conducting surveillances, it might be tempting to sneak onto a person's yard and peek through an open window. Such an action crosses the line from simple trespassing to Peeping Tom. Peeping through the window is probably a violation of the law. Most states have a Peeping Tom law. If you get caught, you might spend the night in the pokey. Sneaking onto another person's property might also get you shot. Most courts are pretty lenient toward the homeowner who shoots someone breaking into his home. In the United States, a man's home is still his castle, and he's allowed to defend it, so be careful.

The police department decided we must have been on to something, though, because they searched the yard for additional bullet casings after warning us off, and found what we were looking for. So our initial suspicions were right. There were more shots fired than originally testified to.

Avoid the Confrontation

Your friend Sally is convinced her husband is cheating on her, and she enlists your aid to follow him one evening. Think carefully before accepting this invitation to danger. If he is unfaithful and the two of you catch him going into a motel, what are you going to do?

Sally's emotions will be redlined to the maximum. Her husband, headed into the motel room, will be very goal-oriented, and if he's interrupted by his wife, he may turn his frustration at being deprived of his goal into anger toward Sally. We learned this lesson the hard way.

Carolyn asked us to follow her husband to what she believed would be a daytime rendezvous. With domestic cases, we usually maintain fairly close contact with the client. Frequently, they can advise us if the behavior we are watching is normal for the spouse or not. This case was no exception.

When we saw Carolyn's husband having lunch with another female, we advised her of that. When the husband left the restaurant and gave the female a hug and a kiss, we photographed it. The two of them drove off in separate cars, but in the same direction. The plot thickens … shortly, both vehicles entered the same motel parking lot. We photographed Carolyn's husband and the other woman going into the same room.

Our mistake here was to call Carolyn and tell her what we were witnessing and which motel her husband was in. Twenty minutes later, Carolyn enters the parking lot of the motel with tires squealing. She races up to the door of the motel room and begins banging on the door. Seconds later, her husband appears at the door with his shirt off, his pants buttoned, but his belt hanging loose.

An argument follows. The husband whips off his belt and begins beating our client. Oh, shoot, what do we do now? As we all know, domestic disturbances may perhaps be the most volatile and dangerous situations for a responding officer. Carolyn had told us that her husband had beaten her in the past.

We called the sheriff's office and then proceeded up the stairs. As is typical in domestic-violence cases, as soon as we approached the couple, they both turned their aggression on us. We backed off, and the two of them took their fight inside the room. The other woman came running out and hid behind us. In a minute, the police arrived, and they needed no directions to the room. The noise from inside was clearly heard through the walls. Both our client and her husband got a free ride in the backseat of the police car.

We made it a policy from then on never to tell a client the exact location of their cheating spouse until the following day. We'll keep them advised of what's happening, but will not tell them where the action is at the moment. Many clients aren't happy with that policy, because they want the confrontation. We don't.

If there's a history of violence in the relationship, consider all of the factors before becoming involved in a similar situation. In this business, though, confrontations will happen, even when you do your best to avoid them.

Jacob was a bookie. He was a heavyset man who drove a large gray Mercedes and paid in cash. He and Martha were separated. A few months previously, Jacob had hired us to follow Martha for almost two weeks straight. I'd reported to Jacob about a man I saw entering Martha's house without knocking. I knew the man. His name was John and he was an attorney who lived across the street from Martha. Still, entering without knocking or ringing the bell seemed a little strange to me.

Jacob pooh-poohed the idea that John could be Martha's lover. He was just a friendly neighbor. Yeah—real, real friendly, as it turned out. I'm sure she was getting good legal advice from John, and at a very good exchange rate as well.

Now Jacob wanted Martha followed some more because Martha had admitted she'd had a fling with John, but that it was over. I've heard that more times than I can count. So had Jacob. We were back on the case. Unfortunately, Jacob had told Martha that he'd had her followed before, so now she was very paranoid and watching for us. In Chapter 19, we talk about paranoia and telephone taps. The same is true for being followed. Just because you're paranoid doesn't mean that somebody's not following you. We were certainly on Martha's tail, figuratively speaking.

One day, about 10 days into the surveillance, I and another investigator were conducting a two-man surveillance on Martha. We followed her down a busy four-lane road. A car very similar to mine was riding her bumper all the way down to an interstate on ramp. When Martha roared onto the interstate, this car still stayed right behind her. This unknown car was the same color and make as mine.

I was staying way, way back, keeping as many cars between me and her as I could while still keeping her in sight. She exited the interstate, and this other car didn't. Finally, it was off her bumper. My other investigator was further back than I was, so I sped up to follow her off the interstate. Once off the freeway, she could have gone any of four different directions, and we didn't want to lose her.

Well, unknown to me, she'd pulled off and stopped and was just sitting there. As I drove past her, she got on my tail. I tried to pull into a nearby gas station, but she whipped around in front of me and blocked my path. She hopped out of her car and jumped right into my face.

"Why are you following me?"

"Lady," I said, thinking as fast as I could. "I'm not following you. I just pulled into here to get some gas and you're blocking my way. Are you okay?"

"I'm fine, damn it. And you are too following me. You've been following me for the last fifteen minutes. I'll tell you why you're following me. You're following me because Jacob paid you to follow me. And you're not very good at it either. How much did he pay you to follow me?"

I just shrugged my shoulders and motioned toward the gas pumps. "Lady, I'm just trying to get some gas."

"Well, I'm going to tell Jacob what a lousy PI he hired. He's wasting his money." With that she jumped back into her car and took off.

What a blow to my ego. Of course, I wanted to tell her that I'd been following her for 10 days straight and she never knew it. And that I'd followed her for over two weeks the month before and she never knew that, either. And the only reason she made me today was because it was a case of mistaken identity. Of course, she was gone, and I couldn't have said those things anyway, but boy, did I want to. I did tell Jacob. He just chuckled about it and paid me in hundred-dollar bills. Of course, what she didn't know was that my partner picked up the surveillance when she took off and we held on to her for a few more days.

Here is a short checklist of what to do if you're confronted by a subject (don't use this list if you're made by the police; that's dealt with in Chapters 12 and 13, both of which deal with surveillance):

- Deny you're following the person who confronts you.

- Don't identify yourself as a private investigator.

- Never reveal the identity of your client or your subject.

- Leave the area as quickly as possible, but not so quickly as to give the impression you are fleeing.

- Stop the surveillance for the day and give it time to cool off.

- If surveillance is reinstituted on another day, utilize different vehicles and, if possible, different personnel.

The Least You Need to Know

- Allan Pinkerton began the private investigative business in the United States in 1850. The term *private eye* may have originated from Pinkerton's company logo, "the all-seeing eye."

- There are many niche areas in the PI arena, and several of them don't require a PI license.

- Successful private investigators must be able to make intuitive leaps in reasoning, a talent that can be learned and practiced.

- Ensure that the investigation is conducted without violating any local, state, or federal laws. If there is any doubt as to the legality of something you want to do, err on the side of caution and don't do it.

- Avoid confrontations with the subject of your investigation.

The Path to the Professional PI

In This Chapter

- ◆ Learning skills to better your chances of being hired as a private investigator
- ◆ Getting the scoop on obtaining your PI license
- ◆ Understanding your liability and insurance needs
- ◆ Organizing to become a super-sleuth
- ◆ Finding a niche and finding the clients
- ◆ Marketing on the web

A career as a professional private investigator can be emotionally rewarding, entertaining, and exciting. It's much better than working for a living. Can it be financially rewarding as well? The answer is yes, under certain circumstances.

If you've decided you want to be a professional PI, this chapter will help you get started, point out some pitfalls to avoid, and increase the collection of those checks. And in reality, collecting checks from clients is probably the only way most of us will ever get to have a Ferrari.

Getting the Experience

The approach you take to starting a PI business from the ground up depends on your previous level of investigative experience. For example, if you're leaving a position with law enforcement, then your years of running criminal investigations should give you a bit of a leg up in this business, at least at the beginning. Such experience is particularly helpful when you begin marketing your services.

Is this one of those catch-22s, where you need investigative experience to get started, but can't get started if you don't have the experience? Not really. How else, then, can you get such experience? One avenue is to spend some time as an insurance claim adjuster. Their training provides good background that would serve them well in the insurance end of the PI business. Military intelligence is another pathway into private investigation. And good on-the-job training can be received by working for another licensed private investigative agency. You can cut your PI wisdom teeth under the auspices of an established group.

This book assumes you have no previous experience in the PI field. If you do, then skip over the basics in this chapter and jump in where appropriate. But even if you're very experienced, you might pick up a few nuggets.

To obtain investigative experience, you'll need to find a job with a licensed firm. This is true in 40 of the 50 states. There are 10 states that don't require anything more than a business license. We'll talk more about that in the next section.

Having run a PI agency for over 20 years, I know it is nearly impossible to find a job in this field without experience. Notice I said *nearly*, not totally. Why? There's lots of competition for very few openings. Becoming a PI seems like a glamorous occupation, and many people think they'd like to try their hand at it.

Alternate Light Source _____

This may not work in all states, but it does in some. So you don't have any experience but you want to own a PI agency and work as a PI. What to do? You can try hiring a fully licensed investigator to work as the manager of the agency. Being a manager does not equal being an owner or president. You'll need a fully licensed PI to be the manager, but you, the novice, can be the owner of an agency. The manager will have to sign on as your mentor or sponsor, but in those states that allow interns to work toward their PI license with on-the-job training, this is one method that does work. It allows you to jump right over the hurdle of finding a job with an established PI agency.

On average, my firm receives three inquiries a week from folks wishing to intern. To qualify for a regular investigator's license in the state of Florida, an applicant must have at least two years' investigative experience, or else a Bachelor's degree in criminal justice and one year of experience. Either way, you've got to get the time under your belt. How do you compete with the crowd for the few openings out there?

Step back for a minute and think about the difference between skill sets and their application to specific jobs. Someone with good skill sets that are useful in a given job can quickly be taught how to apply those skills to another job. On the other hand, those who lack applicable skill sets for the job they want carry with them a double-whammy: they'll need double the training, because they'll need to learn the necessary skills and the right way to use them. This is true in any industry.

When looking for a job with a PI firm, emphasize the skills that qualify you to do the work. Over the years, I've learned it's easier for me to teach a person how to be an investigator (applying the person's existing skills) than it is, for example, to teach him or her the photography skills and research skills that good PI work requires. Come to me already skilled, and I'll teach you how to apply those skills to this line of work. Here's your second investigative assignment: while you read this book, keep a running list of the skills an investigator needs. That ought to strip away some of the TV-induced glamour. Are you already good at each one? Can you take classes to learn, or enhance, the necessary skills? As an employer, my attitude toward a potential employee is favorably affected when I see the initiative the candidate used to improve his qualifications. If he can talk intelligently about *f-stops*, *depth of field*, and *center-weighted and averaged light metering*, his chances of being hired by me are pretty good.

def•i•ni•tion

F-stop refers to the setting on an adjustable, single-lens reflex camera. F-stops are numbers indicating to what degree the iris of the lens is opened or closed. The f-stop setting is one factor in determining the amount of light that passes through the lens and exposes the film. As the f-stop number increases, the iris is then "stopped down" to a smaller aperture, and less light is allowed through the lens. A larger number equals less light, all other factors remaining the same.

Depth of field refers to the apparent range of focus in a photograph. For example, in portrait photography, the background and the foreground may be intentionally blurred or out of focus while the subject, in the center of the photograph, is in focus.

Many single-lens reflex cameras have built-in light-metering capability that automatically adjusts the f-stop and the shutter speed. A good photographer will know if his **light meter averages** the measurement of the light over the entire surface of the lens, or if it **center-weights** the average, giving more importance to the amount of light coming through the center of the lens, where the important image is presumably located.

The lesson here is to make yourself attractive to the firm where you're seeking employment and to be persistent. The skills that were necessary 20 years ago are still as important today. The problem is that the skill set required has increased.

Here is a list of tips and skills you should acquire before applying with a PI firm:

- Experience in 35mm photography, digital photography, and video photography.
- Good skills in computer programs, especially Microsoft Word, Access, Excel, Internet Explorer, and Mozilla Firefox.
- Excellent keyboarding skills.
- Good knowledge of the Internet search engines.
- Know the courthouse and the ins and outs of the clerk's office. Pay particular attention to Chapters 6 and 7.

If a person came to my office possessing all of the above skills, I would hire him on the spot and create a position for her even if I didn't need another investigator.

Alternate Light Source _____

Having your own surveillance equipment will be a big boost to your chances of getting hired. Don't actually purchase the cameras until you get the job, but make it clear during the interview that you've got money set aside for whatever is necessary. Most PI firms don't supply the high-tech camera equipment anymore. Each investigator has to have her own. When you get the job, buy the equipment that your firm recommends—probably digital. Be familiar with both video and single-lens reflex digital cameras. Learn the difference between physical zoom and digital zoom on video cameras.

Obtaining Licenses

Be sure to check with the appropriate governing bodies. There are 10 states that do not specifically license private investigators. Those 10 states are …

- Alabama
- Alaska
- Colorado
- Idaho
- Mississippi

- Missouri

- Pennsylvania (license issued by county)

- Rhode Island (license issued by city or town)

- South Dakota

- Wyoming

Usually, however, at least a business license will have to be obtained. Also, in some of these states, the individual cities might require a private investigator's license in addition to a business license. Some of these 10 states, like Virginia, require proof of training. The PI Directory (www.thepidirectory.com) has a number of useful links, including links to all of the licensing divisions in the various states. Be sure and know what the requirements are for your state by checking with the appropriate licensing authority (www.thepidirectory.com/licensingunits) before you apply for a job with an agency.

As your business expands you might want to acquire licenses in states other than where your principal office is located. If you're working a case in your state and it leads you to a neighboring state, some states will allow you to continue working within their borders as long as the case originated where you are licensed. Others will not. Always check the licensing regulations and reciprocity agreements between states before working a case in a state where you do not hold a license. Use the preceding links and contact the state regulatory body before investigating where you're not licensed.

Twenty-two states will require the PI applicant to pass an examination before granting a license. In order to pass the Georgia test, you'll need to be familiar with the Georgia wiretap and eavesdropping laws, as well as the laws that apply to carrying concealed and unconcealed weapons. In addition, a basic understanding of legal procedure, interview techniques, and basic investigative procedures will be necessary.

Some states like Florida, for example, will require you to possess, in addition to the local business license, three separate licenses issued by the secretary of state, Division of Licensing: an agency license, a manager-of-an-agency license, and a private investigator's license. Of course, there are fees associated with each license. In Florida this is true, whether you are a one-man operation or have 20 employees working out of one location. But hey, there's no state income tax, so they have to generate revenue somehow, right?

In Florida, if you also want to carry a weapon, you'll need two more permits: a weapon license to carry while on duty, and a concealed weapon permit to carry a firearm off duty. In the state of Florida, that makes six different licenses and permits. Do you think that's enough regulation? Maybe we could use a little bit more.

What's the Liability?

Many states will require a PI to carry a liability policy, and they won't issue or renew a license until proof of insurance is demonstrated. Some states require bonds instead of liability insurance. Check your state requirements, they vary from state to state. As of 2006, Florida no longer requires a PI to carry liability insurance. California, however, requires $1 million in liability insurance if you're going to carry a firearm. Firearm-carry regulations for private investigators are often different and more harsh than for a simple concealed-weapons permit. South Carolina requires a $10,000 bond, and Georgia requires a $25,000 bond or a liability insurance policy with a $1 million minimum. Check your own state before deciding how much liability insurance you need. Some states require none, others require a bond, and still others require some sort of a minimum amount.

The Division of Licensing

You will read this cautionary statement in many of the chapters in this book: if you have serious doubts about the legality of any action you're about to undertake, get a legal opinion first, or don't do it.

The policies typically cover comprehensive general-liability coverage for death, bodily injury, property damage, and personal injury coverage, including false arrest, detention or imprisonment, malicious prosecution, libel, slander, defamation of character, and the violation of the right of privacy. Let's see, I think the kitchen sink is in there, too, but at least they had the courtesy to leave out the toilet.

The fact of the matter is, if you're trying to capture big corporate clients and convince them to use your services, it's not unusual for them to require one or even two million dollars in insurance coverage. They also will want to be named as an additional insured. If you want to go after the big fish, you've got to use big hooks.

In nearly 20 years in the PI business, we've never been sued for any action that came out of our investigative effort, the only exception being a couple of automobile accidents. Despite that, in today's litigious society, only a fool would work as a PI and not carry insurance, especially if you consider the violation of privacy issue. Kind of ironic, then, that we're called *private* investigators. That's what a PI seems to do: violate the privacy of others—or at least that's what they'll claim when you catch them in some illegal or immoral act.

Privacy?

So what about this privacy thing, anyway? What's the boundary line between acceptable and invasive PI work?

Surveillance is such a large part of many private investigators' practices that, to avoid being sued, it's important to understand when a person has a reasonable expectation of privacy and when he or she doesn't. A general rule is, if the activity being observed can be seen from a public area, or an area open to the public, then the subject would not have a reasonable expectation of privacy.

A couple kissing or making love in front of an open window that can be seen from a parking lot would be fair game. How about a window with the blinds down? Many times, I've sat in one of our surveillance vans and shot video of cheating couples through second-floor blinds, because the miniblinds were shut in such a way that, from the ground-level parking area, a person could see into the apartment. If you have miniblinds, play with the slat angles, and you'll see exactly what I mean.

Did that couple have a reasonable expectation of privacy? Some would say yes, because they made an attempt to close the blinds. The fact is, I could observe and photograph the activity with ordinary, off-the-shelf photographic equipment. In my opinion, they may have thought they had privacy, but they didn't close the blinds properly. Their lack of proficiency in closing the blinds negated any claim they might make for an expectation of privacy.

Finding the Clients

Many agencies bill themselves as "full-service agencies." That's fine. Take whatever business you can get. A word of caution, though: it's difficult to be all things to all people. The successful agencies find a niche they are good at and then exploit the devil out of it.

When the Brown Group Inc. was marketing insurance surveillance work heavily, it was billing between $80,000 and $90,000 a month. This was in the early 1990s from a single location in northern Florida.

Sure, they did domestic work and some electronic countermeasure work, but their major market was insurance defense cases. They marketed that niche by staffing their own booths at workmen's compensation and insurance liability conventions, where they gave away promotional material and freebies to insurance adjusters and attorneys working insurance defense cases.

C. J. Bronstrup, a long-time private investigator and expert marketer in the PI industry says:

> Beware: lack of "technical" knowledge is not the leading cause of failure. Many fine investigators with 20-plus years of law enforcement backgrounds go belly-up every year. The major cause of failure is not having enough business. Take the time to learn how to market your business. It can propel your agency from making peanuts to a steady six-figure income almost over night.

Even with mediocre skills and a good marketing plan, you'll do better than an investigator with 20 years experience and no marketing effort.

You see, the more tightly defined your area of specialization is, the more you are perceived as an expert in that field. Thus, you can command higher fees than the generalist PI. Who charges more, the general practitioner or the heart surgeon? The heart surgeon, or the heart surgeon who specializes in angio-catheterizations? You get the idea.

In my own firm, we got tired of doing insurance defense work and moved away from that to skip tracing. For five years, we skip traced over 2,000 people a month. Recently, I was able to sell the skip-tracing portion of the business.

In the first paragraph of this chapter, we asked the question: can this business be financially rewarding? The answer was yes, under certain circumstances. There are three ways to make the PI business financially successful:

1. Run the business yourself. Build it up until you have 6 to 12 investigators working for you. You will not make a six-figure income working cases by yourself. Do the math. If you work 40 hours a week, you'll be lucky to bill 24 of them. Twenty-four hours billed at, say, $65 per hour results in weekly billings of $1,560. Fifty weeks of those billings gives you a gross income of $78,000 a year. Subtract all of your expenses, and you'll be lucky to net 50 percent, or $39,000. It is very hard to succeed as a one-man operation.

   With six men whom you pay $20 dollars an hour, billing the same 24 hours a week, all of sudden you are bringing in about $325,000 a year after meeting your investigative payroll. Sure, overhead will increase, but you should still end up with a net well into the six-figure area.

2. Use the "make-it-up-in-volume" strategy. Find a high-volume niche that needs little manpower, such as skip tracing or background investigations. Each case might only gross $50 to $100 dollars, but if the volume is high and the costs are low, a nice profit can be made. If the net profit on your high-volume, low-cost product is, say, $35, and you are processing 500 of them a week, the gross profit will be over $900,000 a year. Not too shabby, huh?

3. You can make a six-figure income working high-dollar cases where the overhead is low. You can see a good example of this spelled out in Chapters 21 and 22. Consider due diligent adoption searches. The cost of working those type of cases is practically nothing. Maybe $50 max per case, but you'll charge your client $750. A net profit of $700. If you do three a week, you're netting over $100,000 a year.

There may be other ways to make high dollars in the PI business, but these are three proven ones for me.

Exploiting the Full Potential of the World Wide Web

Don't forget the Internet in your marketing strategy. Bronstrup indicates that your online marketing program and website can easily account for 60 percent or more of your business in your first year alone. "Those who ignore this advice may wake up one day to find their biggest client just got lured to another PI firm by some kid sitting at the kitchen table in his Harley boxers using a laptop computer."

In starting our new business, I've already had clients tell me that they are using a large national firm with an Internet presence. How do they know this firm is large? All they see is the website, the toll-free number, and the claims on the website. It's not a large national firm. It's that damn kid in the underwear. Excuse me while I hit the stores in search of my own Harley boxers.

I had one of the original PI websites early in 1992. At that time, there were about seven private investigators on the web, and we were the only ones taking case assignments directly over the Internet. Our bank, with whom we'd done business for years, would not give us a MasterCard and Visa merchant account because the Internet was so new and they were afraid of it. We had to go elsewhere to set up our merchant account. Of course that sounds silly now, but that's how early our presence was on the net.

Even at that early stage, we were bringing in cases from all over the United States, and our bottom line began to increase because of our website. There's been a lot of shaking out in the industry since then, but a good, well-designed website can increase your business, even if you are working out of your kitchen.

Look at private investigators' sites on the web. Do they all look alike? Many of them do. They have copied their ideas from each other. Bronstrup calls this "marketing incest." This is one mistake you don't want to make. Find a good designer with original ideas.

Choices on a web page should be kept to a minimum. Too many choices makes it easy for a prospective client to pick the wrong one, get frustrated, and leave your site entirely. It would pay to find a good designer who also knows the private investigative business.

The Least You Need to Know

◆ Becoming a licensed private investigator is a popular dream. Making it a reality requires learning certain skills before applying to an agency, and then pursuing the dream with persistence.

◆ Forty states require PIs to be licensed. Twenty-two states also require a minimum passing score on a licensing examination. The test covers state laws on weapons, privacy issues, and general legal knowledge.

◆ Liability insurance and bond coverage is typically required by the states prior to issuing a PI license. Also, many clients require proof of insurance, often up to $2 million, before assigning cases to a PI.

◆ The business structure of PI firms generally falls within one of the following: sole proprietorship, partnership, C corporation, subchapter S corporation, or limited liability company (LLC). Each has different tax and liability consequences and advantages.

◆ The most successful PI businesses have found their own niche, and market that niche heavily.

◆ Don't forget to explore the World Wide Web as a marketplace. Internet traffic can substantially increase the bottom line for a PI firm.

Tools of the PI Trade

In This Chapter

- ◆ Choosing the right vehicle
- ◆ Getting the right camera to get the shots
- ◆ Selecting the right computer and internet connection
- ◆ Making a case with good binoculars
- ◆ Success is in the details—get 'em recorded

Private investigators produce a product just as surely as candy makers pull taffy and cook fudge. The product in either line of business has to, first, be pleasing to the eye of the customer, and second, be sweet and satisfying to his taste.

Every professional in every profession uses tools. Some of the tools in a private investigator's toolbox are mechanical, others may be digital or analog.

Other tools are intangible, such as skills or techniques that are learned as one matures in the trade, and whose quality directly affects the quality of the product produced. We'll learn a few of those in this chapter.

The Ferrari in the Garage

In the television show *Magnum*, *P.I.*, Tom Selleck played the lead role of Thomas Magnum. In the show, he drove a red Ferrari. It wasn't unusual for Magnum to use the Ferrari while attempting to keep a person under a moving surveillance. Now, I don't know about you, but if I saw a red Ferrari in my rearview mirror, I think I would recognize it when I saw it again a few minutes later, or a few hours later. That's television for you—that's fiction.

We talk some about surveillance vans in Chapters 12 and 13, but let's examine the whole car issue here. Unless you own a whole fleet of cars, you're probably like the rest of us and have only one or two cars available to you. An investigator will have to use his car for both surveillance and marketing.

Selection of a good vehicle for a PI is problematic. A PI should avoid anything that looks like a police car. Likewise, a black van with dark-tinted windows, sometimes called a "kidnapper van," makes people suspicious.

Remember, people will see you. The idea is to stay far enough away so the *subject* doesn't see you. More horsepower is better in surveillance vehicles. An underpowered four-cylinder car is going to make it rough when trying to catch up with the subject when he's two blocks ahead of you and moving out. Actually, pickup trucks make pretty good surveillance vehicles in suburbia. Stay away from the real flashy sport cars.

If the PI has only one vehicle as an option, go for the four-door, eight-cylinder, earth-tone–colored auto. It'll blend in better in most parking lots and give you room to take your clients to lunch.

Getting the Shots

Photography plays a huge role in the PI business. Whether you're working domestic cases, criminal defense, insurance defense, nursing home abuse, homicide and suspicious suicide cases, or employee theft, the quality of the photography matters. How much? Enough to make or break some cases. About the only portion of PI work where it might not be a necessary tool is those cases that don't require you to leave your desk: skip tracing, diligent adoption and estate searches, and pre-employment backgrounds.

In nursing home cases, and almost all cases where we perform face-to-face interviews for attorneys, we ask permission to photograph the person we're interviewing. It helps us later to refresh our memories of the interview, and many of our clients want to see what this potential witness looks like. Of course, the nursing home patient is photographed to document his or her injuries. Likewise, in parental or spousal abuse cases, documenting the injuries and noting the time and date of the photograph and the time the injury occurred can be important. Skin bruising progresses through certain recognized patterns, and to a limited degree the approximate time of the injury can be established.

You'll use a camera to photograph crime scenes, areas where a slip and fall occurred or the intersection of a traffic accident. With domestic cases, a camera's use is obvious in catching the cheating spouse in a compromising embrace. You may wish to document two cars parked together in front of a motel or apartment.

What kind of camera equipment do you need? There are three types of cameras that each investigator should have and also be proficient using:

- Digital single-lens reflex (SLR) still camera

- Digital video camera

- Cell phone cameras

Digital still cameras have come of age, and any professional investigator should have the best one she can afford. Frankly, most investigators are cheap and will try to make their digital video camera do double duty, since digital video cameras are capable of taking still pictures as well. It's hard enough to get an interviewee to sit still while you talk him into having his photo taken with a still camera. Pull out that video camera, and he's likely to get up and turn his back on you. As far as crime scene and traffic accident photography are concerned, you'll want to take both video and stills of the scene. Sure, you could edit the video and capture stills off of it, but that's a lot more work than just shooting digital stills and uploading them to your computer. Most digital video cameras have single-shot capability as well. And just to confuse the situation, some digital still cameras and cell phone cameras have limited video capabilities.

The features to look for in digital still cameras are the number of *pixels*, the storage media, and the zoom capabilities.

def•i•ni•tion

Pixels are little points of light on a computer screen or a television screen that, when combined, are perceived by the naked eye as one large picture. The more pixels, the smoother the picture, yielding a better-quality photograph.

A good digital camera will have at least 7 million pixels. Older and less-expensive digitals have 3 to 5 million pixels. Like everything else in the computer world, electronics get better and less expensive pretty quickly. Ten-million-pixel and higher cameras are already out and will be standard issue soon.

So where do those digital still cameras keep all those photos you shoot? Rather than traditional film negatives, the digital still camera's memory is called "magnetic media." Some brands have their own proprietary type of storage media. Sony, for example, uses a Memory Stick. Cannon and some others use a Compact Flash card, and others use SmartMedia. Larger digital cameras use PCMCIA cards.

To access your digital photos, you have to download them to a computer. So before buying a digital camera, it'd be smart to decide which computer you're going to use and make sure the camera's magnetic storage media is compatible. For example, many laptops have a PCMCIA card slot, which can accept a Compact Flash card with a simple and inexpensive adapter. Newer desktops have combination slots that will accept compact flash, SD, mini SD, and memory sticks. Another techno detail to watch for when playing matchmaker between a computer and a camera is whether the magnetic media contains a controller chip. If it doesn't, as is the case with SmartMedia cards, than you'll have to program the camera to recognize the card. This can get to be a real pain, unless you're a control-freak type A personality.

All the different cameras allow downloading directly from the camera to a computer via cables. The drawback to this method is speed. Cables are slower than direct digital input from a storage media. And, too, the camera's battery charge seems to rapidly dissipate during the downloading. It's a better idea to remove your storage media from the camera and insert it into your computer rather than use cable downloading. Evaluate your complete system, and this includes your digital video camera, before you buy. A good overall plan will save you heartache later. Software to manipulate your photographs once they're on the computer is a whole book by itself. However, most computers come preloaded with photo-editing software and digital cameras usually come with digital manipulation software, some of which are excellent. For digital video, Windows Media Player that comes with Windows XP is a pretty good program. Apple has its own photo and video software.

With digital cameras, both still and video, check the power of the optical zoom and go for the vroom zoom. The higher the power, the better. When surveillance is covered in Chapters 12 and 13, we talk about techniques to help the investigator remain undiscovered. The farther away the investigator is from his subject, the less likely it is that the subject will become aware of the surveillance. The catch-22, of course, is that the greater the distance to your subject, the more difficult it becomes to get good photographs. This means you'll need a pretty good zoom to capture the images you need to make your case.

For your photographs to be effective in court, the subject must be identifiable. This means you have to get good, clear, well-focused shots. In addition to optical zooms, digital cameras, both still and video, will have a digital zoom feature. The digital zoom works very well, up to a point. In purchasing your equipment, all other things being equal, go first for the camera with the highest *optical zoom*, and then consider the power of the digital zoom. One more aspect to consider with the magnetic media is that some media can record images faster than others. When you're shopping for still cameras, buy the media storage that allows for faster storage. You can take quicker shots and won't miss the critical photo while waiting for the previous shot to be saved.

def•i•ni•tion

Optical zoom on camera lenses refers to the focal length achieved by physically moving the lenses further apart from each other, thereby achieving a greater focal length (hence the term "zooming out" with a zoom lens) and increasing the relative size of the image as it appears on the film or recording media.

Digital cameras have a "digital zoom" that magnifies the image through digital technology. All other things being equal, an optically zoomed image will be more clear because the image hasn't been altered or "blown up" through the digital process.

Except for the workers' compensation–type cases, which require the video camera, a quality SLR camera is still the heavy-duty wrench in the private investigator's toolbox. Admittedly, this type of camera is being challenged by the versatility and light-gathering ability of video cameras, but the advantage of *single-lens reflex (SLR)* cameras is the ability to change lenses. The working lens for most PIs is a 100–300mm zoom lens. You can add a doubler between the lens and the camera body to get an effective focal length of 600mm. Anything longer than that, and you'll need to zoom in on a business loan to pay for it.

def•i•ni•tion

A **single-lens reflex (SLR)** camera is a camera where the light (the image) passes through the lens and is reflected by a mirror to the viewfinder, where it is viewed by the photographer. When the shutter button is depressed, the mirror flips out of the way, and the image passes directly to the recording medium. The advantage of SLR cameras over other cameras, in addition to their lens-changing capability, is that the photographer sees the exact image that will be captured.

At 600mm, you'll need a tripod to steady the camera to avoid blurring the picture. A fast shutter speed will also prevent blurred pictures, but with a super-long lens on the camera, the amount of light that enters the lens is reduced, so slower shutter speeds may be required. But with a good *image stabilized* lens (think big bucks here) you can probably get your shot.

def•i•ni•tion

Image stabilization is a function available with almost all digital video cameras and incorporated into many newer SLR camera lenses. The camera or lens digitally stabilizes the image to reduce blurring from a not-so-firmly held camera. An image stabilized lens on an SLR camera means you can open the iris as much as four extra stops (good for low-light photography) when the image stabilization is turned on.

When after-dark photography is needed, there are three choices, neither of which requires flashbulbs or spotlights:

1. An investigator can use a 35mm camera with extra-fast film. Kodak makes Tmax film, a black-and-white product with a speed of 3200. It can be shot at 1600, 3200, or 6400, if needed. Most cameras cannot be set for film higher than 6500. However, finding a place to process black and white can be difficult. Most larger cities will have some photo shops that can do it, or that will at least send it out to a national processing center. You won't get it processed at a one-hour developer, though. Keep that in mind if you're going to need the prints right away.

2. When it comes to nighttime photography, video cameras have come to the PI's rescue. The light-receptive chips (charged, coupled devices) used in video cameras are more sensitive to light than is standard 35mm film. Therefore, after dark a video camera will probably capture a better image than a 35mm one, unless you're using a flash, which will flush you out of hiding and put your flesh at risk.

The Division of Licensing

If you're using black-and-white film such as Tmax or any other film and you push the film to a higher speed, then be sure to tell the processor at what speed it should be processed. If you don't, the film will come back grossly under- or overdeveloped and will be practically useless. This, of course, is not a problem if you've converted to digital.

3. Infrared. Yep, Sony has an infrared-night-shot capability on many of its video cameras. It works pretty well at close range and you can buy an optional infrared light that should work up to a hundred feet. Canon's night shot is not infrared, but it increases the gain on the receptors in the camera. It, too, works well, but if the subject is moving, then the image will blur and be streaked. Gives a new meaning to subjects streaking.

Alternate Light Source

Cell phone cameras have their uses. They're quick and handy to use and you can be sneaky with them. When next purchasing a cell phone, compare camera features. Be sure and buy one that has a removable memory media. Then, don't forget to program the cell camera to save your photos to the removable media. Otherwise, the photos will be saved to the permanent memory of the camera. With removable media, you can slide it out of your camera and right into the appropriate media slot in your computer to be ready for printing, e-mailing, or including in your report.

If you're familiar with cameras in general, then go to one of the search engines we recommend in Chapters 4 and search for "digital cameras." One good site for comparing digital still cameras is www.dpreview.com. It has reviews of all the cameras, plus ratings. That site also has a pretty good learning center, where you can look up unfamiliar terms.

For digital video cameras we suggest going right to the manufacturers' websites to read and compare the specifications on the cameras. Then, go to your local electronics store for a hands-on feel of the camera and personalized answers to your questions. Now, where can you find the best price for the camera equipment you want to purchase? Sounds like a question for an aspiring PI to solve. Shop around, though, because most of the brand names have a street price considerably lower than the suggested retail price.

Computer Equipment

You can't run and manage a successful PI business today without a computer and fast Internet access. If you're not computer literate, don't hang out your shield until you are. That's the bottom line. Even if you want to handle everything on paper and a typewriter, you can't do justice to your clients' needs without access to the databases that are available to help you. And the databases don't accept collect calls for assistance. Chapters 4, 5, and 8 explore the wonderful world of information that is available to the PI. Come on into the twenty-first century.

Your computer should have the fastest processing chip, the largest hard drive, and the most memory (*RAM*) you can afford. Isn't that what all the guys say about the computer they want to buy? Sure it is, but in this business we're talking tools, not toys. Why does it have to be so powerful? Thirty days after you've bought your new state-of-the-art computer, it'll be outdated and a newer, faster, larger computer will be on the market. By starting with the best product *du jour*, you'll get about four good years in before you'll want to think about replacing it.

def•i•ni•tion

> **RAM** is an acronym for **Random Access Memory.** It is the memory that the computer accesses when it processes information and runs programs. If there is not enough RAM in a computer, then the information being processed is swapped back and forth to the hard drive, which slows down the processing speed, causes programs to lock up and the computer to crash, and can actually hasten a hard-drive failure.

If you're going to skimp at all, skip the hottest new chip and get the day-old version. You can sometimes save a considerable amount of money by not buying the newest, fastest chip available, but the next to the fastest. The sometimes-slight differences in performance are not that big. Don't, however, skimp on the hard drive or the memory.

I don't recommend throwing good equipment away and having the newest just to have it. But faster, larger, and more is better when it comes to chip speed, hard drive, and memory.

Computer programs get larger and require more RAM every time a new version is issued. If you're having stability problems, programs are crashing, or the computer is locking up, try adding more RAM to your computer. Increasing RAM can solve a whole host of problems. In your new computer, include the most RAM you can afford, and make sure it's at least one gigabyte.

What Are the Bells and Whistles?

There are lots of bells and whistles you can add to your computer, but don't tell your wife *The Complete Idiot's Guide to Private Investigating, Second Edition*, suggested the high-quality soundcard with the subwoofers. Not true. Do, however, add CD and DVD burners.

We sometimes ship reports with embedded photographs to our clients on CD. Likewise, you can put short video clips onto a DVD instead of duplicating tapes. Your clients can look at the video clip and get a good idea of the degree of fraud in an insurance defense case. The client can do this from his desktop computer and not have to fool with finding the remote to the television and the other remote for his VCR or DVD player.

Using Microsoft Access, we developed a database for one client where we had hundreds of potential witnesses. Each witness record included a complete copy of the interview and an embedded photograph of the witness. We put the database on a CD, and with each change, we'd send the client a new, updated CD that contained everything. If we were doing that today, we'd consider putting the database on DVD. But DVD is not perfect and not all DVD players will play the DVD you burn from your computer. But almost all computers will read any CD you burn. Don't expect your client/attorney's office to have the latest computer equipment. Most attorneys are less computer literate than you are.

A fast color printer is a necessity. You've taken the digital picture and now you want to give a copy to your client. You can run down to your local photography store and wait an hour, and they'll print it for you. Or you can run back to your office and print it yourself, if you have the right equipment. A high-quality color printer, using premium photo paper specifically designed for color printers, will give you a print nearly indistinguishable from a print made at a photography shop.

The Division of Licensing

The only problem we've found with sending CDs containing our reports, photos, and video to clients is that sometimes the client's computer hardware is not up to date enough to play the CDs! We've had to encourage clients to upgrade their version of Access before they could run the databases we've developed for them. Nevertheless, even if the client can't use the CD you send him, he'll recognize you as a top investigator, who is above his peers in professionalism and on the crest of new technology. That's a good impression to leave with a client.

Applying the Bells and Whistles to a Case

It was 11:30 at night on Friday, May 10. The lights in the apartment I'd been watching had gone out about a half hour before. My client's husband, Jonathan, from whom she was separated, had taken their three-year-old son with him for the weekend. Part of the separation agreement was that Jonathan would not cohabit or otherwise spend the night with single females while he had custody of the child.

I'd followed Jonathan to the girlfriend's apartment complex and watched him and the little boy enter. His SUV was parked in front of the apartment, and the girlfriend's car was parked next to his. I walked up to the vehicles and, using a large, black, permanent felt-tip marker, I drew an inverted V on the sidewall at the very top of the right rear tire on both cars. If the vehicles departed and then later returned, I would know it by checking the position of the V. It would be nearly impossible for the V to be in the exact same position relative to the fender as when I drew it.

Next, I backed off a ways behind the cars and took out my trusty Canon digital SLR which allows me to set the aperture for low-light situations. I took three shots of the two cars and the front of the apartment. My objective was to record both vehicles and the address in the same photo. An advantage of digital cameras is you can see immediately if you got the picture you wanted. Then I scooted out of there. Back at the office, I inserted the date and time onto the face of the photographs. I ran off two high-quality prints of the photographs, one for my client and one for her attorney.

At 7 the next morning, I was back at the same apartment complex. Both cars were still there. The inverted V was in the same relative position as I'd left it. There was dew on both car roofs and front windshields. I felt the grill area on both cars, and they were cold. My conclusion? Neither car had moved since 11:30 the previous night, indicating that Jonathan had spent the night with his girlfriend, son in tow.

I shot two more photographs of both cars and hustled back to my office. This time, I inserted "May 11th 7 A.M." onto the prints. Three or four weekends of this, and we had what the client wanted. The case went to court and Jonathan's attorney agreed to the facts in my report without me having to testify. The client told me that out of all the money she'd spent going through the divorce, she thought the most productive use of her money was what she spent with my firm. Gotta love those satisfied clients— and gotta love those digital cameras.

In the Internet Beginning

If you're going to be doing a lot of Internet searching, maybe professionally, then secure a broadband connection for your home, home office, or office. A broadband Internet connection is measured in the number of bytes (usually in thousands) of information that can be downloaded from the Internet. A normal computer modem plugged into your telephone line will transmit information in either direction at 56K, or 56 thousand bytes of data per second. Sounds like a lot, right? Wrong. For text documents that will be fast enough. This entire book (about 380 pages) is about 2,400,000 bytes (2.4MB), not including the graphics. (Normally referred to in terms of megabytes. One megabyte [MB] is one million bytes.) So on a 56K modem, you could download this book in less than a minute.

def•i•ni•tion

Bandwidth for our purposes means the amount of data that can be moved along a line of transmission in a certain time. The wider the bandwidth, the more data is moved.

However, graphic files (photographs), video, and audio files will run way into the megabyte territory. The bigger the file, the longer the download.

Your average DSL "broadband" connection will allow transmission speeds of about 2,000K (or 2MB)—much faster than a 56K modem. However, your typical cable modem will promise download speeds between 4MB and 8MB—two to four times faster than DSL. A full *T-1 line* downloads about 1.5MB.

def•i•ni•tion

A **T-1 line** is usually a fiber optic line (it can be copper) that can carry 24 digitized channels or telephone lines, about 1.5 Megabits of data per second. If you have a large enough business, you can have a T-1 line installed and use it to make all of your calls. A single T-1 line can be split so you can have 12 phone lines and the other half of the capacity can be used for your Internet service as well, at about 750 Kbps.

Why all this emphasis on download speed? Because, as an investigator searching through property appraiser files on the computer, time is money. Do you want to spend an hour waiting for a computer page to load? Or wait 10 seconds?

Okay, you say you understand the need for download speed, but what about upload speed? Is there a difference between download and upload speeds? You're going to want to upload video surveillance clips to your clients and probably reports with photographs.

Typically, cable modems are limited in their upload speeds to a fixed rate between 350K and 750K. If you're going to be sending out a lot of spam or can't compress the files you want to send, then you ought to consider buying a T-1 line because upload speeds will be faster than DSL or cable. But I find that a cable modem and compression software works fine for the limited number of uploads I do. Download speed is the all-important issue because most of my computer time is spent searching and downloading, not uploading.

The Division of Licensing

Cable modems and broadband cable Internet service is not perfect. At times it may be slower than DSL because during peak usage all of the cable subscribers in your area may be on the Internet at the same time. There is only so much bandwidth, and everyone in your neighborhood shares the same bandwidth. You can figure out your download speed by using the free test at www.speakeasy.net. Click on "speed test" in the bottom-right corner, choose the server nearest to you, and watch it go. The website will measure the download and upload speed of your ISP. And the best part, it's free.

Binoculars: The Better to See You with, My Dear

There are two other pieces of gear that are essential to a private investigator. One of those is a good pair of binoculars. Some investigators try to use opera glasses. These are small binoculars that fold and will fit in a small purse or pocket. The size has its advantage, for sure, but it's outweighed by the lack of quality. A good pair of binoculars will make you a more productive investigator.

The binoculars should be 7×50s. At that power and that size, the image does not "bounce" around too much. A good set of binoculars will be filled with nitrogen or some other inert gas. This gas is injected into the binoculars between the lens and the eyepieces. This prevents moisture and dirt from getting into the binoculars.

Don't spare the expense on the binoculars. There is a big difference between an inexpensive pair and an expensive one. It might not be noticeable when you're inspecting them in the store, but the light-gathering aspects of binoculars vary significantly, usually in proportion to the price tag. On a nighttime surveillance, quality binoculars will gather more light and actually make it easier to see your subject's activities.

Some binoculars have a compass built into the viewfinder. Knowing where north, south, east, and west lay is very handy. If you're in radio contact with another investigator and your subject is on the move, you can tell the other investigator exactly which direction the subject is moving or toward which direction the activity is shifting. It's a lot clearer to say "The subject is moving east around the end of the shopping center" than to say "The subject is moving toward my right, around the end of the shopping center." The other investigator probably doesn't know which way you're facing and will be unsure as to which direction he should be looking.

My friend and long-time investigative associate Robert Plance was working a case with me on the island of St. Croix, in the U.S. Virgin Islands. Our subject, the plaintiff, was a claimant in an insurance case. The subject had a set of corrals and several horses stabled there toward the east end of the island.

There were two viewpoints we could use to get good video of the subject working around the barn. One was in a clump of brush, just off a dirt road that passed the corrals. From there, Bob could see one side of the corral and the barn. I climbed a hill, quite a distance across the main road, and concealed myself in the brush there. I could see the other side of the barn and corral that Bob couldn't see.

The subject had six sons ranging in size from small to extra large. Without good binoculars, we would have shot hours and hours of videotape of the two older sons, who looked very much like their father. Wouldn't we have been embarrassed going into court with video of the wrong person?

As it turned out, we obtained lots of good video of the father and not the sons. The case was settled for a nominal amount. In the process of following the father, we inadvertently stumbled upon a love nest he had with a female other than his wife. We always wondered what his wife would have thought if we'd gone to court and she'd heard the testimony about that. Perhaps that love nest played a role in the claimant's quick settlement.

Recording the Facts

One aspect of PI work is the report writing. You've heard this in a previous chapter and you'll hear it again before the book ends: PIs produce a product. A private investigator's clients only see the written or photographic results of our work. They don't see the gallons of sweat on the floor of your car after a hot afternoon surveillance. They don't feel the fear of a near collision on the freeway when your subject exits suddenly and you have to jump three lanes of traffic to stay behind him. To them, your product is your report. That's all they'll see—that and any evidence you collect.

The written report needs to appear professional. We talk in greater length in Chapter 23 about formatting your reports. Here, we'll discuss the process of getting the facts down so they're not lost or forgotten.

Some surveillance investigators handwrite their surveillance logs. That works, but it is tedious. A better way is to have a micro cassette or digital recorder and dictate the surveillance as you go along. With that method, all of the details—license plate numbers, right and left turns, and the rest—are captured as they happen. Nothing important is left out or forgotten. You'll have a more-detailed surveillance log. Down the road, that may become important. People really are creatures of habit, and as you work a subject, his patterns will develop. If this is all laid out in your surveillance logs, then the next guy working him will have the benefit of your experience.

Alternate Light Source

A digital recorder has some advantages over its older cousin, the micro cassette. With a digital recorder you can download the dictation directly to your computer and burn copies to a CD. If it's a recorded statement you have on there you don't have to fumble with tape-to-tape copying. In the very near future you'll be able to use voice recognition software like Dragon Speaking Naturally to transcribe the dictation without anybody actually keyboarding it in.

Even with a recorder, though, I'd recommend you keep a pen and paper ready for quick notes. You should always jot down any important license plate number as you see it, because sometimes, in dictating, we transpose numbers. Write it down immediately. You may need to call the tag in to your office and have the registration run. You don't want to have to listen back through your entire surveillance log to find a tag.

As long as we're on the topic of surveillance logs, here is one piece of advice you won't find in any other book. Back at the office, take the surveillance videotape you've just made and watch it on a monitor. Dictate while the tape is running. In your dictation, note the times of significant activity. When the claimant picks up that 50-pound bag of fertilizer, note that in your log. You don't have to mention every bend and each motion of his body, but do enter into the log the time of any activity you think is important.

When you show these tapes in court, the judge will not want to watch the entire thing. After a few moments, he'll ask you to fast-forward the tape to the "good parts." With the time and date on the tape, and the same time and date in your typed log, you can go right to the good parts and skip over the long, boring, and unimportant parts. We'll discuss this some more in Chapter 24.

If you're just beginning a business, you might not have a secretary. I'd suggest not hiring one until you find that the volume of report typing you're doing is actually keeping you from working on cases. At that point, hire a part-time secretary, and you'll become more profitable.

The importance of producing a high-quality product cannot be stressed enough. The candy maker's fudge must first look good enough to eat. To keep clients coming back, the fudge has to taste even better than it looks. Likewise, your product should look professional, and as the client reads through the report and views the photographs, the contents should be even more pleasing to him.

In one of the examples in this chapter, we talked about Jonathan spending the night with his girlfriend while having his three-year-old for the weekend. Who do you think his wife, or her attorney, is going to recommend the next time somebody asks them for the name of a good private investigator? In fact, his attorney, recognizing my good work, now refers clients to us. The product looked good and tasted even better. Success, in this case, is sweet.

The Least You Need to Know

- An investigator needs a car that is practical for both surveillance and carting clients to lunch.

- Three important tools of the trade are a digital SLR camera, a digital video camera, and a cell phone camera. Important factors for digital cameras are the optical zoom and the number of viewable pixels.

- It's impossible to run a PI business without a computer. In buying a new computer, it's recommended to purchase the computer with a recent processor, a very large hard drive, and as much RAM as you can afford. Also, a fast color printer and a CD and DVD burner should be at the top of the list.

- Use tools to save time. Choosing the Internet connection with the greatest bandwidth might be your most important tool.

◆ An investigator should have a good pair of 7×50 binoculars.

◆ Use a good-quality micro cassette or digital recorder to dictate during a surveillance rather than handwriting a surveillance log. Do keep a pen and paper ready to jot down license plates, as well as dictating them.

◆ A high-quality finished product will please your clients and fatten your bottom line.

Part 2

Getting the Scoop

Now that you've decided exactly what you're looking for, it's time to learn where to find it.

In this part, we'll examine the sources of information that PIs use around the country to get the scoop on the subjects of their cases. You'll learn how to skip trace on the web, and prowl the courthouses and get access to federal, state, and local records. We'll also show you how to log on to those secret private databases that professional PIs use.

Chapter 4

Skip Tracing: The Basics

In This Chapter

- ◆ The genesis of the web
- ◆ Determining where to begin your search
- ◆ Deciphering the name game
- ◆ When and when not to use the free white pages
- ◆ Establishing long-distance relationships
- ◆ Finding that Aunt Mary might be your most productive search

There are many misconceptions about skip tracing and the Internet. Almost daily, someone says to me, "You can find anything on the Internet, right?" Well, wrong. If you want to know about Great Black-backed Seagulls, you can probably find all you'll ever want to know about them. But if you want to dig up the maiden name of your husband's mistress because you wish to check her criminal record, and she's been married three previous times, then the answer is a definite maybe. In this chapter, we'll touch on a few not-so-basic Internet search techniques and some pitfalls to avoid.

Zeroing In on the Right Search

There are as many factors in locating a person as there are fruits in a farmers' market. When searching on the web for a person, you can spend your time tracking down every person that has the same name as the individual you're looking for, or you can narrow it to just that one person. It seems elementary, I know, but you'd be surprised how even seasoned investigators have a hard time narrowing the focus of their search to the right party.

As an investigator, for profit or just for yourself, you need a variety of tools in your toolbox. Using the right tool at the right time marks the difference between an apprentice and a true craftsman. This book is designed to raise your level of craft from apprentice to artist. Experience by itself won't get you there. You'll need a mentor. And this book can be your mentor.

I had an experienced investigator call me and indicate he had a deep-pocket client (the best kind). The investigator and the client's attorney wanted to fly into Jacksonville, Florida, to interview a potential witness in a case. The witness had previously lived in another mid-southern state and the investigator found some indication that the witness had relocated to my area. He'd searched some of the pay databases that we talk about in Chapter 8 but couldn't find a definite address for the witness. Could I search the Florida driver's records by name and date of birth and see if the missing witness had a Florida license?

While we talked I brought up on my computer a public database, open to any person who has access to the Internet, and found his witness in less than thirty seconds. When we finished the discussion, I told him where his witness lived, how much his new house was appraised for, how much the witness paid for the new house, and that he'd purchased it about six months ago.

This seasoned investigator said to me, "Man, you're fast." Now why did I find his subject and he didn't? When you can answer that question, you can call yourself a real investigator. Just joking. The reason I found him so quickly was because I understood which database to search. I knew I could go online to the county property appraiser's website and search property ownership records, while the investigator that hired me had spent his time searching "pay" databases. I could do it while I was on the phone with him. Later in this chapter we'll talk more about property appraiser's databases and how to find them.

This is a common problem in the private investigative industry today. Many investigators haven't learned the basics and rely solely on "pay" databases for searches. Wrong.

Learning how to search public records, as you'll learn in Chapters 6 and 7, is the fundamental key to a successful investigation.

In the previous case, I'll still go to the tag agency and see what vehicles are registered to the subject and drive by the house to make sure that he is in fact living there before the attorney and his investigator fly in to do the interview. So I'll earn my money. But the big mystery of his location was solved, and I look like a superstar to this out-of-state investigator.

What's in a Name?

A person's name and date of birth seems pretty basic. You have to know whom you're looking for before you can began looking. But you may not have a complete name. If you have a partial name and a complete date of birth, you're a long way toward your goal. In the United States, a country of over 300 million people, we have a lot of duplicated names. So a name by itself, unless it's very uncommon, is not sufficient data to perform a thorough locate.

Criminal records, which we'll talk more about in Chapter 21, almost totally rely upon name, sex, race, and date of birth; not name and social security number as many uninformed believe. And if you're not sure of the sex or race, the name and date of birth will probably suffice.

Okay, so you have the name, but most of us don't know our old friends' dates of birth. Shoot, I sometimes can't even remember my own kids' dates of birth. So what are we to do? Let's start with what we have. The name.

Name Games

The population ethnicity of the United States and Canada is diverse. Consequently, not all cultures treat names the same way. The U.S. Census figures indicate that the native Spanish-speaking population of the United States has grown from 20 million in 1990 to 30 million in 1998, about 12 percent of our population. By the year 2010, it is projected that 15 percent of the United States will be Spanish-speaking, and by 2020, it could exceed 20 percent. Spanish is tied with English for the second-most-popular spoken language in the world (both English and Spanish are far behind Chinese). Some studies predict that by the year 2050, half of the population of the United States will be Spanish-speaking. What does this mean for private investigators and skip tracing?

It means you have to understand the structure of names originating in the Spanish language. This is how it works:

The architecture of the Spanish name is different than Anglo-Saxon names. Most Anglo-Saxon names have a first name or given name, a middle name (but not always), and a last name, which is taken from the child's father (although now we're getting a lot of hyphenated last names with females keeping their maiden name). First, middle, and last. Simple, right?

Hispanic names include a first name (given name), a middle name, a last name taken from the child's father, and a second last name, or fourth name, which is taken from the child's mother's maiden name.

When I was assigned with the FBI to the San Juan, Puerto Rico, office, my name was Steven Kerry Brown Bellamy, Bellamy being my mother's maiden name. I still have credit cards from down there that read "Steven B. Bellamy." Try explaining that to a clerk in the department store when he wants to compare my driver's license, last name Brown (hence the B in the credit card), with the credit card showing Bellamy as the last name.

Most databases only have three fields for names: first, middle, and last. These databases are going to have to accommodate the Spanish name structure or they'll have very poor search results, like they do now in Puerto Rico, south Florida, and the southwestern states, because of the large number of Hispanics living in those areas.

Don't believe me? Try searching the Puerto Rican Court System (see Chapter 21). You have to have the mother's maiden name (the fourth name) in order to search it. When clients request a criminal check in Puerto Rico, the first thing I ask for is the subject's fourth name.

Another potential problem is that many people are known by their nicknames, and you might not even know it's a shortened version of their names. For instance, I knew a Peggy I wanted to find from high school. Did you know Peggy is short for Margaret? Or Jack can be short for John? This one will throw you for sure: in the fifties, many male children were named Carroll and the nickname for that? Charlie. If you're not absolutely sure of the person's full or correct given name or how it's spelled (Steven or Stephen?), thumb through a name book at a local bookstore or the library before you begin your search. This one clue might save you hours of fruitless searching.

It's a Family Affair

The absolute easiest way to find a skip or a lost love is to ask someone who knows your subject and knows where he is. Sounds basic, right? You'd be surprised how many hours are wasted on Internet searches and telephone directory calls when you could just pick up the phone and ask your old high school buddy's parent where your old pal is now.

I had a client that asked me to find a skip. The client was an attorney, and his client wanted him to sue the subject for $500,000. They had no idea where the subject had gone. They'd heard rumors he was living on a sailboat in Florida, which is why they called me. I tracked down the rumors, which were about a year behind the subject, and actually found the owner of the boat that the subject had been living on. But our subject had moved to locations unknown by then.

So I had the attorney subpoena the subject's cell phone records. Frankly, I was hoping that the records would show us a new billing address that we didn't already have. But no, as luck would have it, the cell service records we'd subpoenaed showed that the service had been disconnected six months previously. I expended multiple dollars on different PI databases and nothing current showed. Even the most expensive pay databases available (we'll get into those in Chapter 8) didn't disclose any newer addresses.

I did track down the subject's parents who lived in another state and tried several different pretexts to develop his current whereabouts, but they wouldn't fall for any of them, claiming they didn't now where he was.

Where in the world was this guy? Most private investigators would have stopped at that point. If you have the time, sometimes stopping is a good move. Wait a few months and one of the data suppliers might pick up a fresh scent.

I didn't have the luxury of waiting. We needed to get this guy located and served, now. So I picked up the phone and starting calling numbers that showed up more than once on the subject's cell phone bill. Old numbers. Numbers he'd called a year ago. On the second number I dialed I hit upon a friend of the subject in New York City. In about fifteen seconds I had the subject's new cell number, which originated out of San Diego, and his address in Cabo San Lucas, Mexico. Plus, the friend told me where he was working in Cabo. The next knock on the subject's door in Cabo was not the tortilla delivery man but the process server. Surprise!

There are three lessons in that story. One, don't underestimate the power of a subpoena. Two, cell phone records are a great source of information. Without those cell phone records we wouldn't have found that subject. Three, don't forget to try the obvious first. Call your subject's friends, relatives, acquaintances, and neighbors.

Telephone directories, Internet search engines, pay databases: none of them keep up with people's movements as well as do relatives and close friends. If you can't find any relatives, then drive around the old neighborhood and knock on a few doors. If the doors you need to knock on are across the country, there's a way to do that, too.

Making Friends Cross Country

There are numerous free telephone searches on the Internet. They are for people whose time is worth less than a dollar. Nevertheless, we'll go over them, because a lot of folks out there think they can't afford a pay telephone directory service. By pay directory, I'm not talking about your *RBOC* directory. I can't afford that one either. But first the free ones.

def•i•ni•tion

RBOC stands for Regional Bell Operating Company. That is the generic term we'll use for all of the standard landline telephone companies, even though there are a number of independent companies and major carriers not associated with the Bell Companies. Corporations change, names change, one company gobbles up another, but we'll just call the landline carriers the RBOC.

Following is a list of websites that provide free "white page" searches. I'm not including sites that make you believe it's free and then refer you to other vendors who ask you to pay $14.95 for the search, though even these will forward you on to pay sites for more information on your subject. (In the next chapter, I'll give you three sites that might cost you as much as 25 cents for a search, although one is only 15 cents. That's a heck of a lot cheaper than $14.95.) When cruising these "free" searches, don't let yourself be scammed. I can't tell you how many times I've had clients spend hundreds and hundreds of dollars starting with these free searches. When they finally come to me and show me copies of the reports they've purchased off the Internet for $150, it breaks my heart to tell them I would have charged them $45 for the exact same information.

- www.argali.com (You have to download the program, but it's free and it searches multiple free sites at one time. Offers reverse-by-number or by-address, which is a big plus. Many private investigators use this as their main free site. You can pay $29.95 for the professional version, which comes without the sidebar of ads that the free version has.)

- www.whitepages.com

- www.msn.com (powered by whitepages.com)

- www.superpages.com (Verizon sponsored, powered by whitepages.com)

- www.anywho.com (AT&T, reverse lookups)

- www.dexonline.com (Qwest)

- www.switchboard.com (data by Acxiom, reverse lookups)

- www.infospace.com (This infospace search does have one nice feature: reverse lookups. After you get your results, you can "find neighbors" with one easy click.)

- www.canada411.com

- www.btcbahamas.com (Bahamas white and yellow pages by the Bahamas Telephone Company)

- www.phonevalidator.com (A brand new phone search by Crime Time Publishing. One of the best searches for determining if the phone is a cell- or landline, the cell provider, city of origin, and a reverse search powered by whitepages.com.)

I hesitate to suggest which of the above are the best. Try them out yourself by testing them on your own name and your own phone number for the reverse searches. You'll figure out pretty quickly which search algorithm works best.

In searching these or other databases, free or pay, sometimes less is better. For example, for a free search, Anywho.com works pretty well. But when I search it by my complete name and zip, it didn't find me. Use the reverse number search and it finds me right off. Input only the first initial of my first name (S) and my last name and it found both of my listed numbers with my complete name. So if you're getting negative results, try providing less information. You might get more back.

The search at www.phonevalidator.com is a good place to start for reverse searches because you'll know right off if the number is a cell phone or a landline. If you're a professional investigator and want to subpoena phone records, the service provider for the number in question is provided, and that's where you're going to want to send the subpoena.

Maybe your subject moved six months ago and you don't know where. Try the neighbors. Argali.com and Infospace.com have searches where you can input an address and find listings for neighbors on that same street. Also, the three pay sites I'm going to recommend in Chapter 5 have that same feature. This is a great tool, so don't overlook it. Just call up a neighbor and see if they know your subject. If the next-door neighbor doesn't know him, try the one across the street. How do you know who is next-door and who is across the street? Look at the addresses. Almost universally, odd number houses are on one side of the street and even numbers on the other. You'll be surprised how often neighbors not only know them, but know where they've moved to.

Another way to use these databases is to find the owner of the residence where your subject lived and contact that owner. If the house was rented, then search these databases by address and find the telephone number for the new tenant. Ask them who their landlord is and get the landlord's phone number. I've had good success contacting previous landlords via this method and obtaining the forwarding address. Sometimes the former landlord is a relative, and I always ask that question up front. If the landlord is a relative, you may want to use a different pretext to solicit the information you want.

Alternate Light Source

Before you contact the former landlord, have a good reason for asking for the updated address information. Collecting a bill probably won't get you any information. But if it's an adoption matter, then you'll almost always get it. So plan ahead what you're going to say.

Use the Spouse

If your subject has an uncommon name, consider yourself lucky. A general database search by name may well turn them up. But if you're looking for Steven Brown, you're going to need to have a middle initial and some other data to help you filter all of the S. Browns down to the one you want. But don't give up, there is hope. Many of these free searches list the phone in both of the spouses' names. If you know Steve Brown married Melanie Brown, you might find a listing for Steven and Melanie Brown. There's a good chance you've just found your subject.

In working surveillance on family law cases, sometimes our client's mouth is larger than their brain and they tell their spouse that they've hired a private investigator. I know that sounds stupid, but you'd be surprised how often that happens. Now what does this have to do with skip tracing? Well, when our subject of the surveillance becomes very surveillance-conscious, then we move the surveillance off the subject and put the surveillance on the girlfriend. The end result is the same. We catch them at the motel.

The same principle applies to skip tracing. Maybe you can't find your subject, so stop looking for him. Instead, use these databases to track down his girlfriend or relatives. Remember, the girlfriend, the ex-spouse, and the relatives all will know where he is. They may not tell you, but they'll know and often they will lead you right to him. More than once we'd been looking for a skip, called a relative, and the skip answered the phone.

The Most Accessible Free Public Database

If your subject is a deadbeat, she may not own any real property. Lots of people don't. But lots of people do. In the example above, as soon as the investigator gave me his subject's name I accessed the property appraiser's records in St. Johns County, Florida. I keep all of the Florida property appraiser's websites handy for quick reference (in a folder in My Favorites in a web browser). As we talked, I searched his name (which was not an uncommon name) and found a listing for the property. I knew this was our guy because the property was in both his and his wife's names. Let's call them Richard and Deborah. Some property appraiser's websites are updated daily, some monthly, and some only annually. Normally the website will tell you. If not, then call and ask.

How do you find the local county property appraiser's website? Go to any major search engine and put in the criteria for the search: "Property Appraiser St. Johns County Florida", for example. Now don't click on the first item returned. Usually the first returns at the top of the page are paid listings. Don't bother with them. Look at the URLs. Look for ones that end in "dot US" or "dot gov," or "dot state name dot US."

Most property appraiser's websites offer searches. Not all county property appraiser's search sites are created equal. You can almost always search by name, but sometimes you have to have the parcel number. Usually, you can search by property address as well. Searching property appraiser's records is also a good way to find the landlord of your subject if you need to. If you can't find your subject there, well, what has it cost you? Nothing.

The other great public record search that we'll talk more about in Chapter 6, is the Official Records. Even if the property appraiser's records aren't up-to-the-minute, the Official Records (OR) are, and many, many clerks of the court offer free OR searches from the couch in front of your television.

The Least You Need to Know

- ◆ Query old friends and associates to gather information on your subject before you begin your search.

- ◆ Free white page Internet sites make for good searches, but their data is not up to date.

- ◆ Use the white page searches to find neighbors of your subject. It's effective and free.

- ◆ When skip tracing a person, try locating their relatives instead. Often a relative will tell you where they are or at least forward a message to them.

- ◆ The property appraiser's website usually allows searches by name and is a quick way to locate somebody.

Skip Tracing: Advanced Techniques

In This Chapter

◆ Determining if your subject is dead or alive

◆ Locating prison inmates

◆ Restoring the truncated Social Security number

◆ You're in the Army now: military locators

◆ Finding an e-mail address for your first love

Skip tracing is as much an art as a science. When you're trying to locate somebody, you assemble as much data as you can on the person and then search the logical places. There is a big difference between looking for somebody that you've only lost contact with and looking for somebody who is actually a skip, meaning someone who is intentionally hiding (perhaps from creditors) or who has some reason to keep their whereabouts a secret.

Old high school friends would probably like to find you as much as vice versa. They're not hiding their identity. They haven't put their phone in somebody else's name, and their mail goes to their home address, not some *private mailbox*.

If a person is really on the run, it's highly unlikely you'll find his or her current where-abouts on the free Internet sites. Professional pay sites are a different matter. If some-one owes you money, if you're going to make money by finding the owner of vacant property before it goes to foreclosure sale, or if your time is valuable, read the rest of this chapter and do it yourself for next to nothing, or you can pay someone like me big bucks to find them for you.

def•i•ni•tion

Private mailboxes are commercial establishments, such as the UPS Store. Mail is deliv-ered to their business and then put into a box setup, much like post office boxes at the U.S. Post Office. In addition to the regular street address and box number, for a private mailbox the address is supposed to contain the initials "PMB" (private mail box).

As I mentioned in Chapter 1, if you're going to be a do-it-yourselfer PI or become a professional PI, then you have to "think outside the box," or "sideways." Most folks, when attempting to locate someone, think only of telephone directory information, whether it's on the Internet or on the telephone dial. Due to so many telemarketing campaigns and a growing desire for more privacy, it's becoming more and more popu-lar to have a phone number that is either nonpublished or nonlisted. If you only uti-lize telephone databases, you're out of luck. However, the pay telephone sites I listed in Chapter 4 might show your subject's address even if the phone is nonpublished, just not the phone number. That might be all you need. Also, they have some features that will actually reverse a nonpublished number for you. You have the nonpub number but don't know who it is listed to? Try www.masterfiles.com or SkipSmasher.com or Tracersinfo.com.

There are lots of other databases where people show up. Use them.

Wanted Dead or Alive—Searching the Death Master File

Is the person you are seeking a birth parent, someone who's age you're unsure of and who might be elderly? It's possible he or she is already deceased and you don't know it. It would be a good idea to check that out first before spending a lot of time and money searching for him or her elsewhere.

There are lots of sites on the Internet where you can search something known as the Social Security Death Master File. Some sites will let you search it for free. Others, of course, want you to pay. As in any database search, you need to know exactly what records are being searched and when they were last updated. The Social Security Administration sells that part of its data, and it's not cheap.

I had a new client from another state call me just this week. He asked me to locate a cousin of his that he hadn't heard from for several years. He had her last known address and telephone number, but couldn't locate her through directory information or find anything current about her by using the free white-page searches on the Internet.

I quoted him a minimum price of $250, which he agreed to, and I set about searching for her. First, I called the number he'd given me, and sure enough, it was disconnected. There were lots of directions I could have gone in trying to find her, but since he'd told me she was elderly and lived alone, I checked the Death Master File.

She was listed there. The Death Master File gave me her Social Security number; day, month, and year of death; and county of last known residence. I waited a few days to get back to the client because I didn't want him to think it was too easy. I called him and related the sad news. He could have saved himself $250 if he had bought this book and read it instead of calling me.

Keep in mind that this search is not all-inclusive, and the number of deaths listed before 1980 are not many compared to those after that date. For instance, my father, who died in 1975 and had a surviving spouse, is not listed. My mother, who died in 1988 and did not have a surviving spouse, is listed. Like any database, it is a resource that is not necessarily definitive in all directions. If the person you are looking for is there, then they are probably deceased. But, if their name is not listed, it doesn't mean they're not deceased, nor necessarily alive. It just means they're not in this database.

You can take any search engine and insert "Death Master File" in the search box. You'll get a list of websites that will run the search for you. Some are free, others want to charge as much as $49; several run in the $5 to $15 range. Even one of the best professional pay databases that I subscribe to charges $5 for this search. Many of the free ones are updated very infrequently. Likewise, the pay sites may only update their data every three months, and some only every year.

You can buy the search directly from the National Technical Information Service that handles the distribution of this data from the Social Security Administration. A password for unlimited searches will cost $995 a year. Ouch! A little steep you say? Well, you can buy 1,000 searches from them for just $600. Don't need a thousand searches?

The good news is that you can get the best search of the Social Security Death Master File for free at a site that is updated monthly. Interestingly, it's offered at two different sites, both owned by the same company, but the RootsWeb.com search is better than that of its counterpart, Ancestry.com.

Go to www.rootsweb.com. On the first page look under Search Engines and Databases. Click on the link to the Death Master File. This search is free and by far the best and most current that I've found anywhere. Don't ask me why, but we have done identical searches at both websites, and the RootsWeb.com site performs better. And it's free. It even performs better than the searches on our PI-friendly databases.

Searching the database is fairly straightforward. The more exact information you have, the better. With that said, it's also true that too much information is not good. For example, try searching for my mother, Brookie Bellamy Brown. If you search her full name, no hits are returned. However, if you search Brookie B. Brown, just using the initial for the middle name, you get a hit.

Her last residence is shown as Tempe, Arizona. That's not exactly right. While she did maintain a residence there, that is not where she was residing at the time of her death.

Any information that you receive from databases, whether they are free or you paid big bucks for them, must be looked at with a broad view. Sometimes the information is exactly right, but just as often, the "facts" returned may have part of the truth, but not necessarily all of it. Just as a good mariner doesn't rely on only one source for his navigational data, a good investigator will check the facts through multiple sources before testifying that they are accurate and complete.

The Social Security Master Death File will also return the correct date of birth and, drum roll please, the complete Social Security number of the deceased individual. Why might you want that? Well, suppose you're doing an estate search and need to find the relatives. Plug in the Social Security number of the deceased into one of your pay, PI-friendly databases and you'll get the past residences of the deceased, plus a list of individuals who shared those various residences with her. And you'll get a list of possible relatives.

Curing the Plague of Social Security Truncation

What is Social Security truncation? In 2004, Choice Point, a major data supplier, was scammed by several small clients. The clients were crooks and took thousands of identities from Choice Point data and used it, yep, you guessed it, for illegal gain. Choice Point reacted by deciding not to do business with small companies like most private investigative agencies, which were the foundation of the company. They decided their data was safer in the hands of large companies, like Enron, I suppose.

There were congressional hearings and all of the usual denunciations of big brother, etc. One of the fallouts of this Choice Point debacle was the truncation of Social Security numbers. By truncation, we mean that instead of reporting the complete nine digit number, Choice Point only reported the numbers like this, 123-45-XXXX.

As soon as they began truncating Social Security numbers (SSN), the other data suppliers worried about their liability and followed suit. Well, most, but not all.

The SSN is still a basic component of any skip trace search. The databases all rely on it, but won't reveal it completely to you.

Why do you need the SSN? You can search Steve Brown across the county by name and date of birth and you'll find me and a couple of thousand other Steve Browns. Then you'll have to do some more searching to figure out which one is me. And suppose you don't have my complete date of birth. You're dead in the water. But if you search for me using my Social Security number, you'll nail me the first time out. Probably.

I say probably because it's not unusual to see others associated with my or your Social Security number. How can that be? My son's credit file is sometimes mixed up with mine. Someone might be using my SSN for nefarious deeds. Or some clerk might have mistyped my SSN when I bought a car. Lots of ways for that to occur.

So what is the cure for the plague of truncation? The good news is that there are solutions and you don't even have to be a licensed PI to use some of them.

- One solution is the Death Master File, if your subject is deceased. Find the complete SSN there.

- Official records in your county clerk's office still have complete biographical data: name, date of birth, and SSN. However, note that many clerks are now redacting the SSN from the records that are publicly viewable on the Internet. You may still visit the clerk's office personally and view the complete record. This is more the case on more-recent records than on the older records. Find an old transaction and you'll probably find the complete SSN.

- Subscribe to PI-friendly databases that don't truncate (www.tracersinfo.com or www.skipsmasher.com). Tracersinfo.com has a nice feature that they call the Social Security Number Expander. Input the first five digits of the SSN (remember the last four digits have been truncated), and this search will take those five digits and return the complete SSN if it's in their database. The cost? A whopping ten cents.

◆ Driver's License Data. If you are a licensed PI, you fall under the exemptions provided by the DPPA (this is further explained in Chapter 6) and can go to your local DMV and see what they have on file for your subject. Usually the DMV will have the driver's SSN. Sometimes they won't want to give it to you, so be prepared with a copy of your state law that regulates the release of that information.

◆ PACER, the federal government database explained in Chapter 7 does not truncate SSNs like the rest of the world. PACER lops off the first five numbers and provides the last four. So, a clever person can obtain the first five from almost any database, search PACER, and if your subject has any sort of federal record (civil, criminal, or bankruptcy), you'll get the missing four numbers. Makes you wonder, doesn't it.

Go Directly to Jail, Do Not Pass Go, Do Not Collect $200

One of the unpleasant things you have to consider when searching for someone is the possibility that he or she has been incarcerated, whether in a federal facility, a state prison, or a county or city jail.

Elementary, My Dear Watson

In the spring of 2002, there were a few over 150,000 inmates housed in about 100 different federal detention facilities. The federal prison system only houses individuals convicted of federal crimes. According to the U.S. Department of Justice, Bureau of Justice Statistics, over 6.3 million people were on probation, parole, or housed in federal, state, or local jails at the end of 1999.

To find a federal prisoner, go to www.bop.gov. This is the Federal Bureau of Prisons website. On the left side of the screen, there's a hyperlink to Inmate Locator. Click on that link and there you can search by name. If you are at your computer as you read this, just for fun, search John Gotti or Martha Stewart and see what comes up. Have you ever wondered how old Martha Stewart is? Now you know.

These records not only show you everyone who is currently incarcerated, but also gives their anticipated release date and the institution where they're housed, the institution's address, and its telephone number. The database records date back to 1982 and should show anybody who has spent time in a federal prison since 1982, even if he or she is now released, like Martha Stewart.

I searched my own name and found 12 Steve Browns and 50 Steven Browns (and no, I've never spent the night in a federal prison), and even one Steven K. Brown who is currently incarcerated in the Middle District of Florida, where I live. So be sure and search all possible name variations for the person you are skip tracing.

This database won't show what the crime was that sent them to the federal penitentiary. I'll show you how to find that in Chapter 7.

If you're pretty sure the person is in jail but he or she doesn't show up in the federal prison database, then you'd need to start searching the state prisons and county jails.

You can go to www.corrections.com. At that website, put your mouse over the word "Resources" and click on Inmate Locator, which gives links to the various states and Los Angeles County that allow Internet access to information on the inmate population of their respective correctional institutions.

Many states will also allow you to search for individuals on *probation* and *parole* as well, not just those folks who are still locked behind bars. If you add parolees and probationers to your search, then you're considerably expanding the number of people in these databases. So, when searching the prison databases, don't overlook these options. The databases usually have a separate search or a button you have to click on to include the probation and parole population.

def•i•ni•tion

Probation indicates that a person was convicted of a crime, but rather than sentencing him or her to a jail term, probation is given to see if that person can not violate the law, stay employed, or any other terms of their probation given to them to follow over a specified time period. **Parole** means an individual was sentenced to and actually spent time in jail, but was released earlier than the original sentence called for. He or she also must not violate any conditions of their parole or they face having the parole revoked and being sent back to prison.

The information in the preceding list will certainly change. Most of the state web-based inmate locators work very well. Some states, such as Utah, only allow access to sex offenders, while the other states listed will let you search their entire prison population.

You're in the Army Now—Military Locators

Currently, no websites run by the military will allow the public access to the military locator databases. You can determine if your subject is in the active duty military. The federal government gives special exceptions and some civil relief to active duty military persons. There is a Service Members Civil Relief Act. You can search this site to determine if your subject is active duty military: www.dmdc.osd.mil/scra/owa/home. You will need your subject's complete Social Security number. Is that a catch-22? Government databases are truncating the SSN, but when you want to search them you have to provide the SSN in its entirety.

> ### Elementary, My Dear Watson
>
> In 1918 Congress passed an act known as The Soldiers' and Sailors' Civil Relief Act. It was rewritten and passed again in the 1940s. The act was designed to protect the rights of persons in the active duty military. After 9/11/2001 it was rewritten and signed into law by President Bush. (12/2003) Its new name is the Service Members Civil Relief Act. It provides for a ceiling on home interest rates to a 6 percent max on all FHA-approved loans. Not only home loans but credit card debt can be capped at 6 percent as well. It also provides that active duty persons can not be foreclosed upon or evicted, and it allows for the military families to break a lease if they need to. Often in foreclosure matters, the foreclosing institution is required to prove that the debtor is not on active duty. National Guard members who are called up to active duty are also protected under this act.

There is another method of obtaining a military person's location.

If you are a family member and have an emergency, you can call the numbers that follow and a representative of the specific branch will find your family member for you.

If you are a private investigator or nonfamily member, or a family member without an emergency, you can write to the following addresses, include a check for $3.50 (a fee set by Congress), and give the individual's name, Social Security number, and as much information as you have. Family members do not need to pay the $3.50.

The current exceptions to this method are the Coast Guard and the Navy. The Coast Guard might respond over the telephone and there is no fee. The Navy, due to current security considerations, will not respond, but will forward mail to the individual.

- Air Force
  HQ AFPC/MSMIDL 550 C St. W, Suite 50
  Randolph AFB, TX 78150-4752
  210-565-2660

◆ Army
As of this printing the Army's locator service has been discontinued.

◆ Coast Guard
Commandant
U.S. Coast Guard Personnel Command (C.G.P.C.)
2100 2nd St. SW
Washington, DC 20593-0001
202-493-1697
e-mail: CGlocator@Ballston.uscg.mil

◆ Marine Corps
USMC – CMC
HQMC – MMSB – 10
2008 Elliott Rd., Suite 201
Quantico, VA 22134-5030
703-784-3942

◆ Navy
Navy Personnel Command
PERS – 312
5720 Integrity Dr.
Millington, TN 38055-3120
901-874-3388

Alternate Light Source

Both the Social Security Administration and the IRS may forward a letter to an individual for humanitarian reasons or to inform them that they have money owed to them. Write the letter to the individual, place it in an unsealed envelope with first class postage on it, and then place that envelope in a larger one addressed to either …

Internal Revenue Service
Office of Disclosure Operations
1111 Constitution Avenue NW
Washington, DC 20224

or to:

Social Security Administration
Office of Public Inquiries
6401 Security Blvd.
Baltimore, MD 21235

If you're sending it to the Social Security Administration, include a check made payable to them for $3. I wouldn't hold my breath, but let me know if it works for you.

Putting It All Together

Here is your final exam. Like all of the examples in this book, it is true and from our case files. Now is your chance to test your knowledge of skip-tracing. I'll give you a clue. Be sure and read the chapters on searching courthouse records, and then come back and solve this skip-tracing case.

Mariah Sue, in 2004, needed a new place to live. She had two small sons, was working, and was making a pretty good living. Mariah saw a one-bedroom condominium that she found attractive. It was clean, had a community swimming pool, and was close to work. The owner, let's name her Peggy Ferrar, owned several of these condos and rented them all.

Mariah Sue gave Peggy a check for $2,100 as a deposit to hold the condo for a few days until she could make up her mind if she wanted it for sure. Peggy, said, fine, no problem, if Mariah Sue didn't want the condo, she should call her and let her know within seven days.

Three days later Mariah decided that a one-bedroom condo was too small for her and two boys and called Peggy. Peggy wasn't home and Mariah left her a message on the recorder informing Peggy of her change of mind and requested that she tear up the deposit check.

Fast forward to 2006. Two sheriff's deputies show up at an old address of Mariah's to arrest her on a worthless check charge of $2,100. The people at the old address know Mariah and call her, but don't tell the deputies where she is.

Mariah checks with the district attorney's office by telephone and verifies that there is a warrant for her arrest, and she needs to bring either the $2,100 plus costs down to their office or a receipt from Peggy Ferrar showing that it has been paid.

Mariah is beside herself trying to reach Peggy, but the number she had for her has been disconnected. She tries the telephone directory information but can't find a listing for her. Peggy was an older lady and Mariah is thinking perhaps she is dead. She calls the State Bureau of Vital Records and pays them $30 to search the death records for the last three years plus a $25 rush fee. They promise to mail her the search results within two weeks. Meanwhile, she's drumming her fingers, waiting for the sheriff's ominous knock on her front door.

Okay, now you have the facts. Using what you've learned, how would you find Peggy Ferrar?

As we learned at the beginning of this chapter, there is a quicker and free way to determine if Peggy has passed on, unless it happened within the last few months. So you are correct. First, you'd search the Social Security Death Master File.

You search the Death Master File and it's negative. Okay, what next? In the county that Mariah Sue lived, she could have gone online to the county property appraiser's website and searched by address the ownership of the property she was going to rent. That's what I did.

The property records showed the address was owned by Frank Ferrar and June M. Ferrar. I presumed the middle initial "M" in June's name probably stood for Margaret and Peggy, as we learned in Chapter 5, is a nickname for Margaret.

I went to www.555-1212.com, but you could have also gone to www.masterfiles.com and searched for Frank Ferrar. There was a listing for him at an address close to the condo that Mariah was going to rent. Just for fun, I went back to the property appraiser's records and checked the ownership of that address as well. It showed Frank and June M. owned that property, too.

In less than 30 minutes I'd found Peggy for Mariah Sue. The total cost was one search at www.555-1212.com or www.masterfiles.com. Again for giggles, I searched the free white page listings on the Internet and found the Ferrar family was also listed in the free sections we've talked about. So it could have been a totally free search.

As it turned it out, just in case you're interested, Mrs. Ferrar was not about to forgive the debt and insisted that Mariah Sue bring the money over to her right away. That was an expensive lesson for Mariah, but it could have been a little less expensive if she'd read this book first.

The Least You Need to Know

- The Social Security Administration has maintained a database of deceased individuals, known as the Death Master File, since 1980.

- The Federal Bureau of Prisons has a prisoner locator database, and some states have websites that allow searching the inmate, parole, and probation population.

- Many databases and public record internet sites truncate a person's Social Security number. Often the original record when viewed at the clerk's office is not redacted and the complete number is present.

- Some PI-friendly databases truncate SSNs. Others do not, and TracersInfo has an SSN expander that allows you to input the last four numbers of the SSN and returns the complete number.

- The Defense Manpower Agency has a website that will allow you to search a name and Social Security number to determine if your subject is active duty military.

- Using a little common sense and knowing what databases are available can save you time and money and maybe even keep you out of jail.

Chapter 6

The Whys and Wherefores of Public Records

In This Chapter

- ◆ Using the secretary of state records to find that missing person
- ◆ Obtaining access to state occupational licenses and the information they provide
- ◆ The nitty-gritty of the Driver's Privacy Protection Act
- ◆ Private books and the public library

In an industrialized culture, society lives and dies by its records. Governments control their people by tracking them. They use a census for planning purposes: watching changes in living habits and making sure that every person is taxed appropriately.

The various governments—federal, state, and local—have a mountain of records on each of us. Some of these records are open to the public and some are not. We're all familiar with birth certificates, marriage licenses, driver's licenses, and death certificates. But you may not be acquainted with the multitude of other public records that are accessible to you.

Why Should You Care About Public Records?

Are you asking yourself right now, "Why should I care about public records?"

When a 25-year-old plumber came to me and wanted help in finding his girlfriend, I was a little wary. He explained that his girlfriend lived with her parents and they had moved to another part of the city and wouldn't tell him where. When I asked how old the girlfriend was, he told me she was 16.

In taking cases, I don't usually make moral judgments. I guess it's sort of like being a prostitute; I pimp my services to the highest bidder. There are exceptions, though, and I do have my standards, popular conception not withstanding.

I told the plumber to take his money someplace else. Having teenage daughters myself at the time, I could understand the forces of love for a daughter that would make the parents move the family across town in order to keep her away from this older guy. Me? I would have had him charged with statutory rape, but …. The reality was, if this guy had read this chapter, he could have found them without my help, but I didn't tell him that.

Are you seriously dating somebody? You'd better read this and the next chapter to understand how the records system works so when you get to Chapter 21, you'll know how to run a background check on your bride- or husband-to-be.

And what kind of information, you may wonder, is actually out there?

State Records

States maintain a variety of records that are valuable for background investigations. There will be variations between states as to how the records are organized and where you can locate them, but for the most part, they will follow what we'll set out here.

Corporate Records

Most states maintain records of companies incorporated at the secretary of state's office, division of corporations. In these records you can find the names of the officers and directors of a corporation. Typically the *registered agent* is identified and the physical address of the corporation is given.

Why would we care about the officers of some corporation? Suppose you are looking for Steve Brown in Florida. You might just go online from the computer in your bedroom during a TV commercial break and pull up the Florida secretary of state's website. There you might find your man in a matter of a few keystrokes before the game starts again.

Most of these secretary of state corporate-record websites can be searched by the name of the corporation or by individuals associated with the corporation.

def•i•ni•tion

A **registered agent** is an individual who agrees to be available to accept service, subpoenas, or other legal documents for a corporation. In the event you need to sue a corporation, your attorney will have to physically serve the lawsuit to the registered agent, the person who will accept notice of the suit on behalf of the corporation.

Go to www.sunbiz.org, which is the Florida secretary of state website. The top item on the "Popular Links" on the left hand side (Online searches and document images) will take you to their search area for Corporations, Trademarks, Limited Partnerships, and a host of other options. Click on Officer, Registered Agent Name List, and the search window comes up. Type in Brown, Steven K., and 14 of the first 17 listings that come up are corporations that I've had some affiliation with. If you're actually doing the search and were wondering, no, I never ran a wedding business. That's a lot easier than searching all of the 250 Steven Brown listings on white-page directories, as we saw in Chapter 4.

Of course, if you don't know my middle initial, than you'll have to wade through about 175 listings in the corporate records. Maybe there's a better search if you're trying to find me.

Professional and Occupational Licenses

Many people work in professions that require some sort of state license, from PIs to hairdressers, to nurses, to massage therapists. It's good to know how to check the various state Internet sites and find those licensees. The person you're looking for might be there.

Let's see. You talked to an old high school chum, as I suggested in Chapter 4, and he told you, sure, he remembered Steve Brown. Brown was in the FBI for a while, and last he heard, he'd left the bureau and was running a PI firm somewhere down in Florida. But for the life of him, he couldn't remember where in Florida.

So you go back to another state directory, www.myflorida.com. At the top of that page click on "Find an Agency." Up pops a list of agencies. In that list you'll see the word "Agriculture". This is where you'll find your licensed private investigators in Florida. Us and the rest of the fruits in the state. In Florida, it seems that each state agency now needs to have its very own website, so you'll have to follow the link there to the Department of Agriculture website (www.doacs.state.fl.us). But if you're persistent you'll find us. Click on the link that says "Licensing Permits Reg." and you'll find us private investigators listed right on the same list with pathogens, pigs, pests, and plant seeds. Makes one wonder, doesn't it? Maybe government for once has us classified where we belong. I've never been called a pathogen, but I have been called a pest more than once.

While you're there browsing through the oranges and grapefruits, if you click on "Licensing Home" you'll be able to search for an individual PI or an agency. Turns out that today, I'm the only Steven Brown in the entire state of Florida that is a PI. Well, you found me. But what's that? Oh, darn, you click on my name and a notice appears that says "RESTRICTED. The home address and telephone number for this individual is restricted from public record in accordance with the Public Records Act, Section 119.07(3)(i) F.S." The state of Florida is kind enough not to publish a private investigator's home address and telephone number, thank you very much. This keeps the irate husbands from knocking on my front door. Of course, if they really wanted to find me I'm dead meat, because all they have to do is read the rest of this chapter and any dummy could figure out how.

But perhaps the person you're looking for is a massage therapist, or a nurse, or a doctor, or a body wrapper. The information is all there for you to see. You can go to the Department of Health and search all of the preceding professions by name. It's a great way to find somebody and a very good way to determine if the professional person you're going to see is actually licensed.

Remember, these state sites, like all Internet sites, are prone to changing their menus. So if you don't immediately see what you're searching for, look around the site a little, explore it until you do find it.

> **Elementary, My Dear Watson**
>
> There is much talk lately about identity theft and how to safeguard your Social Security number. The truth is, your Social Security number used to be pretty much a public number. It could be found in your voter's registration information, which is public. You give it out to banks, telephone companies, utility companies, and credit card companies. Eight states used to use the Social Security number as the driver's license number.
>
> But states are now redacting Social Security numbers from public records. Identity theft is a problem if it involves your bank account. It creates a hassle for the victim, but the end result is not usually a large monetary loss for the private citizen. That's because if a bank honored a forged check, then once you sign the forgery complaint they should return the money to your account. And surprise, identity theft cases involving your bank account are usually committed by a relative.
>
> Although credit card companies heavily advertise about identity theft, the real victim is the merchant who provided the goods and services.
>
> Identity theft is a problem for merchants because of the charge-backs from the credit card companies. The merchants may lose big bucks. Your liability for illicit charges on your credit card is only $50. Getting the credit bureaus to straighten out your credit history is another story. The bottom line is, a theft of your identity doesn't usually create a huge liability for you the individual, just a huge nuisance.

Driver's Licenses

Every state issues driver's licenses. The information on a driver's license usually includes the name, address, date of birth, some descriptive information such as height and color of eyes and hair, and previously the person's Social Security number. But that is appearing less frequently. The number usually is in the state driver's license records, however. So if you can access the records, you can usually get the number. Different states have different procedures.

Driver's license information is still one of the single best sources for identification purposes. But frankly, as John Q Private Citizen, it probably is no longer available to you. The Driver's Privacy Protection Act (DPPA) pretty well limits driver's license information to government agencies and licensed private investigators, which has posed a problem to some PIs in states that don't issue PI licenses. Sort of a catch-22 for private investigators in those states. So if you need the DL information because you can't find your subject's identifying information anywhere else, hire a PI to get it for you.

Many database searches require basic data on the person you are searching for besides just a name. You'll need, at the very least, a date of birth and/or Social Security number.

So how do you do that? Easy. Remember the lesson on wild card searches in Chapter 6. With some of the pay databases that we'll discuss in Chapter 9, you can use a wild card search with the driver's license information database and almost always get the Social Security number and date of birth you'll need to search other databases. You may have to remove the truncation of the Social Security number which was done by the data supplier, but we showed you how to do that in Chapter 6.

The Division of Licensing

Most of us have neighbors or friends who work for a police agency. Don't be tempted to ask your police friend to pull someone's driver's license information for you. You'd be asking him to violate several laws, including theft of information, and he'd be guilty of a direct violation of the DPPA (Driver's Privacy Protection Act), which has criminal penalties for this kind of behavior. You and your police friend could be convicted criminally and fined, and your friend would certainly be fired.

Driver's license information is good information. It is almost universally helpful in locating someone or in helping to verify that you have found the right Steve Brown. Most states have laws that require drivers who are licensed in the state to report a change of address to their DMV within 10 to 30 days of a change. Not everybody reports their new address to the DMV, but when they don't, are in violation of their state's statutes. At least every few years when the license is renewed, the newest address is probably used.

Also note that states discourage the use of a post office box or postal mailbox (the kind in those postal packaging stores) as an address on a driver's license. Therefore, if you can legally get this information, at least you will have a physical address from where you can begin your search.

Getting driver's license information is becoming more difficult. You will probably have to go to a professional PI to get it for you. But if you're planning on becoming a PI, you should subscribe to one of the providers we'll talk about in Chapter 8. A PI shouldn't charge you any more than $45 for driver's license information. If he's a professional, he should make sure the use is in compliance with the DPPA, or else he leaves himself open to a civil damage suit including actual damages (set by the statute as a minimum of $2,500), punitive damages, and attorney fees.

Elementary, My Dear Watson

In 1989, Robert John Bardo hired a private investigator to get the home address of actress Rebecca Schaffer, who at that time played on the television sitcom *My Sister Sam*. The PI got the information from the California Department of Motor Vehicles (DMV) and sold it to Bardo. Schaffer was expecting Francis Ford Coppola to come to her door to discuss an audition for his film, *Godfather III*. When the bell rang, Schaffer opened the door and found Bardo there instead. She asked him to leave and closed the door. Bardo went away but returned very upset. He rang again but hid so that Schaffer had to step out of the apartment to see who was there. Bardo shot her once in the chest and fled.

As a result of this incident, the U.S. Congress passed the Driver's Privacy Protection Act. This act prohibits the release of information pertaining to driver's licenses, but included 14 specific exceptions. Licensed private investigators are listed as exception number eight, as long as the information is used for one of the other 13 reasons.

The bottom line is you can no longer walk up to your local DMV and request this information that used to be publicly available.

Driving History

Most states will allow you to have a copy of your own driving record. This will require a trip to your local DMV office, showing some identification, and paying a small fee. If you want the driving history of somebody other than yourself or somebody in another state, again you will need to hire a professional PI who has legitimate access to this information. States do sell driving history information, but usually only in bulk to resellers. Resellers buy this information from the state and sell it primarily to insurance companies and large trucking firms. They download the information from the state daily, which means thousands and thousands of records. The entire department of motor vehicles record database is downloaded or purchased on tape every day. Because of some irregularities they've encountered in reselling the information to private investigators, the resellers almost entirely refuse to provide it to PIs anymore, even though there is a specific exemption in the law for private investigators.

Consequently, these records are now even harder to get than the driver's license information, and not all PIs subscribe to the services that provide this. I wish I had better news about obtaining DMV information, but the Driver's Privacy Protection Act has put the squeeze on it. It is available from these resellers to properly documented pre-employment background-screening companies.

The Division of Licensing _____

Beware, if you're a PI and you're selling this information, you could get busted. Some states like Pennsylvania run tests, sort of undercover stings, to see if their information is being sold without proper safeguards. The state of Pennsylvania canceled its contract with one reseller, who had sold this information to a PI firm, who in turn sold it unknowingly to an undercover state operative testing various websites. Many of the resellers are no longer providing this information to private investigators because these PIs sold this information through their websites without verifying their clients' identity or permissible use. Nevertheless, a good PI will have his sources and be able to get it for you. The cost will probably be in the $25 range over the price of the state fee. The state fees vary from less than $3 to more than $15.

State Records on the Web

As you read in a preceding section, many states have some of their records available for free on the Internet. Your local counties are getting online big time, more so than even your state governments. Get your wallet out, though, because some states and counties are charging for access to their records via the Internet and generating revenue. The process of searching county records online is in the midst of a big change as this book is written. In a few years, the counties will probably find what works best for them and you, their client, and most will likely be pretty standardized. They'll probably polarize at one extreme or the other, pay or free. Often what you'll see is a free search for records, but if you want to actually view the record or a summary of the records, then you'll need to pull out the plastic.

Alternate Light Source _____

Before paying a PI to run a search for you, use the search engine skills you developed in Chapters 5 and 6 to see if what you are looking for is now available on the Internet. More states and counties are coming online everyday.

A fellow named Marty called me and wanted to check a potential tenant's criminal record. The rental unit was in a garage apartment attached to his house and he wanted to make sure the applicant wasn't an ax murderer or worse. The prospective tenant had recently arrived in Florida from Colorado.

Until just recently, Colorado would provide a statewide criminal search as long as we'd mail a letter requesting the information with a prepayment. We'd wait three to five days for the request to be processed and then mailed back to us, which was a pretty decent system compared to many states. But Marty was in a hurry. You can still use the mail system if you want, but what many states are doing now is quicker and cheaper.

We hadn't checked any criminal records in Colorado for a while, so before going through the laborious process of dictating the letter, waiting for my secretary to type it, writing out the check, and waiting until the next day for it go out, I did a little searching on the web.

Guess what? Now all you need to do for Colorado criminal records is go to www. cocourts.com. For a $6 fee, you can access up-to-the-minute information on the complete Colorado court system—every criminal court, including both *misdemeanor* and *felony* charges, is searched in every county with one click of the mouse. It might not show arrests if the charges were dropped, but if the case made it to court, it should be there. Marty paid $45 for that search. He could have paid $6 and done it himself just as quickly as I did. But at $45, it was still a bargain. As you'll see, many other states are coming online with statewide or nearly statewide searches. The administrator of courts in many states is pushing for online access to current and archived data. In Marty's case, the tenant had no felony or misdemeanor record in Colorado. Marty can sleep better knowing the guy sleeping in his garage is not an axe murderer.

def·i·ni·tion

Criminal offenses are categorized according to the severity of the offense. Less-serious crimes, those typically involving a potential penalty of less than one year, are called **misdemeanors**. Crimes that are punishable by a one-year jail term or longer are called **felonies**.

A particularly useful site that you might want to bookmark is www.brbpub.com, run by BRB Publications Inc. Look under "Free Resources" and you'll see a link to "Free Public Record Sites." This is a great place to start your search. You won't find the Colorado court site as I described in the preceding section because it's not a free site, so that simply highlights the need to conduct your own search.

BRB also sells books in the genre of searching public records. You can browse its catalog at the same website.

The Sourcebook to Public Records

Things are changing so fast in the public-record-search area that before the books can even get printed, they are out-of-date. That being said, many of the sites they list will still be functional. The brand-new ones just won't be listed.

There is one book that is essential to have if you are in the business of doing records checks. This book is the *Sourcebook to Public Record Information* published by the folks with BRB. We'll talk about the *Sourcebook* in greater detail in Chapter 21 when we go step-by-step through the process of checking a person's background.

The *Sourcebook*'s current price is $87.95, and the seventh edition of the book is over 1,900 pages of fine print. It weighs about 6 pounds, so make sure you've been working out and gotten buff before picking it up. They do have a web-based version with an annual subscription price of $119.00, or you can buy it monthly as well.

The book tells you where to look for the records you need in each county, state, or federal jurisdiction, as well as how much the record will cost and the hoops you have to jump through to get what you're looking for. It also lists the websites for the various state agencies and county clerks. And the web version, of course, provides the links so you can click your way right into the court system in hundreds of counties around the country.

Federal courts fall into districts, as explained in Chapter 7. The federal records section of the book sorts by state and county. You'll be able to find your county and tell under which federal district and bankruptcy court it falls.

The Canadian section tells you how to get a Canadian driving and criminal history. It also lists more than 200 Canadian universities.

Public Libraries and Private Books

You don't have Internet access, you don't want Internet access, and you don't own or even want a computer. But you do live within the boundaries of the United States or Canada. Chances are, then, you have Internet access and don't even know it.

Your public library probably has computers already online and logged onto the Internet. Using the public library's computers, you can take advantage of all the information in this chapter, the preceding ones, and those that follow. But your library also has other reference books that are invaluable resources.

The two main resources a private investigator uses at the library for skip tracing are, first, the *criss-cross directory* (also known as the *reverse directory*, or the *city directory*). Second, you'd be surprised how useful old telephone directories are.

The main branch of larger library systems have telephone books for not only their own city but for major cities around the country, and also for many other towns within your own state.

If you have a telephone number or street address located in a town other than your own, call the library in that town and ask for the reference desk. If you're polite, the reference desk librarian will look up the address, name, or telephone number you give them in the local criss-cross directory and give you the information. I've never had one refuse a request yet. But then, I'm a nice guy.

The library probably has the telephone directory for your town going back 10 years, or sometimes longer. When skip tracing someone whose address you have is no longer valid, you can look in the library's old telephone books and find out when, within the parameter of a year or so, your subject moved. Next, go to the criss-cross directory and identify the neighbors who lived there when your subject did. Use the current criss-cross to see if any of those neighbors are still living there, and go out and talk to them. They may well remember your subject and might be able to tell you where he or she moved to, and possibly even an employer's name. See Chapter 11, which deals with this in greater depth.

def•i•ni•tion

Criss-cross directories, sometimes called **reverse** or **city directories,** are privately published by Cole, Polk, Donnelly, and others. These directories sort their listings by name, address, and telephone number. You can take a telephone number, check it in the "reverse" listing, and find the subscriber information. Likewise, you can search the directory for an address within the city, and it will give you the person living there and the phone number.

Frequently, these directories give additional information about the person living at a residence, such as how long he or she has lived there, how many people live in the residence, their occupations, and income level. Not all city directories give all of that information; it depends upon the publisher and their research efforts. So if you only have one phone number to check, and don't want to subscribe to either 555-1212. com or the Reach Directory, then try the criss-cross at your library.

Think you know the public library? Think again. Did you know that many libraries have access to pay databases that you can access from home by typing in your library card number? That's right. Databases like Ancestry.com and Thompson-Gale, Criss-Cross directories, and dozens more that most private people have to pay for. Well, your library pays that for you and most of those you can access from your home computer. Sometimes you'll have to access them from the libraries' public computers.

Normally, from your home computer, you'll go to your local library's website and then access the pay sites for free through the library's website. The login will ask for your library card number and bingo! You're in. So check with your reference librarian as to what private "pay" databases they make public to you. You'll be surprised and can even save a buck or two.

Alternate Light Source

In Chapters 12 and 13 we mention not to be distracted on surveillance by reading a book or magazine. Well, many libraries subscribe to www.netlibrary.com. There you can download audio books for free to your portable device and listen to them. Just like listening to a book on tape or CD, only if you're hiding discreetly in the back of a surveillance van you can't have the CD blasting away. But a pair of earphones and a portable player device work great. The device has to be compatible with Windows Media Audio and play WMA files. Sorry, not mp3, as it won't work with your iPod.

The Least You Need to Know

- Secretary of state records are usually public and include officers and directors of corporations.

- State records frequently include license information for professions in medicine, nursing, private investigating, and almost every other occupation licensed by the state.

- Driver's license information is increasingly difficult to get. Your best bet is probably through a licensed PI.

- The library has useful reference books such as criss-cross or reverse directories and old telephone books. You can call a library reference desk in another city and someone will probably look up the information you need.

- The library frequently pays the subscription price to expensive pay databases and you can access them for free. Just as often as not, you can do so from your home computer by using the number on your library card.

Chapter 7

Prowling the Courthouse

In This Chapter

- Locating property-transaction records
- Understanding the lower and higher court system
- Learning how to search for local criminal records
- Examining the federal system
- Obtaining computer access to federal case indexes
- The ins and outs of the bankruptcy court
- Use official records to cancel your alimony obligations

Christine called me last week. She and her boyfriend are getting married soon. The problem is, he's not divorced yet from his first wife. They've been separated for four years but no divorce, hence they've never agreed to any formal alimony or child-support settlements. The soon-to-be ex-wife is asking for more money than Christine thinks she's entitled to. Christine, being no dummy, knows money out of the fiancé's pocket means less money for her.

She wanted to know how much the ex-wife was paying each month in mortgage payments. Christine thought the ex-wife had grossly inflated the figure to bump up the child-support payments. Proof of a lower mortgage payment would result in lower support payments.

I actually was kind of rooting for the kids in this case, but I don't make up the facts, I just report them. So in Christine's case I shrugged my shoulders and took her American Express credit card number over the telephone. She could have saved herself $225 if she'd read this chapter.

> ### Elementary, My Dear Watson
>
> State courts bear a tremendous load when it comes to handling cases. There are approximately 30 million cases filed a year in the U.S. state court system. On the other hand, there are about one million cases filed per year in the federal system. Of those federal cases, about 70 percent are bankruptcies, 20 percent civil cases, and 10 percent criminal.

Need other reasons to read this chapter? Have you ever bought a house? Or might you buy a house in the future? If so, if you're smart, you will want to know how much the seller paid for it, and how much he still owes on his house, before you make your offer. You don't *have* to know those facts, but knowledge is power. Your realtor probably won't know or won't think to tell you if she does. If you've done your research and know the seller has a gazillon dollars worth of equity in the house, then you can submit a low-ball offer and he may just accept it. If you know the house is free and clear, you may ask the seller to finance the house for you instead of using conventional financing.

But if the house has a first, second, and third mortgage recorded on it, the seller probably needs every penny out of the house he can get. On the other hand, though, you also know he is probably desperate to sell since he's making three mortgage payments. Desperation equals lower prices, and if he can't lower the price because there is no equity in the house, he might throw in that riding lawnmower or the pressure washer you saw in the shed out back because he has to get the house sold now.

Have you ever thought about going into business with a partner, a buddy from work maybe? You'd better find out if he has any judgments against him before you sign those partnership agreements. Merrill-Lynch had a slogan that said, "Investigate, then invest." That's still good advice.

Or how about you are paying alimony to an ex-spouse: the alimony is supposed to end upon remarriage of the spouse. She's been dating the same guy for a year, moved in with him, but you're still shelling out the big bucks each month. Now, ladies, don't get peeved with me. More and more of you women are paying alimony to those wimpy ex-husbands so this works for the fairer sex, too.

Ex-spouses remarry all the time without telling their former spouse. And they cohabitate without remarrying thinking that they can continue to collect the alimony without recourse as long as they aren't legally wedded. Well, surprise! Many states have laws that will allow for the reduction or withdrawal of alimony if the receiving spouse cohabitates and receives substantial sustenance from her common-law husband. So read this chapter carefully if any of the above pertains to you and I'll show you how to cut that heavy burden.

The Local County Courthouse

There are four main areas of interest for investigators in the county courthouse, not including the courtrooms where you'll be called upon to testify. We'll cover your testimony in court in Chapter 24. The areas we want to look at are sometimes called different names in different counties, but every county has them.

Making the Official Records Speak

For some reason, searching the official records seems to confuse a lot of my investigator interns. I think they feel it is a waste of time and they should be out on the street following somebody. A good private investigator knows the courthouse and all of its nooks and crannies, inside and out.

Don't just think "databases" and leave your courthouse searching to the computer. You need to understand how the record system works in the courts where you're doing the research. Pay databases are great, but you need to develop calluses from flipping through files to really know your local court system.

Official records are those records that are recorded at the courthouse for all the public to see. By "recorded," we mean the document is entered into the official records in a particular book and on a certain page. In the pre-computer era, a notation was handwritten into a large ledger-type book saying, for example, a certain mortgage from such-and-such a lender was recorded against a particular piece of *real property*.

def•i•ni•tion

Real property is described as anything that is not personal property. Real property is anything that is a part of the earth or attached thereto which can not be easily moved. Think dirt.

The existence of this mortgage was physically entered into a book on a particular page number. An index was made somewhat alphabetically and you could hand search those indexes by year to see if there was a mortgage recorded or not. As the pages of one book were filled up, the county recorder's office would begin a new book. The books were numbered and hence you would find a legal description of a mortgage, noting it was recorded in such-and-such book and on that particular page number.

These book and page numbers are noted, and anybody who may have a claim or want to establish a claim or lien on or to any particular piece of property is free to search through these official records. You'll find notations regarding other mortgages, liens, judgments (or satisfaction of mortgages, liens, or judgments) that might pertain to a particular person or piece of property.

When you purchase a piece of real property, a deed is recorded in the official records of the county. If you borrowed money to buy the property, most likely the mortgage company or bank also recorded the mortgage. The lender does this as a sort of notice to all the public that it has the first mortgage on that property. If it wasn't recorded, and you borrowed some more money on the property, the next bank would record its mortgage and it would have the first mortgage recorded. If you failed to pay the mortgage on the second loan, the second bank could foreclose and the first bank would just be out of luck. This is why when you buy a piece of real property, there should always be a title search to make sure all the mortgages, liens, etc., recorded on that property are paid or satisfied before you take title to the property.

Alternate Light Source

I hear people complain all the time about our public servants. Let me tell you, I've searched for information in courthouses all across the United States. I've never found a more helpful bunch of people in my life than at the local county court-house. They've always been more than willing to show me how to do the search I need, or if I act pathetic enough, they'll even do it for me most of the time.

Now, why do we as investigators care about all of this? I'll show you why. Remember Christine at the beginning of this chapter? The house the ex-wife lived in belonged to her father. All I had to do was go into the official records and search his name to find the mortgage on her house. In fact, I found the house was purchased in 1979 and a mortgage placed on it. I found a satisfaction of the mortgage recorded in 1989 and another mortgage was placed on it. That mortgage was satisfied in 1999 and another higher mortgage was placed on it at that time. On this last refinancing it looked like she pulled some cash out of it and refinanced it for 15 years. The mortgage was for

$72,000. Unfortunately for my client, since this mortgage was for only 15 years, her payments would have been higher than for a 30-year mortgage.

I took a financial calculator and figured out what her payments were for principal and interest based on a $72,000 loan for 15 years. I had to guess at the interest rate because the promissory note wasn't recorded with the mortgage. But it wasn't too hard to go back three years and see what the average 15-year loan was going for in April of that year. Principal and interest came to about $607.58.

Christine needed to know the amount of the mortgage payment. Now I had the first piece of the puzzle, the principal and interest payment.

The Property Appraiser

I went across the hall to the property appraiser's office. (I could have, but actually that's a fib. In our county, as in most counties now, the property appraiser's records are online, and before I went to the courthouse I looked up the latest appraisal on the website.)

The appraiser's office showed the value of the property, the type of construction (which was brick), and this year's current tax amount. In this case the property taxes were about $1,200 annually. This meant the ex-wife's mortgage company would have added about $100 per month to the principal and interest payment for the property taxes.

I called my insurance agent to see what a typical homeowners insurance policy would cost for a brick home. He gave me a figure of about $485, which is about $40 per month. (That was before the parade of hurricanes that hit Florida, so insurance rates are higher now.) Add the three figures together (principal and interest, $607.58; taxes, $100; and insurance, $40) for a total of $747.58.

Bingo. In 30 minutes I had the information Christine wanted. Let's see, $225 for a half-hour's work is what Christine paid me—that's $550 per hour. Better than minimum wage, for sure.

The State Civil Court Systems

State court systems in most states are divided into higher courts and lower courts. Some states have other courts, like water courts and traffic courts, but we won't deal with those here. Criminal courts and federal courts we'll touch on later in this chapter. Don't let the names of the courts confuse you. Some of my investigative interns just don't seem to get it, but it's real easy. Just think of higher courts and lower courts and everything will fall into place. We'll talk about civil cases first.

Higher Civil Courts

The higher courts and the lower courts have different names in different states. In Florida they are called circuit courts and county courts; Arizonans call them superior courts and justice courts; New Yorkers call them supreme courts and county courts. Let's forget the names and just call them higher and lower courts.

The higher courts deal with more-important cases. More-important usually equals more money. Everybody has heard of small claims court. Small claims in most jurisdictions means sums of money where the damages sought are less than $5,000. In some states it is even less. In lower court cases, frequently people do not use the services of an attorney and represent themselves. I'm sure you've heard the old saying that a person who acts as his own attorney has a fool for a client. I've always found this to be true. So if you find yourself in small claims court, you might want to reconsider representing yourself.

Civil actions such as divorces, malpractice, libel, and other suits are likely to involve money amounts over $5,000 and are heard in the higher courts. Petty actions like residential rent disputes will be found in the lower courts.

My client, Mary Beth, whom I'd known on a personal basis for a long time, called me. She said her husband was in jail on charges of spousal abuse (toward her) and she had a restraining order against him. He'd blackened her eyes, dragged her around the house by her hair, and beat her with a clothes hanger.

Mary Beth had been married to Lionel for just under a year. She wanted to know if he'd had physical altercations with any of his previous three wives. Where do we go to look?

Right, to the office of the clerk of the higher court. I reviewed all three of the previous divorce files. There was one restraining order in one of them alleging physical brutality. I found the personal data on the ex-wives and tracked them down. Each of his ex-wives told me Lionel had been physically abusive to her. In fact, he had been arrested multiple times for abusing each one.

Lionel's relationship with his second wife was a little different. She told me they used to beat each other up. Now that was a new one for me.

If Mary Beth had come to me before she married Lionel, she would have known about his propensity for violence and perhaps been prepared to diffuse it or even not marry him at all. At least now she knows it was probably not her fault. It amazes me, though, how few people do any sort of prenuptial background investigation, especially when we're talking second, third, and fourth marriages. In this case this was Lionel's fourth marriage and Mary Beth's fifth. I also checked the criminal records for Lionel and we'll talk about what I found there in the following section on criminal courts.

Mary Beth is still married to and living with Lionel. He goes to anger management classes every Tuesday night. I told her to lock up the clothes hangers but she didn't think it was funny.

Lower Civil Courts

We conduct background investigations for a local landlord. This fellow rents high-dollar furnished homes located in a golfing community on short-term leases. One of the checks he insists on before renting a house to a prospective tenant is to search the lower court records from whatever county the renter previously resided in. He's been involved before with tenants who will pay the first month's rent and then begin some kind of action in small claims court, and end up living rent-free month after month until he can finally get them evicted. If we find any previous litigation where they were the *plaintiff*, he refuses to rent to them. If they were a *defendant*, he wants the details of the suit and then makes a decision.

This commercial client figures even though it costs him a little bit more to have us run a civil-records search, he saves big bucks in the long run in attorney fees and loss of rent.

def•i•ni•tion

Legal actions require a minimum of two parties. The **plaintiff** is the party who initiates the action or lawsuit. The **defendant** is the person on the receiving end of the action.

In most court actions the plaintiff's name is listed or shown first on the complaint. The defendant is being sued or arrested by the plaintiff. In criminal cases the plaintiff is the government and the person being charged with the crime is the defendant. Usually you'll see a criminal case listed as, for example, *the State of Florida V. Brown*.

Cases are indexed in the state court system by the plaintiff's name and cross-referenced by the defendant's name. In *Kramer V. Brown*, Kramer is the plaintiff and Brown, the defendant. In a court index you might find the notation, Brown adv. Kramer. "Adv." stands for adverse, the reverse of versus. In that case, Brown is still the defendant and Kramer is still the plaintiff. In some states, instead of "adv.," the abbreviation "ats" is used. "Ats" is an acronym for "at the suit of."

Lower court records are also at the county courthouse. Large counties may have annexes or sub-courthouses in different locations around the county for the convenience of the taxpayer. Usually the annex will have computer links to the entire courthouse system so a check can be run from any annex. When in doubt, ask if a search at an annex will search all of the records in the entire county. If not, then go to the main courthouse. In smaller, less-computerized counties you'll probably have to go downtown to the county courthouse. There the clerks working in the clerk of the courts office can direct you to the records you're looking for and will gladly show you how the system is organized.

Miscellaneous Civil Courts

In addition to the higher and lower courts, as described in the preceding, there are also in many jurisdictions other courts such as traffic court and municipal court, depending upon the state, county, and city. You'll need to do a little research in your city of interest to see what the courts are called there. The easiest way to remember is to think in dollars. The higher dollar value at risk, the higher the court. The more serious the offense, the higher the court. Fewer dollars at stake means the item will be heard in a lower court. Traffic violations, less serious still, move on down to the traffic or municipal court.

State Criminal Courts

State criminal courts, not including the appellate courts, are divided into higher and lower courts just like the civil courts. We will deal with some with these courts in Chapter 24.

The criminal courts usually carry the same name as the civil courts. In Florida they are the circuit court (higher court) and county court (lower court); Arizonans call them superior court (higher court) and justice court (lower court).

Remember Mary Beth from the preceding section on higher civil courts? Well, when she was downtown shopping, prior to marrying Lionel, had she only paid a visit to the courthouse and checked the criminal records on her husband-to-be, she would have found that charges against Lionel were still pending, even as she walked down the aisle at her wedding. She didn't make the stop, so she never knew it.

Elementary, My Dear Watson

Cases in the state criminal courts are usually prosecuted by attorneys working for the local or county government. They are sometimes called state's attorneys, district attorneys, or county attorneys. They are, in fact, attorneys for the state, district, or county, which is the plaintiff in criminal actions. These are often elected positions. Most states have a state attorney general's office that may get involved in prosecuting cases. Those cases usually originate from state law enforcement bureaus, as opposed to the local police or sheriff's office.

I can't stress enough the value of checking criminal records on your husband- or wife-to-be prior to getting married. You have all the tools right here in this book to do it yourself. If you grew up with your intended spouse, high school sweethearts and all, then maybe you know all there is to know about the person. You think.

But do you know their money management habits? Have they ever written a bad check? You'd be surprised how many people have 3, 5, or sometimes as many as 15 bad check charges against them. Often there are even warrants out for their arrest for insufficient fund checks and they don't know it. They should know it. They probably received a letter from the prosecuting attorney's office but they never responded. Hence, the warrant is issued. Usually the sheriff is not going to beat down their door (or if you're married, your door) at midnight and arrest them. But don't be surprised when they call you from jail because they got stopped for speeding and the policeman found warrants outstanding for the insufficient funds checks. Happens all the time. A 10-minute search through the court records will alert you if your spouse-to-be has this problem.

I know one woman who wrote a bad check for her wedding dress. Imagine her husband's surprise a year later when he had to pay her bail and pay for the wedding dress, too. When he asked me to look at it, I found that she'd had numerous other bad check charges against her, all dismissed because she'd paid them before the wedding.

Especially if you're from different towns and states, spend the few dollars or whatever it takes and find out for sure. If you don't want to do it yourself, then hire me or another PI to do it for you.

There is no magic bullet that can guarantee a long, peaceful, and happy marriage. We all know that. But you can sure improve the odds a lot on the peaceful part of the equation by doing your homework before you wed. Mary Beth wouldn't be wearing sunglasses today to cover her black eyes had she taken the trouble to check into Lionel's background. It's not hard.

Federal Courts

The federal judicial system breaks down a little differently than the state systems. Excluding the federal appeals court and the United States Supreme Court, the three basic federal courts are the federal civil, federal criminal, and bankruptcy courts.

The U.S. government also has its attorney, similar to the district attorney within the state system. This federal government attorney is a political appointee and he will be out of a job if a rival political party wins the next election. He has the title, appropriately, of the U.S. attorney (USA). The cases are usually prosecuted by an assistant U.S. attorney (AUSA), who is usually a career employee. There are several different methods available for checking federal records. Other than walking into the nearest federal courthouse, the answer to your problem is the PACER (Public Access to Court Electronic Records) system.

Elementary, My Dear Watson

Each part of the United States, Puerto Rico, Guam, and the Mariana Islands is broken down into federal districts. There are 94 federal districts in the United States. Districts do not cross state boundaries. The districts are also broken down into divisions along geographic and population lines.

The federal courts have been developing an electronic search system, which is available via the Internet. If you plan on requesting even a few federal court searches, subscribing to PACER is the way to go. You must first register, which you can do online for free. It takes about two weeks to receive your system password by mail. They will not e-mail or fax it to you.

Thereafter, there is a charge of 8¢ per downloaded page. Not all district courts are on the Internet system. The government will invoice you once every three months for usage of the system. If your bill for using the system is less than $10 per year, it will forgive the debt and not expect payment. (It would most likely cost more than that to physically bill you.) Each court maintains its own database, so they are all a little different. You can access the PACER system by going to http://pacer.psc.uscourts.gov.

After registering for PACER, be sure and register for the U.S. Party/Case Index. This is a national index of almost all of the district court cases. It is updated each night. By utilizing this index, you can conduct a nationwide search (except for the few courts which don't participate) for federal court cases involving whatever individual or entity you are interested in. If you find a case that piques your interest, you can go to that file through the PACER system and view the contents. Fees are the same as for the PACER system.

The U.S. Party/Case Index is a great tool if you don't know for sure where a particular case may have been filed. In addition to civil cases and bankruptcy cases, you can also search for federal criminal cases. Federal criminal cases are those cases brought by the FBI (Federal Bureau of Investigation), DEA (Drug Enforcement Agency), ATF (Bureau of Alcohol, Tobacco, and Firearms), the Secret Service, Homeland Security, and other federal agencies when they allege a violation of federal law.

By searching the U.S. Party/Case Index (USPCI), you can basically perform a national federal criminal conviction and national federal civil and bankruptcy search. Don't confuse this with an NCIC (National Crime Information Center) rap sheet. We'll talk about rap sheets and the NCIC in Chapter 21.

 **The Division of Licensing**

The only U.S. federal district court that is not on the PACER system as of this printing is the New Mexico District Court. Also, there are four courts of appeals that are not on the system. The Second, Fifth, Seventh, and Eleventh.

The Bankruptcy Courts

Filing for bankruptcy is a federal matter. Personal and business bankruptcies all fall under federal statutes and therefore are handled in a federal court. The bankruptcy law was designed to give individuals and businesses a "fresh start."

Bankruptcy courts are organized differently than the other federal courts, have their own set of rules, and actually trace their origin back to a different part of the Constitution.

Searching the records at the bankruptcy court is similar to searching the district courts. Most of the bankruptcy courts are on the PACER and USPCI systems.

To understand the records you review, it would be helpful to know that bankruptcies are filed under four different chapters:

- ◆ Chapter 7, liquidation: for individuals and businesses
- ◆ Chapter 11, reorganization: for larger corporations
- ◆ Chapter 12, reorganization: for family farmers
- ◆ Chapter 13, reorganization: for individuals and smaller businesses

Liquidation means all of the assets (with some allowable exceptions) are disposed of and all debt (with some exceptions, like debt to the government) are discharged.

Reorganization stops collection activity on the part of creditors and gives a business or individual a chance to breathe while working out a plan of action in coordination with a trustee appointed by the bankruptcy court.

I get requests to perform due diligence searches all the time. This can be a check of an individual, but more often of a company's reputation, ability to perform under contract, and verification that there are no liens or judgments filed against the company.

A good due diligence search will also encompass any lawsuits, pending or potential, or other current or potential areas of liability, such as a pending bankruptcy. There are some private investigative agencies that not only specialize in due diligence searches, it's all they do.

Most clients request a bankruptcy check as part of a due diligence to determine if the person with whom they are going to be doing business has filed for bankruptcy in the past or may be in the middle of a bankruptcy now.

If you're thinking about doing serious business with a company or individual, you should check the appropriate bankruptcy court before signing any contracts.

Reducing the Alimony

So you were the bread winner and your jerk ex-husband sued for alimony after he left with the new girlfriend. How are you going to get that bum out of your life and off your payroll?

Ralph went to his attorney and posed that question. Florida has a relatively new law that allows for the cessation of alimony (Florida Statute 61.14 (1)(b)) which states:

> (b)1.The court may reduce or terminate an award of alimony upon specific written findings by the court that since the granting of a divorce and the award of alimony a supportive relationship has existed between the obligee and a person with whom the obligee resides. On the issue of whether alimony should be reduced or terminated under this paragraph, the burden is on the obligor to prove by a preponderance of the evidence that a supportive relationship exists.

In English, the above means that if your ex-spouse is in a "supportive relationship" with another person, your attorney can petition the court to reduce or terminate your obligation to pay alimony. We have recently successfully completed a number of these cases. So how do you show the supportive relationship?

If the ex is living with another person, before you pay a lot of money for surveillance, check the public records. See who is paying the utility bill. Find out who owns the house they're living in. In Ralph's case, we didn't know who the boyfriend was or where Ralph's ex was living. So we put a two-man surveillance team on the ex-wife, Carolyn, and followed her home from work. Not rocket science. In about an hour the boyfriend shows up. We get the tag off of his car and call it quits, planning on returning at 5 the next morning (not my favorite time of day) to document that she spent the night there and was in fact living with this guy.

I decided to do a little background on the boyfriend, to see who he was. Did he have a criminal record? Did he own the house where Carolyn was now living? Ralph's ex, Carolyn, owned another house in a different county that she was renting out since she had moved in with the boyfriend six months previously.

I searched the official records in the other county and found that three weeks earlier Carolyn had refinanced her old house, pulling over a hundred thousand dollars in cash out of it. On the new mortgage she declared she was a single woman.

In looking through the official records in the new county I saw that, guess what? One week after Carolyn refinanced her old house, she and the boyfriend closed on the purchase of the house where she was living with the boyfriend. And as a sweetener, on the deed and the mortgage they declared themselves to be husband and wife, even though she kept her old married name.

So somewhere in that week, between the refinance of the old house and the purchase of the new one they'd gotten married. She hadn't told her ex, she hadn't told her children, but who did she tell? The clerk of the court and the entire rest of the world. Ralph's alimony agreement, like many, included an agreement that the alimony would cease upon Carolyn's remarriage. Slam dunk, and only one afternoon of surveillance.

The Least You Need to Know

- Real property transactions such as sales and mortgages are recorded in the official records of the county and are public records that can be reviewed.

- State court systems have higher courts that deal with more-important cases (think higher dollars) and lower courts, which handle less-important cases (think lower dollars).

- The criminal divisions of the state court system are nearly identical to the civil divisions. Higher courts handle felonies and lower courts deal with misdemeanors.

- The federal court is divided into districts. Some states have only one federal district, and others have several, depending upon population and geography.

- A national search can be conducted in the federal court system by using the U.S. Party/Case Index, available through PACER.

- Some states allow for reduction or cessation of alimony payments if the ex-spouse is in a supportive relationship with another person. Searching public records can help establish the relationship.

8

Under-the-Radar Databases

In This Chapter

- ◆ Credit headers
- ◆ The composition of credit reports
- ◆ The Fair Credit Reporting Act (FCRA)
- ◆ Using credit reports in asset searches
- ◆ Choosing the right database

The single major aspect of investigative work that separates the true professional from the amateur is the professional's access to proprietary databases. These databases are not generally open to the public. If you're serious about a career in the private investigative field, then this chapter is for you.

An attorney client of mine called me as I was writing this chapter. A female friend of hers who was trying to get a divorce had spent all of her money on one attorney who'd skipped town. My client/attorney wanted a favor. Before they sent divorce papers to be served on this woman's soon-to-be ex-husband, whose last known address was in Upland, California, she wanted to make sure that the address her client had was still accurate. Could I do her a favor? *Pro Bono?*

def•i•ni•tion

Pro Bono derives from the Latin, *Pro Bono Publico,* "for the public good." Usually it's shortened to just "Pro Bono" and means legal work undertaken without expectation of payment.

I had his name, date of birth, Social Security number, and last known address. How hard could this locate be? The name she'd given me was not very common. Let's call the soon-to-be ex David Morph. I went to my favorite pay telephone database, www.masterfiles. com or www.555-1212.com, and searched his name in Upland. No David Morph listed.

I used the pay telephone database again and did a reverse search. I searched the address I'd been given to see if any telephones were listed at that address. The address was a large apartment complex and there was one listing for a Jack Morph, but not a David. The telephone companies in their directory listing don't give apartment numbers, so I wasn't sure if this was the right phone number or not.

Not including my time, so far I'd spent maybe 40 cents on this search. My client/ attorney had referred some pretty large (think dollars) cases to me in the past and was a continuing source of referrals. Still, since I wasn't getting paid for this locate, I didn't want to be out of pocket a lot of money.

def•i•ni•tion

A **Social Security trace** is the searching of a database by Social Security number. The search normally returns residence addresses connected to your subject.

My next step was to run a *Social Security trace.* I went to one of my favorite under-the-radar databases, IRB (International Research Bureau: www.irbsearch.com), and plugged in the subject's Social Security number. In 30 seconds and for the cost of one dollar I had verified the current address for the subject. The same address my client had given.

The nice thing about these databases is that often you'll get a date that the information was reported so you'll have a pretty good idea of how current the reporting is. In this case it reported the date as the preceding month. But because the phone number was in a different first name, I wasn't 100 percent certain that this was the primary residence of my subject. It could have been his father's or some other relative's and he was just using it as a mailing address.

So I needed to call there and be sure that this was a good address, enabling my client to have him served.

I made the call and asked for David. He answered and confirmed this was his residence. I did not use a pretext like we talked about in Chapters 4 and 5. Since they'd been separated for two years and by 3,000 miles, I figured this guy would probably be just as happy to get the divorce over with as would his wife. I told him outright why I was calling. He seemed fine with that and indicated we could serve him at that address.

My total cost for the locate was $1.40 and 30 minutes of my time. The key to efficient locates is using the professional databases and pay telephone sites we're going to learn about in this chapter.

The Division of Licensing

Addresses reported by these databases is information gleaned from a variety of sources. Credit headers, the pizza database, telephone company records, public records, and forwarding records from the post office. When a person is intentionally trying to hide his whereabouts or is traveling or is perhaps a student, she'll often give an address that is a family address, like her parents' residence. Or some permanent mailing address where her driver's license can be mailed. It doesn't necessarily insure that your subject is physically residing at that address. You'll need to do some additional verifying to insure that the subject is actually there.

As a professional PI, you'll want to subscribe to a variety of data providers. Each data provider has strong points and weaknesses. In this chapter, we'll examine several of the more-popular providers that serve the professional private investigative industry. There are some data providers that have located themselves out of the territorial boundaries of the United States to avoid the prosecutorial jurisdiction of the U.S. federal government. You can read between those lines as you wish, but I'm not going to discuss them here.

Look at these databases as tools. Just as there are different types of hammers for different jobs, there are different databases a PI will utilize, depending upon the job requirements. You wouldn't use a sledgehammer for putting a tack up; you'd lose all of your profit repairing the hole in the drywall. Likewise, if an investigator uses his most-expensive data provider for a $25 case, he won't last a year in this business.

The Credit Bureaus

Before 1985, the Credit Bureau was the only real database available which showed a subject's employment, residence, and telephone numbers, as reported by the Credit Bureau's members. Then, as now, it was not "officially" available to private investigators. The credit bureaus had contracts with life insurance companies to perform reputation-type checks on potential purchasers of larger-dollar-amount life insurance policies. They used an affiliated company named Retail Credit Corporation to perform these checks, sending RCC investigators to telephone neighbors and determine the lifestyle of the potential insurance customer. For this reason, the credit bureaus considered private investigative agencies as potential competition and refused to allow PIs to subscribe to their services or become credit bureau members. As the larger credit bureaus gobbled up the smaller local credit bureaus, this refusal became the industry standard and continues to this day.

Where to Look

A resourceful private investigator will have developed credit bureau sources and be able to pull credit reports for *permissible purposes*.

def•i•ni•tion

> **Permissible purpose** refers to 1 of 11 (depending upon how you count) legal purposes for pulling a credit report as defined by the Fair Credit Reporting Act last updated by Congress in 2004.

A lot of information that goes into private databases is derived in one way or another from credit bureau files. The three main credit bureaus are …

TransUnion (www.transunion.com)

Equifax (www.equifax.com)

Experian (www.experian.com)

Credit bureau files contain, of course, information about payments on credit accounts. Negative information stays in your credit file for seven years with the exception of bankruptcy, which will remain in your credit file until ten years after the discharge date.

Credit bureaus have different reports formatted in different manners, depending upon the needs of their customers. A credit report run for pre-employment purposes will usually not include the *credit score* because the prospective employer is not issuing credit. The credit score is an integral part, if not the major focus, of the credit report for home financing or car purchasing.

def•i•ni•tion

Credit score refers to one of several types of numerical rating systems devised by credit companies to give a credit grantor an instant evaluation of a person's risk as a credit applicant. FICO (Fair Isaac Corporation) is probably the leading company in credit scoring. And while reportedly the three bureaus all use Fair Isaac, they market them under different names. Experian names their score "Experian Fair Isaac." Equifax calls theirs "Beacon." And TransUnion uses the name "TransUnion Fico Classic."

While all three credit-reporting agencies report credit scores, not all of their scores are created equal because they are using different data: data from their own credit bureaus, not data from combined bureaus. Scores may run from 350 to 850, but you as a consumer will probably have a different score with each of the three bureaus, even though they're all utilizing the same scoring model.

The Division of Licensing

Private investigators are not usually in the position of granting credit to clients and normally do not have a permissible purpose for pulling a subject's credit report. Be aware that credit-reporting agencies monitor and audit their accounts to insure that reports are pulled for permissible purposes.

In Chapter 21, we'll talk at length about securing access to credit reports with permissible purposes. However, while those services are offered by some private investigative companies, most private investigators do not provide those services and do not have access to credit bureau reports.

Why to Look

When might an investigator get a request or have a need for a credit check? I regularly get requests from ladies who are dating men and the relationship is turning serious. Is this a permissible purpose? Well, yes and no. The Fair Credit Reporting Act (FCRA) governs access to credit information. You can read the act at www.ftc.gov/os/statutes/fcrajump.htm.

Basically there are two reasons that might qualify, although I doubt you'll find universal agreement in the credit or the PI industries. Those two are:

(E) intends to use the information, as a potential investor or servicer, or current insurer, in connection with a valuation of, or an assessment of the credit or prepayment risks associated with, an existing credit obligation; or

(F) otherwise has a legitimate business need for the information

Is marriage not a legitimate business need? Certainly it's governed by civil laws and involves financial transactions between the two parties. Still, I doubt that you'll want to ask your fiancé for a release to pull his credit report. What to do? What to do?

The Division of Licensing

Pulling premarital credit reports probably does not violate the restrictions of the FCRA. And if more people pulled their prospective spouse's credit report before they got married there'd probably be fewer divorces. But the FCRA doesn't take that into account. There are two reasons for PIs not to pull premarital credit reports. First, an inquiry will show on the prospective spouse's credit report and your client might have to explain to her fiancé why she doubted him. Second, there is a very good chance the credit bureaus will yank your access if they find out you pull premarital credit reports, because they may not agree that it falls within the permissible-purpose rules of the FCRA.

What You Might Find

Other than the credit score, what else do we find on the credit report?

- Creditor's name
- Creditor's account number
- Date this information was reported
- The date the account was opened
- High credit limit
- Remaining balances
- Past due amounts

- A credit rating for each account determined by how many times the account has been late

- History on each account showing how many times the account was paid over 30, 60, or 90 days late

- Current monthly payment for each account with a balance owing

We also find the subject's current address; previous addresses; an identification section which compares the name and date of birth associated with the SSN that was queried; and a profile summary of subtotals of his accounts broken down by installment accounts, revolving, real estate, and other.

You'll also get any negative public records in the credit bureau's file such as *judgments*, tax liens, and bankruptcies.

def•i•ni•tion

A **judgment** is a final determination by a court of competent jurisdiction setting forth the rights and liabilities of the parties in a lawsuit. Usually the term refers to a money judgment where the court may decide that a plaintiff is owed money by a defendant in a case. These judgments are recorded in the official records at the clerk of the courts office and are generally public records. Credit bureaus review these records on a regular basis and include them as part of their credit report.

Okay, now that we know what the credit report is, how do we, as PIs, use it? We use it in asset searches for the purpose of collection of judgments. Well, now you ask, "The credit report shows who your subject owes money to, but it doesn't show any of his assets, like bank accounts or real property, so how does that help us find his assets?"

I thought you might ask that question. If your client has a judgment, then there was/is a court case. You then get your client's attorney to subpoena the records of your subject's creditors. Be sure to include in the subpoena the application for credit that your subject completed.

Generally, when people are applying for credit, they make themselves look as solvent as possible so they'll list their bank accounts, their equity in real property, and other assets they hold. Bingo! As soon as you get that information, you've got the location of their bank accounts and can garnish those accounts as well as place liens on their property, and even have the sheriff seize their vehicles and boats.

Alternate Light Source _____

The technique of subpoenaing credit applications and then following the leads to bank accounts and other assets works particularly well in family law cases, where your client (one of the spouses) doesn't really know what assets the other spouse has. You don't have to have a judgment to subpoena credit applications. Just an ongoing civil case, like a divorce, will do. Start with one bank or credit card that the spouse is aware of and go from there.

When subpoenaing bank loan records, in addition to the application, don't forget to ask for copies of checks and bank transfer records, both transfers in and out, as well as copies of all deposits. Wire transfers and cancelled checks will tell you a lot about a person's finances as well as facts about their lives, like personal travel and payment for a girlfriend's rent, which may be germane in your family law case.

The Genesis of Data

In the early 1980s Compuserve was one of the first "gateways" that provided data access via office or home computer to public records. They secured a contract with several states, including Florida, and resold driving history and vehicle registration information.

Credit Headers

Even though the credit bureaus won't sell their data directly to private investigators, they are in business to sell the data in their computers. The bureaus do possess data that is not directly related to credit and is not governed by the FCRA. This is called "credit header information." Since they're in business to make a buck, they sell this data to "data suppliers" who in turn sell it to private investigators.

That data includes:

 ♦ Name and previous names or "also known as" (a.k.a.)

 ♦ Date of birth

 ♦ Social Security number

 ♦ Current and previous addresses

 ♦ Current and previous employers (sometimes)

 ♦ Telephone numbers

 ♦ Relatives

The reason credit-header information is so valuable for private investigators is that it is updated often. It's not just updated when you apply for new credit, but every time you call your credit card company, mortgage company, or any other creditor, they verify your address and phone number. Your creditors report any changes and if there are no changes they report the date of last verification. So the information can be fairly current, which helps a PI tremendously when searching for their subject.

Into the Database Mix

Many databases buy their information from the same sources, so you might as well throw a dart and pick any one. But not all databases are created the same. Some are stronger in some areas of data than are others. Other data besides credit bureau data goes into these databases. This is what makes choosing a database so difficult. Here's what else goes into this stew:

- Magazine subscription lists with addresses and names
- Telephone directory information
- Postal change of addresses
- Licensed drivers
- Book club lists
- Registered vehicles
- Boats and trailers
- Cell phone users
- UCC listings
- Corporate officers and registered agents
- Internet search engine results
- Pizza delivery names, addresses, and phone numbers
- Public postings of liens and judgments
- Public notices of bankruptcy and foreclosure
- Names which appear in newspapers and magazines
- Public professional licenses
- Traffic accidents
- Criminal charges

When you combine all of the above, and there are others I'm sure I've omitted, with a good algorithm and a fast computer server, it's amazing how much information can be correlated and reported on one individual.

The computer doesn't always get it right, especially with common names, but just think about this. Take your last known addresses. They're in the computer data mix somewhere. Throw in the time frame when you were there as reported by your credit card company and then ask the computer, who else shared that address with you during that time frame? That's how these databases generate reports that show relatives and roommates, by comparing addresses with time. Then expand that exponentially to show current addresses on those relatives and former roommates and pretty quickly the PI, even if he can't find you, can find your mother or brother or former roommate and call them, perhaps getting a lead on your whereabouts.

The Pay Databases

"Which database provider is the best? The cheapest? The most accurate?" Below is a list of the databases that market to the private investigative industry. Many of these will allow a PI firm a free trial period. If you're a professional private investigator, I strongly suggest you try as many as possible before narrowing your subscription down. Hey, there might be no free lunch but there are free trials.

The Pay Databases

Alternate Light Source

IRB resells data from Accurint. As of this writing IRB and Merlin Data Services have signed a letter of intent to merge. So if you're reading this and you can't find IRB or Merlin, they'll be around, but perhaps under a different name.

- ◆ Tracers Information Specialists: www. tracersinfo.com

- ◆ IRB: www.irbsearch.com

- ◆ Skipsmasher: www.skipsmasher.com

- ◆ Merlin: www.merlindata.com

- ◆ E-infodata: www.insightamerica.com

- ◆ Locate Plus: www.locateplus.com

- ◆ Enformion: www.enformion.com

- ◆ NDR Querydata: www.querydata.com

Many of the above databases have "no hit no fee" searches. When you input the name, Social Security number, or other data, if they can't locate any records on your subject you might not be charged. Then again you might. Be sure and compare this feature when looking into which databases you want to subscribe to.

Another feature that bears examination is the monthly charge. Some databases have a minimum monthly charge. The strange part is that some charge the minimum if you use the database and some charge it even if you don't use the database during the month. Some apply the minimum monthly charge to your bill so that if you use say, five dollars more than the minimum, then your bill will be the minimum plus five. Each database provider seems to like to deal with this in different ways. Some, like Tracers Info, don't have a minimum charge, so give those a good look. And to complicate it just a bit further, some give you an unlimited amount of basic searches (usually older data) for a flat fee.

I usually find it beneficial to subscribe to at least two and usually three databases at any one time. They each have different strengths. Some truncate the Social Security numbers and some don't. You need to have at least one that doesn't truncate because, let's face it: most of the identifying data is more easily sorted by Social Security number than any other way. Just think how many Steve Browns there are in the country. There might be several with my same date of birth, but there's only one with my Social Security number.

Alternate Light Source

A factor to keep in mind with these data providers is that generally they began as suppliers of data in different regions of the country. When they first started business, they acquired data within their own state and then expanded to a broader coverage area. Even the credit bureaus have different regional strengths. If you've just set up shop as a PI and the paint is still wet on the sign over your door, keep geographic coverage areas of a potential data provider in mind. It can make a significant difference in the effectiveness of your work and your bottom line. How do you know their strong areas? Look to see where their corporate headquarters are and you'll have a good indication of the section of the country where they have the most depth of data.

Following are some of the searches that these different databases make available to private investigators. Generally the database companies will require you to show proof of investigative licensing. However, they do sell their product to non-PIs and other companies for collection purposes and human resource departmental needs.

The different databases charge different amounts. I could do a whole book on each database, their searches and their charges, and it'd be out of date before it ever went to the printer. So I'm going to give you a list of searches available from these database companies.

You'll find that most of these pay databases offer similar menus. However, they each perform differently in different searches. Like the credit bureaus, they may have similar records, but they're not all searching the same records. They offer searches such as:

Public Records

- Bankruptcies, judgments, and liens
- DEA registration
- Fictitious business names
- U.S. aircraft
- U.S. vessels
- U.S. air pilots
- Professional licenses
- Hunting and fishing licenses
- Concealed weapons permits
- Voter registration
- Federal firearms and explosives
- Court records
- Traffic accidents
- Marriages and divorces
- UCC searches
- Official records
- Social Security Death Index

Proprietary Data

- People locator searches
- National phone directory

- National property searches

- Phone directory—real time

- Social Security number verifier

- Employment searches

- Internet domains

- Dun and Bradstreet

- Delaware Corporation Search

- Motor vehicles

- Driver's licenses

- Patriot Act search

- Sexual offender search

The Least You Need to Know

- Database information that includes credit-header data will usually have a date that the information was reported, and it will often be fairly current.

- The three major credit bureaus all have a credit-scoring system based on Fair Isaac, but the score is pulled from their own data, so you will probably have a different credit score with each of the bureaus.

- The credit bureaus will not normally sell their data directly to private investigators or attorneys.

- The Fair Credit Reporting Act (FCAR) governs the release of credit information. There are occasions when a PI might have a need for a credit report that falls within the purview of the FCRA.

- The private databases use algorithms to match up addresses with people with dates. By so doing, they can often report current addresses for relatives and previous roommates of your subjects.

- The data in the private databases includes credit-header data, public-record data, and other proprietary data.

Outmaneuvering the Telephone Companies

In This Chapter

- ◆ Outflank the telephone company's defensive line
- ◆ Slash directory information costs in half
- ◆ Phone breaks, pager breaks, and cell breaks
- ◆ Finding the elusive nonpublished number
- ◆ Determining a pay telephone's location

The telephone is a tool. I know, all this time you thought it was a voice instrument used primarily for ordering pizza. Surprise, surprise, it's really the most basic tool in the private investigator's toolbox. A competent PI can find out more information using the telephone than any database can possibly provide. A PI may not always have access to his computer, but he should be able to lay his hands on a pay phone or a cell phone—unless he's in the Virgin Islands, where the pay phones don't usually work anyway.

We're going to examine the ins and outs of using the telephone to enhance your PI career. In order to make the best use of the phone, sometimes you have to outwit the person you're calling, and frequently you have to outsmart the telephone company itself.

The Secret to Verifying Nonpublished Numbers

In the private investigation business, sometimes knowing where your subject lives is just as good as knowing his or her telephone number. If the PI wants to conduct surveillance on an individual, he doesn't necessarily need the telephone number, but he does need the address so he can get out of bed in the dark, well before dawn, and venture out into the cold, while every sane person is still sleeping (isn't PI work fun?), and set up the surveillance on the residence prior to the subject leaving for work.

The PI has run the subject's name in the databases and they show an address for him, but he's not sure if the address is current or not. The databases are not infallible, and as we discussed in Chapter 8, the databases pull a lot of the information from credit bureau files. Not everybody applies for credit every month, so the address might not have been updated for six months or more.

Next, you, the PI, check directory information, where you can get a phone number as well as an address. If you call 411, the recording and the live operator might both report the listing you want is nonpublished. What do you do? You certainly don't want to get out of bed and go to the wrong address. You can run all of the other checks we talked about in the skip-tracing chapters (Chapters 4 and 5), but here is the easiest way to verify the address when your subject has a nonpublished number.

With a possible address in mind, and knowing the subject's telephone number is nonpublished, mumble your way through the 411 computer until you get the live operator. Next, tell the operator you'd like her to check a listing for you. You think the number is nonpublished but you'd like to verify the address.

The operators don't get this request very often because most people don't know you can verify an address on nonpublished numbers. Be prepared to have her say she can't give you the address. When she says that, you tell her that's okay; you already have the address, you just want to verify it. Give her the address where you think the subject is living. Either she'll confirm it or she'll tell you no, it's a different address. She might not be willing to give the address to you, but she does have it in front of her on the screen, and she can and will verify it for you if you give it to her first. If you've got the right address, then set the alarm for about 4 A.M. and go to bed early.

Elementary, My Dear Watson

Some long-distance companies use third-party subcontractors to handle directory assistance inquiries. Sometimes these subcontractors will not verify addresses on nonpublished numbers. If you're using any of the Regional Bell Operating Companies (RBOC), you shouldn't have a problem. If you run into one of these subcontractors who refuses to verify the address for you, then simply hang up and dial 1 plus your subject's area code and 555-1212. That should put you into the RBOC directory information network and you should get an RBOC operator who will verify the address. Also, there are other private telephone companies out there besides the Bell System companies, and they may have different rules. Altogether, the technique in this section works 99 percent of the time.

Area codes seem to change within some states every week. Here are two good area code locators; www.555-1212.com and www.mmiworld.com/telephone.htm. There is no simple solution to keeping up with the area code changes, but these two websites help.

Breaking the Number

Obtaining a *telephone break* can be one of the most challenging and exasperating problems facing a private investigator. A wife will come to you with a telephone number she found in her husband's billfold or coat pocket. The wife suspects the number may belong to a female, and she wants to know for sure.

In obtaining a telephone break, you have to first satisfy yourself that the client means no harm to the subscriber. The very last thing a PI wants is to find that, by breaking the phone number, he has enabled his client to go to the subject's address and attempt to physically harm that person.

Next, arrange the price with your client. On a listed number, the price should be about $25. It's hardly worth the paperwork if you charge any less. A nonpublished number, cellular number, or pager number break should cost the client about $125.

def•i•ni•tion

A **telephone break** is the process of taking a telephone number, with no other identifying information, and obtaining the subscriber information, including name, the service address if it's a landline, or the mailing address if the number rings to a cellular telephone or pager.

The Division of Licensing

Data brokers and information brokers have their place. Be cautious. The laws change and some of these data brokers may use illegal methods to obtain the data you're requesting. Recently some states have made it illegal to obtain another person's cell phone or long distance records, or to request a person to obtain this information, or to even be in possession of it if it was obtained through illegal methods. Don't bury your head in the sand. These data brokers are using pretexts of questionable legality. There's no question about it now. It's flat illegal and the United States Congress has several bills pending making it a federal crime.

Start with the easy checks. Go to www.masterfiles.com or to www.555-1212.com and run a reverse search on the number. There's a good chance the number will be a regular listed number and you've just turned a 25¢ search into an extra $25 in your pocket.

If those two searches come back as "no record," then you'll know that, in all probability, you've got a nonpublished, cellular, or pager number. But there are some other possibilities. For example, if the client had picked the number off of her caller ID instead of finding it in her husband's billfold, it could be a trunk-line number, such as a T-1 line, from a commercial establishment. A quick search at www.phonevalidator.com will tell if you're dealing with a cell phone number or a landline.

Your next step is to call the phone number and see who answers. In this day of voice mail and answering machines, there's a 50-50 chance you'll get a recorded greeting, and more often than not, it will include the subscriber's first name, or even last name. And if the number is assigned to a pager, you'll know that right away, too.

If you find out your number is a pager, nonpublished, or a phone, *data brokers* and *information brokers* are useful tools, too. The next few sections will explain more options.

def•i•ni•tion

Data brokers, also known as **information brokers,** are individuals or companies that have access to specialized sources of information or use advanced techniques to gather information and then resell the information to the private investigator. An example of this would be asking an information broker to obtain a nonpublished telephone number or a list of credit card charges that the PI couldn't get himself.

Breaking the Pager

If the number goes to a pager, as a PI you have two possibilities:

◆ You, the PI, can go to an information broker who specializes in telephone numbers, pay him $50 to get the subscriber information, and turn around and charge the client $125.

◆ You can page the number and wait for the return call. If you decide to page, here are four rules:

1. Use a phone that has caller ID.

2. Use a *safe phone* that you can answer with a "hello" (not a business phone).

3. Use a phone that is neither your home phone nor a number that anybody associated with you would recognize.

4. Consider paging the number later in the evening so that the page is returned from the subject's home.

Now, when the page is returned, answer the phone with a business name. Make one up, but not a PI firm name. Pretend you are the switchboard operator of a very small company. The person returning the call will tell you that she was just paged from your number. She will probably ask you what kind of business you're in. Your response to her question is very important and can make the difference between her hanging up and your getting the information you want. Tell her, "Oh, it's complicated, give me your name and I'll see who paged you."

def•i•ni•tion

A **safe phone** is a telephone that has the following characteristics: it is not traceable back to the user; it does not reveal its number to the caller ID services on outgoing calls; it does have caller ID service for incoming calls; and it is set up in such a way that it can be answered in any manner necessary and is used for only one case at a time. As a good PI you should have one of these phone lines available in your office at all times.

Eight times out of ten, you'll get the name. The other two times, the person will hang up. If she does hang up, wait 15 minutes, and page again. If she calls back, this time she'll give you her name. If she won't return the page again, then hopefully the caller ID will give you a lead. I would immediately run a reverse on the number from the caller ID. If you wait until evening to page the number, there's a good chance your subject may call from her home. You should get what you're looking for right there. If you didn't take my advice because you couldn't wait until evening, then she may have called from a business telephone. Give it 30 minutes and then call the number from the caller ID and see who answers. If it's a business and she answers, you've got her. If she doesn't answer, ask the person who does whether any salespeople just left, because somebody returned a page from there about 30 minutes ago but didn't leave her name. Does anyone, by chance, know who that might have been?

Breaking the Nonpublished Number

Getting subscriber information for nonpublished numbers is difficult. A PI can always resort to a telephone information broker, pay the $50, and get on with his life. But if you're not a licensed PI, most of these data brokers won't deal with you.

So here is a technique, a pretext call, that works most of the time. Actually, in my 20 years in the business, I don't recall it ever having failed. In Chapter 15, we talk at length about the do's and don'ts of pretext telephone calls. You need to read that section before attempting this particular pretext call.

The pretext goes like this: you call the number from a safe telephone. When it is answered, identify yourself as a representative of a major pizza home-delivery company (be specific—use the name of a pizzeria in your local area that the person you're calling will recognize). Tell him if he'll answer three quick questions, you'll send him a coupon for a free large pizza.

The questions are …

1. Have you ordered home-delivery pizza from (insert the name of the company) within the last three months?

2. If so, how many times per month do you call for home delivery? If never, do you know where the closest home-delivery outlet is?

3. Are you familiar with Sicilian-style pizza and have you ever ordered that?

Now, you don't give a hoot about the answers to the preceding questions, so just get through them as quickly as you can. Next, thank him very much for his time. Tell him you'll send him a coupon for a free large pizza and thank him again for his participation in this survey. To what address should you send the coupon? If he's gone this far with you, he'll always give you his address. And what name should you address it to? Bingo, you've got his name and address. If he wants it to go to a Post Office box, take the box information (it might come in handy later), but tell him that these coupons can't be mailed and the delivery folks will drop one off, so you need the street address and apartment number, if any.

The Division of Licensing

Pretexts, pretexts, pretext. Pretext is really another word for lie. Didn't your mother tell you never to lie? Well, pretexts are sometimes the heart and soul of the methods used by private investigators to obtain information from a person in such a manner that they freely divulge the information when they might not have so freely given it if asked directly. The real division of licensing in the various states recognize that a PI can not always identify herself as such and be successful in obtaining the information needed. So at this time there is no push to make "pretexting" illegal. However, stay abreast of the laws. This one may change. Never engage in any investigative activity that is illegal or unethical. The view from behind those skinny little bars is not nearly as good as the one out your own window.

Breaking the Cell Number

Again, the easiest way for a PI to get a break on a cellular telephone number is to pay the information broker. It is quicker for me to fax the number to my phone guy and get a fax back from him the next day with the information I need. The client is footing the bill, anyway.

Elementary, My Dear Watson

I've been told by people in the telephone directory assistance business that cellular phone directory information will soon be available. Why the change? The industry's announced reason was that cellular time was so expensive, the cellular providers didn't want their customers to be bothered with spurious calls. The real reason was they didn't want to give up their customer database because of the fierce competition between cell phone companies. But now, with the explosion in cell phone use, the thinking is changing, and in the future you might find cellular directory information available at different sites on the web. I'm sure you'll be able to do a reverse search as well.

Why the turnaround by the cellular companies? The regular carriers are making big bucks selling their directory information to resellers. With the intense competition in the cell phone market, the cell companies want in on that same kind of profitable action. It'll generate another revenue stream for the almighty bottom line.

If you're not a PI and don't have a "phone guy," then you'll have to go to a PI to get it done, or call the number and pretext it. You can use the same pizza pretext that we used for the nonpublished number, with a few changes in the questions. Start like this: "We know we've called you on your cell phone, but this will take less than 60 seconds and we'll send you a coupon for a free large pizza from (name the pizza company) if you'll answer two questions for us:

1. Have you ever used your cell phone to order a pizza from us?

2. Have you ever used your cell phone to order any other type of carryout food, so that it would be ready when you got there? If so, what type and how often?

"Thank you very much for your time. At what address should we send you the coupon for the free pizza? And what name should we address it to?"

We've had pretty good success with this pretext for cell phones. It is not unusual for the person answering to say they don't have time to talk right then. If they say that, ask if it's okay if you call them later. There's no gimmick and you're not trying to sell them anything, so most people are willing to cooperate.

Sources for Nonpublished Numbers

Just because your telephone number is nonpublished doesn't mean I can't get it. "Nonpublished" simply means the telephone company won't give it to me willingly. The subscriber has requested the phone company not to release his phone number for publication. Fair enough.

What we find, however, is while the subscribers have made that request to the telephone company, they violate their own instructions by giving it to the cable company, the electric company, the water company, the pizza delivery company, the newspaper for home delivery, service and repair companies of all kinds, the credit bureaus, their employer, the schools their children attend. The list of folks who have the "nonpublished" number goes on and on and on.

As we discussed in Chapter 9, in many locales the utilities are publicly owned and so their records are public. All you have to do is go to the source, examine the records, and you can get the infamous nonpublished number.

If the utility records where you live aren't public, then look at your list of friends and see if any of them or their spouses work at the cable company, the newspaper, or any other place where your subject has probably left his number. If you think of someone, ask him or her to get the number for you. But there are a couple of reasons why you don't want to ask this favor of anybody you know who works for the telephone company.

First, it is a violation of the telephone company rules for employees to divulge proprietary information, and second, it could be considered theft of information. The likelihood of either you or your friend being prosecuted for it are nil, but still, your friend could lose his or her job.

If you can't find a friend who can get the nonpublished number for you, and you can't con it out of the cable company, then call your local PI. She'll go to her broker of telephone information and get it for you. It'll probably cost you about $125. If she wants a lot more than that, find yourself another PI.

Pay Phones: Location, Location, Location

My client's 16-year-old son ran away. Anybody who has dealt with a teenager would think my client should be ecstatic. The kid's finally out the door; but no, the client wanted him back. And the kid didn't even take the family car with him. Go figure. This particular runaway is someone I've picked up and returned to his family four times in four years, so I knew the kid's friends and haunts pretty well.

This time, the boy apparently headed south to a city 200 miles away. The girlfriend cooperated with us to some degree because she was more mature than the boy and was genuinely concerned for his safety, though she wouldn't rat the kid out entirely. She never told us exactly where we could find him. She did say he would routinely call her from pay phones and she would turn around and call him back because he didn't have any money.

We got the incoming phone numbers from the girlfriend's cell phone bill. I then ran a reverse search on the numbers. Pay phones frequently have repeating numbers or a successive series of numbers in their phone number, such as 305-768-9999 or 305-768-3456. However, that's frequently but not *always* the case, so don't count on it. After running the reverse search, it was pretty easy to figure out which numbers were pay phones and which weren't. Next, we needed the physical address for the phones because we wanted to stake them out to find the boy. We'll talk more about how to find runaway kids in Chapter 18.

Sometimes the direct and honest approach works just as well as being sneaky. The locations and phone numbers to pay phones, while not published in the telephone directories, are not a secret. In this case, I called the telephone company business office and told them I was a private investigator. I explained the facts of the case and in a few minutes, after the customer service representative checked with her supervisor, she gave me the street address where the phones were located.

I took the street locations and plotted them out on a city map. They all fell within about a three-block radius in West Palm Beach, Florida. You'll have to read Chapter 18 to see if we found the runaway boy, but now you know how to find the location of a pay phone if you have the number.

The reality is, in the twenty-first century cell phones are rapidly putting pay phones out of business. But, there are still some out there and I get requests for finding their location regularly.

The Least You Need to Know

- ◆ Directory assistance operators will verify a nonpublished address if you give them the address, but they will not give you the address outright.

- ◆ Phone numbers, pager numbers, and cellular numbers can be broken by use of pretext phone calls.

- ◆ Nonpublished numbers can be found in public record information and retrieved from sources other than the telephone company.

- ◆ The phone company representative will provide you with the locations of pay telephones if you convince him or her you have a good reason.

Part 3

On-the-Job Training

Once you've learned how to search the public records and the private databases, it's time to learn actual investigative techniques.

In this section, you'll learn how to conduct successful surveillances. You'll uncover the tricks PIs use to get nonpublished numbers, cell phone numbers, and subscriber information. Methods of conducting investigations that provide proven results are taught to you, step-by-step, to help you with your own case. You'll see how to conduct an interrogation and how to use GPS-equipped tracking devices.

Techniques of Interview and Interrogation

In This Chapter

- ◆ Learning preparation techniques
- ◆ Getting the most out of a witness
- ◆ Handling informants
- ◆ Outsmarting the suspects into confessing
- ◆ Taking notes in the interview
- ◆ Principles behind recorded statements
- ◆ Digital cameras and the witness interview

Obtaining information from people is almost always the largest part of a private investigator's job. Attorneys ask investigators to track down witnesses and take statements from them. Insurance companies want accidents investigated. Businesses ask investigators to solve internal thefts. Parents need their runaway teenagers returned. Each of these types of cases involves interviewing witnesses and potential witnesses, and interrogating suspects.

A witness is an individual who may have testimony pertinent to an investigation. A suspect is an individual who may have committed or aided the commission of a crime that is under investigation.

In this chapter, we'll examine some techniques and methods that will aid you in extracting the information from witnesses and make it possible for you to get those suspects who have the most to lose, the guilty ones, to reveal the details of their crimes.

Be Prepared

There has never been better advice for debriefing a witness or interviewing a suspect than to be prepared. Before beginning an interview, the PI has to be completely familiar with all of the facts of the case.

Attorneys and insurance companies will usually call with a new case assignment or fax or e-mail the assignment to you. It is a good practice to go to the client's office and review the entire file concerning the case before beginning the investigation. I made a practice of this whenever possible for two very good reasons.

First, you're the investigator. You know what will help you locate your witness much better than your client. There may be nuggets of information in those files that your client doesn't even realize are important, such as license tags, phone numbers, dates of birth, and Social Security numbers. Employment data for your witness may be in there, but the client didn't relay that to you. If you want to set up an appointment with the witness, it's usually easier to contact him or her at work first. Most people would rather be interviewed at home, but sometimes finding them is difficult. If you know where they work, you can at least contact them there and set up the interview for after hours.

Second, going to your client's office and reviewing the file gives you an opportunity to meet face-to-face. I can't tell you how many additional cases I've picked up by going to an attorney's office and walking past other attorneys in the practice. They see me going down the hall and invariably I hear, "Well, since you're here, I've got a case I could use some help on." It never fails. Even the attorney or claims adjuster you originally came to see will frequently find additional work or other files for you to review. Whenever it's feasible, go to the client's office.

In making your preparations for the interview, write a list of the items you need to cover. Sometimes the interview takes an unexpected turn; the witness reveals some information of which you were unaware, and in the heat of following the new lead, you forget to ask everything you needed to ask about the facts you had to begin with. That's why you should always make a list of the topics you want to cover. If the interview gets really exciting for some reason, be sure to go over your list before you leave the witness. That way you're sure to cover every topic you originally intended.

Just last week, I sent one of my investigators to a small town, a three-hour drive away. When I went over his report, I saw he forgot to ask some really pertinent questions. He didn't make a list before he left as I'd taught him to do, so he had to drive six hours round-trip to redo the interview on his own time and at his own expense.

Get Them to Like You

In conducting interviews, you have to give the person you're interviewing a reason why he or she should tell you what you need to know. Logical reasons why the witness should cooperate are actually the least effective. Emotion works better than reason. One of the best emotional reasons for him or her to cooperate is because your witness likes you and wants to help *you*.

If you're interviewing a driver who witnessed a car accident, she really doesn't care about helping some attorney win a case where the attorney is going to take 30 or 40 percent of the settlement. Most people don't like attorneys anyway. Her dealings with attorneys have probably always been negative and she considers them a subspecies of the human race. Her sympathies may lie with the other side. She certainly isn't interested in helping a big insurance conglomerate save a few bucks at the expense of some poor old guy who ran into another person's car accidentally. So why should she help you at all?

The answer is to make her like you. Become her friend. Once a friendship has developed, she's now invested time and emotion in this relationship. Now by helping you, she unconsciously feels she is helping to improve the relationship between the two of you.

When you knock on the door, greet her with a smile and genuine warmth. Once inside, survey your surroundings immediately. There are two reasons why you want to do this:

1. Glance around the room when you enter to make sure that there is no danger present—nobody hiding in back of the couch or behind the front door, for example, with a weapon. You may think this is a paranoid thing to do, but you just never know what was going on in that house or apartment at the time you knocked on the door. You could be walking in on a drug deal or a violent domestic dispute and the couple stopped in order to answer the door. It is better to err on the side of caution.

2. People surround themselves with what's important in their lives. Look around to find some common ground or an interesting hobby that your witness has. If you can discover her passion, what really motivates her and makes her life worthwhile, then you are on the road to making a new friend.

Find a common element with her life. If you're a sailor and she has a picture of a sailboat on the wall, talk sailing. If the woman you're trying to interview is busy cooking dinner and the kids are screaming, pick up the screaming baby and keep her occupied while you talk to the mother. If you can make friends with the child, the mom will be your friend, too.

Talk about her problems, her life, what interests her. Be charming and witty if you can. Once she's told you what is going on in her life, you've succeeded in subconsciously tying yourself to that part of her life that makes life worth living. Now, instead of being an outsider, a representative of one of those "damn insurance companies," you're a real person with a tie to the better part of her life. And most importantly, she's now emotionally involved with you, even if she's not actually aware of it.

Once you've established that bond of trust, the witness will tell you everything you want to know, as long as your questions don't break that bond.

At one time during my career with the FBI, I was assigned to the Phoenix division. I had a road trip that covered three Indian reservations: the Pima, the Maricopa, and the northern part of the Papago. Early every Sunday morning, I'd receive a telephone call from the tribal police indicating that some federal crime had been committed, typically burglary, rape, assault with a deadly weapon, or homicide. I'd leave my bed and travel to the reservation. Generally, by mid-morning the crime would be solved, the perpetrator arrested, and the prisoner handcuffed with his hands behind his back and strapped into the front seat with the seatbelt where I could keep a close eye on him. I'd transport the prisoner, a two-and-a-half-hour drive, back to the Maricopa County jail in Phoenix.

The suspect's rights would have been read to him and usually he would have waived those rights, signing a document to that effect. During this drive to the jail, I'd engage him in conversation. Invariably we'd talk about his life on the reservation and his frustrations with life in general. Before the trip was over, he would have told me how some part of his life made him commit the crime I'd arrested him for. It was never his fault, some outside force or inner demon made him do it, but he always confessed to the act itself. Because of the ironclad confession I obtained during the drive to the jail, I never had one of those cases go to trial. Every one of them pled guilty.

There was no rubber hose, no coercion, just concern for the suspect's troubles and his life. You know, some of these guys committed the most heinous of crimes, brutal, body-mutilating crimes, sometimes against their own mother. But during that drive I always found a redeeming side to each one of them. I never arrested a man I didn't grow to like during that ride back to Phoenix. And I think the feeling was mutual.

Informants

Working with *informants* has similarities to interviewing witnesses, but there are differences as well. You must first develop the same level of trust and rapport with an informant as we talked about in the preceding section. Informants usually have some motivating factor, something that drives them to help you besides the bond you develop with them. This could be a secret desire to be a private investigator themselves. It's good to kid with your informants about "putting them on the payroll." It feeds their need to live an exciting life vicariously through yours.

def•i•ni•tion

> An **informant** is an individual that cooperates, usually without the knowledge of others involved in the case, by providing information during an investigation. She might or might not be a witness or a participant in the particular case under investigation. Frequently, an informant may receive compensation, or other benefit, for her information, whereas a witness never should.

Forget what you've seen on television about police and informants. The tough-cop routine, slamming the informant against the wall, threatening him, and then expecting him to work for you is ridiculous and just pure fiction. You should never call an informant a "snitch." It's derogatory, and if you think about him in derogatory terms, your actions, mannerisms, and tone of voice when speaking will betray your true thoughts. He will sense your demeaning manner and you can kiss that informant good-bye. Remember, the informant is a friend first, an informant second.

When Does a Private Investigator Use an Informant?

An informant can simply be a neighbor of a subject in a domestic case under surveillance who will let you know when the subject arrives home. This informant may call you when your client's wife, who is supposed to be at the gym, just showed up for a different kind of workout. To motivate this informant, you must build the bond we spoke about. The chances are, however, that the two neighbors have some sort of ongoing dispute. It could be something as trivial as your subject's dog relieving himself on your informant's front lawn every morning. Regardless, whatever the reason, your informant is probably using you to get even with your subject.

Can You Pay Informants?

Money and informants seem to go hand in hand. You can perform favors for informants. You can pay informants. But you can never pay an informant if that person may be a potential witness in a case. A witness may hint to you that for a little money her memory might improve. After all, her testimony might save your client, an insurance company, millions of dollars. Regardless, you can't pay her.

If a witness were to be paid by a private investigator and then actually be called to testify, her testimony would be thrown out. You might see witnesses paid on television. No matter. You can't do it. Now, with law enforcement and criminal cases, the story changes. Police can pay informants, but civil cases have different rules than criminal law. There's no quicker way to be embarrassed in open court in a civil matter, lose the case, and lose a very good client at the same time, than by paying a potential civil witness. Don't do it. The exception to that rule is the "expert" witness, who can be paid.

Interrogating the Suspects

Do private investigators ever get involved in criminal investigations? Absolutely. Some PIs make a career out of working criminal-defense cases. Our firm usually has some criminal cases ongoing at any given moment. Frequently, in the defense of a *premise liability* case, we will be investigating rapes and assaults that were alleged to have occurred on our client's property. We'll talk more about premise liability cases in Chapter 11.

def•i•ni•tion

A **premise liability** case involves the allegation that a property owner was negligent by not curing some default in the premise or real property owned or managed by the defendant, and this negligence led to the harm of the plaintiff. An example of this could be the plaintiff alleging that the defendant failed to provide adequate exterior lighting and the ensuing darkness caused a rape or assault inflicted upon the plaintiff.

When interviewing suspects in criminal cases, it may not be easy to establish a bond of trust. Most criminals are street smart and believe in their hearts that they are smarter than you, the investigator. For certain, they may have more street smarts than you do. A good investigator can turn the criminal's "smarter than you" self-image to his advantage in interrogating the suspect.

After a high-speed chase through downtown Phoenix, I arrested Daniel Black for interstate transportation of a stolen motor vehicle and assault on a federal agent. He'd assaulted my partner and fellow FBI agent who'd accompanied me to interview Black concerning his attempt to obtain false identity papers.

A week or so later, Daniel called me from the county jail and requested I come down to talk. He claimed concern for his wife who'd escaped during the chase, but whom we later identified and charged as well. Previously, he'd had shoulder-length hair, but when he entered the interview room, I noticed he sported a completely shaved head. I ignored the change in his appearance and listened to his stated concerns about his wife, who'd made bail for herself, leaving him in jail. I think he actually called for the interview (he was represented by counsel, but since he'd initiated the contact, I could talk to him without his attorney present) to try to find out how much we knew about his numerous and varied criminal activities.

After a few minutes, he couldn't stand the fact that I'd asked nothing about his shaved head. In order to show how "smart" he was, he admitted he'd shaved his head so when he was put into a lineup, his appearance would be radically different and the witnesses wouldn't be able to identify him. That statement constituted an admission of guilt and I used it at his trial to convict him. He got eight years in the federal penitentiary because he just had to demonstrate how much smarter he was than the young FBI agent.

Whatever the case, if you can figure out what motivates your suspect, you can successfully interrogate him. A client called me just about a month ago. This client held a fairly high political office. His home had been burgled three days previously and a safe containing over $40,000 in cash had been stolen.

The facts were as follows: my client and his wife, the Smiths, returned home one evening to find a glass panel in the front door broken. A baseball bat lay on the front stoop. Wisely, rather than entering the house, they called the police. The officers arrived and found the door locked. They reached through where the broken pane had been and opened the door. When the police entered the home, the burglar alarm sounded. The police inspected the house and found the burglar was not present. The Smiths entered the home and discovered the safe, which had been in a hall closet, was now missing. They reported to the police the safe had held $20,000 in cash, but insisted to me the figure was really closer to $40,000.

Who committed the burglary? After interviewing my clients, the Smiths, I was convinced that there had indeed been a burglary, the Smiths were actual victims, and that this was not just an attempt at insurance fraud. The facts of the case and the burglar alarm being armed when the police arrived gave me three good clues as to the identity of the thief. Can you guess what they are?

- Whoever broke in and took the safe knew the alarm code, turned it off when he entered, and reset it when leaving with the safe.

- The reason he took the entire safe was, while he knew the alarm code, he didn't know the combination to the safe and hence couldn't open it on the spot.

- The psychology behind rearming the alarm when he left indicated to me the burglar had concern for the Smiths and didn't want anybody else to burglarize the house while the Smiths were out; that, or else the burglar set the alarm out of force of habit.

Evaluating those three reasonable deductions, I decided the thief was a regular visitor to the house and probably a family member.

We can make other deductions based upon the facts I've given you, but those are the important ones. I went through the list of possible suspects with the Smiths and pretty well narrowed it down to their 21-year-old unemployed son Luke.

Luke lived in a trailer park with his girlfriend, whom the Smiths did not approve of. I went to the trailer park to interview the prime suspect. Luke was a thin white boy, who was unsuccessfully trying to grow a mustache. A bare whisper of straggly dark hair grazed his upper lip. I showed my private investigator's identification to Luke and asked him to open the trunk of his car. He didn't balk at the request and didn't ask why. I knew then he was good for the burglary because if he'd been innocent he would have protested. Protesting wouldn't have necessarily made him innocent. A guilty man might have protested, too, maybe even more, but not protesting combined with the other facts, certainly convinced me he did it. When he opened the trunk I also knew the money wouldn't be in there or he never would have opened it so readily.

I went through the motions of searching the car, just in case he'd left some of the money hidden there. Nothing. Luke told me his girlfriend was pregnant, but his folks didn't know about the pregnancy. Luke appeared vulnerable and I knew he wouldn't fare well in the state penitentiary.

Elementary, My Dear Watson

On occasion, a case may arise that lends itself to some sort of a percentage for a recovery rather than an hourly rate. In most civil cases, private investigators are prohibited from working on a percentage because they are supposed to be "finders of fact" and if their fee is dependent upon the success of the case, it could lead to a conflict of interest. This is especially true if the investigator will be a witness in the case.

However, if the case is similar to the Smith safe burglary described in this chapter, then a percentage of the monies recovered would be an acceptable fee arrangement. Use the sample contract in Appendix C and modify it at the beginning of the case to delineate the fee agreement before you begin the case. The risk though is, if you don't succeed, you won't get paid.

I asked him if the police had been there yet. They hadn't. "The police are coming," I told him. "They'll be here shortly." I explained to him very graphically and in great detail what life in prison is like for young men of his slight build and complexion. Next, I put myself in a position to help him, to become a friend with his best interest in mind. I told him the only way for us to keep him from that fate was to get the money he'd stolen and return it to his parents before the police got there. Once the police had him, there was nothing his parents or I could do to help.

After my clear description of prison life and his alternatives, it took Luke about 30 seconds to step to the side of his trailer and begin digging with his bare hands. In a few minutes, he'd dug up a plastic container filled with bills. We took it inside and counted it together. I photographed him with the money, wrote out a receipt, and had him sign it. Together, we took it back to his parents.

The police had a three-day head start in solving that burglary. It took me a little over an hour. Why was I able to solve it when they couldn't? First, the use of a little deductive reasoning. Second, I was able to read what would motivate Luke into confessing. Lastly, I was more motivated than the police, because I needed results to justify my rather large bill to my client. The police get paid whether they solve the crime or not. It's not unusual in a case like this to use *results billing*.

def•i•ni•tion

Results billing is the practice of charging more than a standard hourly rate if the results achieved justify a higher bill or a higher hourly rate.

Copious Notes

When interviewing witnesses or suspects, always take copious notes. You should have a yellow legal pad or other type of notebook to record as much as possible of your interview. It's not necessary to write down the questions that you ask the witness, but you should record in a personal shorthand or scribble how the witness responds.

Next, you should initial your original notes, date them, and, after using them to write your report, the original notes should be placed in an envelope and maintained in the case file.

There are three very good reasons for this:

♦ Memories are not perfect. The interview will be absolutely clear in your mind when you leave the witness, but it may be a day or two before you write or dictate your report. In the intervening time, you will forget some of the facts the witness had related to you. Your detailed notes of the interview will refresh your memory and make the report you deliver to your client more accurate.

♦ A witness will change her story. Six months to perhaps four years later, you may be called upon to testify as to your interview with that person. The witness also will be called to testify. Her memory of the accident will have been colored by what she's read, or seen, or been told by other people. Sometimes a witness will change facts intentionally; sometimes she just can't remember.

♦ Your attorney, the opposing counsel, or the judge will ask you to produce the original notes. Your original notes are considered documents produced in the normal course of business, and as such, are admissible into court. They carry considerable weight in our judicial system. When the witness's story, four years later, conflicts with your reporting, your attorney or the opposing attorney may ask you to produce your original notes. If your notes have been dated and initialed and are clear on the point in question, your testimony will be considered factual, not the witness's. When a case is won because of your professionalism, charge the client more. You deserve it and he will pay it.

A successful resolution to a case makes the client happy, the attorney happy, and you should be happy, too. The attorney who hired you will usually suggest that you get your bill to him right away so that he can submit it to the client for prompt payment. If the case was a big win for the client, and you don't have a signed contract with him, you might at that time want to bump your rate up a notch. Nobody will balk because you're worth it. You may have just saved your client a million dollars. If you're a successful PI and produce winning cases for your clients, you should consider raising your rates anyway.

Recording the Interview

Attorneys use investigators to locate potential witnesses and interview them because it's cheaper for the client to pay the investigator than it is to pay the attorney. It makes no sense to have the attorney running around interviewing folks who may or may not have any information about the case.

Once the investigator finds a witness that has information germane to the investigation, then the attorney may schedule a *deposition* for the witness. Depositions are expensive and time-consuming and require that a court reporter be present to record the questions and answers. Also, the opposing counsel is present. An attorney would not want to be deposing everybody on the block where the accident occurred. He'd only want to depose the folks who actually witnessed the accident and who will help his case.

def•i•ni•tion

A **deposition** is a statement made under oath by a witness, usually written or recorded, that may be used in court at a later time. If there is the likelihood that the deponent will not be available later, for instance, due to illness, it is not uncommon for the deposition to be videotaped. The deponent is the witness being deposed.

For instance, you, the PI, might find a woman who can testify that the driver of one of the vehicles involved in an accident you're investigating was drunk when he left a party. Later, that driver caused the accident. The witness, although she didn't see the accident, could testify to the driver's condition shortly before the accident when he left the party.

The Division of Licensing

Unfortunately, the law in civil cases is not always about truth, but more about which side can present its view of the truth most effectively. The PI should not take sides in a case. He should report the facts accurately. If the facts are not good for his client, then that's too bad. Report the facts and let the chips fall where they may. If you start skewing the facts, your client will not be happy and you will tarnish your reputation and quickly lose clients. If there is information out there that is going to hurt your client's case, he needs to know about it, because you can be sure the other side will bring it up. At least your client can be prepared for the worst.

You, the investigator, need to get all the facts, good or bad, to your client. But your client, the attorney in this case, doesn't want the opposing side to know there is a witness out there that will hurt his case. If he deposes a witness harmful to his case, the other side will be at the deposition and obviously know it.

In order to make sure you have all of the facts and don't omit anything from your report, you should consider recording the interview. We talked in Chapter 3 about the advantages of a digital recorder. Digital or analog, the PI has to have the permission of the witness to record the interview. Getting permission is not always easy.

One approach that seems to work is to tell the person you're interviewing that recording the conversation would really save you a lot of the trouble of taking handwritten notes. Would she mind? Don't make a big production out of it. If the approach is low key and seems to be the normal thing that you always do, most people will not object. But if you make a big production out of setting up the recorder, the witness may change her mind.

Once you have the witness's permission to record, there are four items that have to be done at the very beginning of the recording:

1. State your name and occupation.

2. State the date and location where the interview is taking place.

3. State the witness's name and indicate that she has given you permission to record this conversation. "Mrs. Brown, you are aware that we are recording this interview and I have your permission, is that correct?" Make sure the witness verbally says yes to that question. A nodding of the head can't be heard on the tape when you produce it in court two years later.

4. Indicate the subject matter of the interview: an accident that occurred on such and such a date at a certain intersection.

Don't give the original recorded statement to your client. See Chapter 23, for details on handling recordings and maintaining the chain of custody on the evidence. Some clients will ask for the original tape. Give them a duplicate. Besides violating the chain of custody on the evidence, attorneys are notorious for losing things. Produce the original tape when you go to court.

The Least You Need to Know

◆ Never go to an interview unprepared. It's better to go to the client's office to review the file, because the investigator knows better what he needs out of the file than the client does.

◆ The best way to gain a witness's assistance is to befriend her. Have the witness invest in your mutual relationship and then you'll have her help.

◆ Informants should become your friends and be treated with respect. Do not be demeaning to an informant and then expect his complete cooperation.

◆ Successfully interrogating a suspect requires the PI to outsmart her and to understand what will motivate her to confess.

◆ During a witness interview, it is imperative to take complete notes and retain the original notes, as they may be called into evidence later at a trial.

◆ With permission, recording a witness interview is a good idea. Never give up the original recording in case you have to produce it in court.

Chapter 11

The Neighborhood Investigation

In This Chapter

- ◆ Learning the steps to neighborhood investigations
- ◆ Searching for the know-it-all neighbor
- ◆ Weaving neighborhoods with liability investigations
- ◆ Matching talents with assignments
- ◆ Fibbing to the neighbors
- ◆ Checking out the dirt … literally
- ◆ Finding other crimes, other times

At some point in your life as an investigator, you will inevitably have to perform what is termed a "neighborhood investigation," usually referred to in the trade as just a "neighborhood."

If you're investigating a burglary, for instance, and you are going to "do a neighborhood," you'll want to knock on every door in the immediate area and interview the neighbors. If you have the time and the budget, you should check with neighbors up to several blocks away. Why? Because burglars don't usually park their cars in front of the home or business they're burglarizing. If you want a description of the burglar's getaway vehicle, it's not going to come from the guy across the street from the victim.

There are several techniques and important methods to conducting neighborhood investigations. If the PI is going to go to the effort to do this type of investigation, he or she might as well do so effectively. A neighborhood investigation can be one of the best investigative techniques a professional can use, and yet the inexperienced PI or lazy law enforcement detective frequently overlooks it.

The Mechanics

A neighborhood investigation really involves several steps. The most obvious is to knock on doors in the neighborhood where the accident took place, or the home was burglarized, or from where the child was kidnapped. This should be done as shortly after the inciting incident as possible. If the case is a kidnapped child, chances are the police will have beaten you there. If it's a runaway teenager, the police probably won't be involved at all. In a number of jurisdictions, the police won't respond to a home burglary where the items taken amount to less than $5,000. If your case does have police involvement and the police have already done a neighborhood, do it again.

There are three steps required to conduct an effective neighborhood investigation:

1. Knock on doors.

2. Check out the vehicles.

3. Consider the getaway car.

Performing these steps on a neighborhood investigation will be the subject of the sections that follow.

Knock on Doors

The key to success in this type of investigation is to talk to every person who was home on the day and at the time of the incident.

Let's take burglaries as an example. Chances are that when the PI arrives on the scene, it is going to be some time after the burglary occurred. Remember the son in Chapter 10 who stole the safe from his parents? The police didn't do a neighborhood investigation in that case. Had they done one, they might have found that the neighbor across the street had seen the boy at the home during the time of the burglary. We'll never know, though, because the police didn't ask. I didn't do one either, in that case, but I would have come back and done it if the son hadn't confessed to the crime.

Obviously, you have to narrow down the time frame of the offense. You do this by interviewing the victims, their family, and the immediate neighbors to get a fairly specific idea of when the burglary occurred.

Once the approximate time has been established, you have to figure out the point of entry and exit. These two points are not always the same. If the burglars entered through the back door and there are neighbors across the back fence, then that should be the first door you knock on—not because they're suspects (although you need to keep an open mind), but because they might have noticed someone cutting through their backyard and climbing the fence to get into the victim's yard.

Alternate Light Source

Take good notes while you're talking to the neighbors. Keep track of whom you've talked to, what they saw, who was home at the time of the burglary, and who wasn't home at the time you knocked on their door. If a wife tells you she wasn't home when the burglary occurred but her husband might have been, make a note of it. You're going to want to go back and talk to that husband, even though the wife says the husband didn't see anything.

The only way to do a thorough neighborhood is to talk to each and every neighbor, not just a representative from each home, but every person who may have been home at the time of the burglary. That's a lot of work and will require multiple trips through the subdivision. A PI can cut a corner in a neighborhood investigation by getting the phone numbers of each home he talks to. Then, instead of going back to the residences to speak to those who weren't home on the first visit, he can call and conduct the interview over the phone. A face-to-face interview is better, but the budget may not allow for repeated trips back to do the neighborhood.

Don't forget the kids. Kids are all over the neighborhood, riding bikes, walking to friends' houses, inline skating, and skateboarding. Kids notice strangers and strange goings-on. Be sure to speak to all the children and not just the parents when you're conducting the neighborhood investigation.

Consider the Getaway Car

Most criminals use some sort of transportation to flee the scene of their crime. Certainly, if it's a planned crime, getting to and away from the scene of the crime is an important part of the plan. Now we all know that criminals are not always the smartest folks, but usually they try to think a little bit ahead. In solving burglaries or property crimes, the PI has to put himself into the mindset of the criminal. If you were a not-very-bright criminal, how would you make your escape? Where would you have parked the getaway car?

Examining the list of items stolen can give the PI an idea of how far away the getaway car may have been. If the burglars stole a big screen television, they didn't carry it very far. If they only took jewelry and small items, the car might have been several blocks away.

Why do we care about the getaway car? In movies, the getaway car is always stolen and not traceable back to the criminal, anyway. In real life, most getaway cars belong to the criminal or to an associate. When the getaway car is identified and the license plate run, you'll probably catch the criminal.

Once the investigator has identified where the getaway car might reasonably have been parked, he knows how far out to conduct the neighborhood investigation. It's possible that the getaway driver, sitting in the car with the engine idling, was spotted by a neighbor who wrote down the license number.

Find the Nosy Neighbor

In almost every neighborhood there is some person, a little old lady or gossipy man, who just has to know what is going on all of the time. It's not unusual for that type of person to be peering out her window to see what the fellow across the street is doing.

At one point in my PI career, we were moving the office from one rental space to a newer one. While waiting for the new space to be readied, I ran our operation out of my home. My wife, who worked in a medical facility, had to leave for work by 6:30 every morning. A female assistant, who drove a little red sports car, would come to the house around 9. After about six weeks of this, my next-door neighbor made a point of asking my wife if the cleaning lady who drove that little red car and came to our house everyday was any good. She needed somebody to clean her place, too, but not as often as we did. My wife, of course, knew we didn't have a cleaning lady daily and it took her a minute to realize to whom my neighbor was referring. Women have to stick together, you know, and my neighbor was just doing her duty, making sure my wife knew that after she'd gone to work, some strange woman came to our place and always left before my wife got home.

The FBI is big on neighborhood investigations, and so am I, because they work. Sure, they're manpower-intensive, but they can produce good leads.

While I was still with the bureau, I had a case where I was doing a neighborhood where I had an interest in some people at a certain address. I went to the residence and noticed the house stood vacant. The mailbox by the front door was stuffed with letters. Don't tell the postal inspectors, but I thumbed through the mail, writing down the return addresses. After walking around the house and not seeing anything of further interest, I began knocking on doors and interviewing neighbors. Eventually, in doing this neighborhood investigation, I arrived at the house directly across the street from my subject's residence. I'd noticed that at this house, the drapes were drawn. I thought perhaps nobody was at home, but there was a car in the driveway. As I started up the walkway, I noticed the drapes in the front window moved a little.

I rang the bell and this little old lady came to the door. I identified myself and showed her my credentials. She opened the door and invited me in. Next to a chair by the front window was, no kidding, a pair of binoculars. When she saw my glance toward the binoculars, a sheepish grin spread across her face. After explaining the interest I had in her former neighbor's comings and goings, she produced a lined pad of paper. On it were written 45 license plate numbers. These 45 cars had all visited her neighbor across the street during the last month the house was occupied.

I've never found anybody that nosy, or that conscientious, since. But I have found a lot of very good neighbors who write down license plate numbers of suspicious cars they see in their neighborhood.

I have developed many, many excellent leads and solved numerous cases by executing the laborious and tedious task of a neighborhood investigation. If the circumstances warrant it, there is no better investigative technique.

Premise Liability Cases

In Chapter 10, we briefly touched on premise liability cases. These cases always involve an allegation of negligence on the part of a property owner and some sort of an injury to the plaintiff. The underlying incident that starts the whole case rolling may be an assault, a rape, a homicide, or something as simple as a slip and fall on a banana peel or a dog biting a neighbor.

If the inciting incident of a premise liability case is a slip and fall in a grocery store, then a neighborhood investigation is obviously not warranted. Hopefully, the store manager will have taken the names of a number of customers and store employees who witnessed the accident.

However, in most premise liability cases that take place outside of a commercial establishment, such as in a parking lot or an apartment complex, a neighborhood investigation is definitely warranted. Keep in mind that for our purposes, the neighborhood does not have to be residential. Employees of neighboring stores make good witnesses.

One such case I worked involved the alleged abduction and rape of a young girl from her residence. It was in the heat of a southern July, at about 2:30 P.M. Julie, a 15-year-old girl living with her stepmother in a large apartment complex, was brought into the hospital emergency room. She had been beaten about the face and her bottom lip was swollen and bloody. She was alleging rape. Physical examination confirmed her allegations, and the sheriff's office began an investigation.

Julie stood only 4-feet, 10-inches tall. Her mother had gone to the store for cigarettes and told her daughter not to let anyone into the apartment while she was gone. Julie said that while her mother was out, someone knocked on the door. She thought it was her mother returning. She went to look through the peephole installed in the door, but the hole was too high for her to see through, even standing on the tips of her toes. She opened the door and an unknown male grabbed her by the hair, dragged her through the apartment complex to a wooded area behind the apartments, and proceeded to rape her.

Her father and mother, as her guardians, were suing the apartment complex, alleging that the peepholes were installed at such a height as to make the apartments unreasonably unsafe.

The crime scene in the wooded area indicated a struggle may have taken place there, and articles of the girl's clothing were still there, as well as a packet of spilled cigarettes. At the time we were called in, nearly six months after the incident, the crime was still unsolved.

I began interviewing neighbors and came up dry. Nobody had seen or heard anything. Several of the people I talked to had been home at the time of the assault. It seemed unusual that the girl had been dragged, kicking and screaming, past the swimming pool, through the apartment complex, and down a hundred yards or so through an asphalt parking lot, and nobody would admit to having heard or seen any of it. Perhaps this might happen in New York City, but I found it unlikely in this southern town.

Some of the people I talked to had been at the swimming pool, but were not there continuously. They had gone inside to get drinks and such, so the girl's story could have been true. Nonetheless, I smelled a rat.

In talking with the apartment residents, I had several tell me they knew the girl had been friends with a couple of boys who hung out at a certain corner market. They gave me a good description of those boys. I spoke with the manager of the market. Of course the boys weren't there, but the manager said they came in every afternoon between 2 and 5 P.M. It was already after 5, so I went back the next afternoon at 2 and waited. Eventually, two boys came in that matched the description I'd been given.

I spoke with the two youths and they admitted that they knew about the assault. In fact, those two and a third boy had been in the woods smoking pot with Julie at about 2 P.M. the afternoon of the rape. The third boy, let's call him Leroy, had wanted to have sex with Julie for a long time. When Leroy began putting the moves on Julie, these two told him to leave her alone, as they knew she was underage. Julie seemed mildly co-operative but my two informants didn't want anything to do with that particular scene, so they departed, leaving Leroy and Julie alone smoking more pot.

It's apparent that Julie probably got scared and changed her mind, but Leroy was determined and finally beat her and raped her. It was a terrible crime, but it didn't happen because the peephole was too high in the apartment door. It happened because Julie had some questionable friends.

The rape didn't actually occur on the apartment grounds, so my client, the owner of the apartment complex, was off the hook. I provided a copy of my report to the sheriff's office and Leroy was eventually charged with the crime. Why was a PI able to solve this case when the sheriff's office couldn't do it with all of its manpower and forensic evidence? Because the investigating detectives didn't perform a thorough neighborhood investigation. Remember, my neighborhood investigation was done six months after the incident and I still got a good lead from it. Suppose I'd been able to do it the day of the rape or the following day. Had the sheriff's office executed a proper neighborhood investigation, they probably would have found Leroy hanging at the corner market still bragging about what a good time he'd had.

Discretion with the Neighbors

Interviews are successful if you build the bond of trust with the person you're interviewing. Part of that bond of trust is that the interviewee is confiding in you and expects you to exercise discretion with the information he entrusts to you.

Almost without fail, during an interview the subject will say something like, "Well, I don't really want to get involved. I have to live in this neighborhood, even after your case is over." And that is very true. He knows that if he rats out the lady across the street, then she may try to get even with him at some point. That's a very real fear people have. You'll be long gone, but he's still living across the street from her.

Going to Court

If you promise the subject that what he says is "just between you and me," he won't believe it and he will know you've just lied to him. If you say that, you've just broken the bond you've worked so hard to build. He knows you've got to report the results of your interview to your client. He knows there is a lawsuit going on and he may end up in court testifying.

How do you handle that situation? By being completely honest—well, almost—with the interviewee. Tell him that most of these cases never go to trial. Ninety-nine percent of the time, these types of lawsuits are settled out of court. You, of course, have to share the information that you get from him with the attorney for your client, but you will not share it with anyone else. Unless the case actually goes to court, the other side will never know what your interviewee says. If it does go to trial, then he will likely be *subpoenaed* and will have to testify anyway. By cooperating now, he might help settle the case, which would prevent him from going to court and testifying.

def•i•ni•tion

> A **subpoena** is a command from the judge of a court requiring that the person or representative of an institution named in the subpoena appear in court at a certain time. A **subpoena deuces tecum** is a subpoena that requires the individual or institution to provide documents to the clerk of the court as outlined in the subpoena. A subpoena could require both an appearance and the retrieval of documents.

Keep in mind that some people might enjoy going to court and testifying. Your interviewee may get a big kick out of saying what he has to say about his neighbor across the street and doing it in front of her. If that is the case, then play on that. Encourage him to tell you all he knows now and if it is good enough, you can practically assure him of his day before the judge. In order to have success here, you have to evaluate whom you're talking to, determine what motivates him, and manipulate him accordingly.

Arbitration

There are occasions where the interviewee's information might get reported back to the client without the case going to trial. In the settlement process, a case might go to arbitration. Arbitration refers to a process where the plaintiff and the defendant in a civil lawsuit meet with a third party, known as a professional arbitrator.

The arbitrator is skilled in negotiating, and it is his responsibility to try and help the two different sides come to an agreement. This process reduces the number of cases going to trial and helps clear the court calendar for cases that cannot be settled.

If your report contains some really hot stuff, a smart attorney will use those statements as leverage to encourage a better settlement. It's possible that those statements might be reported to the subject of the investigation, the neighbor of your interviewee, even though the case is settled before trial. It's not likely, but it's certainly possible. So the neighbor might find out what was said by your interviewee, regardless.

Usually, if a settlement is not reached by arbitration, the case is scheduled for trial. This does not preclude a case from settling later, even though no agreement was reached during arbitration. However, some contracts provide that in the event of a dispute, the parties must submit to binding arbitration. This means that a settlement *must* be reached during arbitration. If the parties cannot decide upon a settlement considered fair by all, then the arbitrator, after being fully informed of the facts, will reach what he considers a fair conclusion. But his determination is binding on both parties.

Keep an Eye Out

One last major factor to consider in conducting neighborhoods is the "other crime" aspect. Be aware of your surroundings and what the folks you speak with are telling you. You have to be intuitive and sensitive to the meaning behind their words. Many times people will try to tell you something but are afraid to come right out and say it, so they allude to it rather than by being direct. You need to have your antennae up all of the time.

By listening carefully, you may become aware of other factors that have a bearing on your case. Remember Daniel Black from Chapter 10? He was the fellow who shaved his head in an attempt to fool the witnesses at a lineup. We later obtained a search warrant and conducted a search of his home. In his garage we found, in addition to the stolen motor home he was driving when we arrested him, a stolen Volkswagen and a stolen Porsche. In talking to his neighbors, they all mentioned that some items around their homes had gone missing. We were able to return bicycles, a lawn tractor, numerous personal items, credit cards, and traveler's checks, all belonging to the neighbors. Daniel was a thief. And it didn't matter to him whom he stole from.

As a PI, most of your neighborhood investigations will involve some sort of criminal or fraudulent activity. You might be talking to neighbors about an insurance fraud case. Most investigators don't consider performing a neighborhood in those cases for two reasons:

1. They just plain don't think of it, or don't know how to do a neighborhood investigation.

2. If they do consider it, they're afraid that the neighbors will alert the subject to the investigation and this will spoil any chance they have of getting "good" video of the subject's activities.

We spent a lot of time trying to catch a man who was the subject of a workmen's compensation fraud case. We knew he was physically capable of working and had been told that people saw him performing all sorts of physical feats that he'd told his employer he could no longer do, yet we rarely saw him leave his house.

We decided to do a neighborhood investigation. We talked to his neighbors on either side of his house and the ones across the street. Those interviews were all negative. Finally, I went around the block and spoke to the family that shared the back fence line. It seems they would see him through the fence nearly every morning chopping firewood. You can guess where I was the next morning with the video camera. When peeking through fence holes, be sure to have a good understanding of "reasonable expectation to privacy." Private investigators would normally consider a person's reasonable expectation to privacy in terms of surveillance matters. But the expectation to privacy matter can be applied to neighborhoods, surveillance, crime scene investigations, and there have been a number of court rulings lately on expectation of privacy in the work place. As a PI, if you're conducting an internal theft investigation for an employer, you need to know what this is all about.

The expectation of privacy is really handed down to us from the U.S. Constitution, the fourth amendment protecting us from unreasonable search and seizure. We have a reasonable expectation of privacy if a reasonable person would believe that what she says or does will not be heard or seen by others. How do you establish what is reasonable? Several factors of importance to the PI play out here, including the sophistication of equipment used to "invade" the private space and the vantage point from which the investigator is viewing or hearing.

In an earlier chapter we talked about a Shipyard case where we used a two-story apartment complex with a view over our subject's eight-foot privacy fence to video him working in his backyard. Our subject never considered that a resourceful investigator could gain legal access to the apartment that had the view. But just because he didn't consider it didn't mean that he had a "reasonable expectation of privacy." If the apartment had been two blocks away and we'd had to use super-long lenses and digital zooms, then maybe we would have crossed into his area of reasonable expectation to privacy. But then again, maybe not.

Always be alert to this privacy problem. It extends well into the information-gathering area including not only physical, but electronic and financial data.

In working any case, you have to use your judgment as to whether or not a neighborhood investigation might bear fruit. Put the neighborhood in your toolbox and put it to use when appropriate. A well-done, thorough neighborhood investigation, although possibly labor-intensive, is a good technique. If the FBI is fond of it, you know it has its merits. Most investigators don't like doing them because they don't want to spend the effort or have never been taught how. Now you know more than they do.

The Least You Need to Know

- ◆ Every neighborhood has a resident that is nosy and knows everything going on in the area. Find and interview that person.

- ◆ Conducting a neighborhood can further your investigation on a premise liability case, rape, assault, or slip and fall.

- ◆ Assigning investigators who will "fit in" in that particular area can enhance a neighborhood investigation. Be aware that you're asking people to open their doors and their homes to you.

- ◆ Be honest with the people you interview. If they feel you're lying to them, they will not be forthcoming. You can promise them anonymity only to a certain degree. Cases most often settle out of court (sometimes using arbitration), and usually their identity is between you and your client.

- ◆ Be aware that your subject may be guilty of other crimes besides the one you are investigating. His neighbors may know about his other activities. Or, in speaking with the neighbors, you may piece together facts that implicate your subject in additional criminal behavior.

Chapter 12

Stationary Surveillance

In This Chapter

♦ Choosing the type and picking the site

♦ Planning the cover story

♦ Handling the nosy neighbor

♦ Staying cool if you're busted by the cops

♦ Keeping your secrets to yourself

♦ The price of goofing off

If there is one aspect or technique most people associate with the professional private investigator, it is surveillance. An investigator's entire practice may be criminal-defense work, which almost never requires surveillance. But let him be introduced as a private investigator at any cocktail party or business luncheon and the first statement made is something like, "I suppose most of what you do is following husbands and wives, that sort of thing, huh?"

Depending upon an investigator's clientele, that may or may not be true. Many PIs spend a good deal of their time doing surveillance. For example, there's always the insurance company that doesn't believe the workmen's compensation claimant is really injured. Those cases are 99 percent video surveillance, with maybe a little judicious neighborhood investigation thrown in, like we talked about in Chapter 11.

Number two on the PI's list of FAQs, after it's learned that he's a former FBI or other law-enforcement type, goes like this: "I suppose being a PI is not as exciting or as challenging as being a cop, is it?"

Nothing could be further from the truth. When the FBI tails a subject, they frequently have eight men in six cars doing the surveillance or a GPS transmitter, which is not legal for PIs to use in many states. Plus, it's not at all unusual for the bureau to also use airplanes. It is the rare—very rare—client that would pay for that much manpower.

def•i•ni•tion

Being made means that a covert operation like a surveillance has been exposed and its presence made known to the subject of the operation. It's a clue you've been made when the person you're following gives you the finger.

It is much more challenging and rewarding to conduct a one-man surveillance and not *be made*, than to utilize eight men, six cars, and an airplane. In this and the next chapter, you're going to learn how to conduct a successful one-man surveillance, and how to most effectively utilize additional manpower, if it's available.

Picking the Site

There are two methods of stationary surveillance:

◆ Fixed surveillance

◆ Fixed-mobile surveillance

In a fixed surveillance, the location used by the surveillance team is usually an apartment or house that has a clear view of the subject or the subject's property. In a domestic case, the PI is more interested in what the subject does after she leaves her house than her activities at the residence. In that case, then, a fixed-surveillance site might be set up some distance from the subject's location, but along the path of the subject's egress in order to alert mobile units that the subject is on the move.

By far the most common in the PI business is a fixed-mobile surveillance. This is a surveillance set up in a temporary fixed site, such as a surveillance van or other vehicle. In this case, while the surveillance takes place from a mobile vehicle, the purpose is to gather evidence at one specific location.

Fixed Surveillances

An attorney for a department store chain contacted us and explained that a man who claimed to have slipped and fallen in one of their stores had filed a lawsuit. Because of the fall, he alleged he'd hurt his neck and could not work. The plaintiff was, by profession, a commercial underwater diver. He'd been working on drilling rigs off the Louisiana coast. It was a coincidence that the slip and fall occurred about the same time as the oil drilling business hit a new low and the diver was scheduled to be laid off.

The diver was supposed to be living temporarily with his folks. We spent a little time watching the parents' house but never saw the guy there. We did a pretext (see Chapter 14 for a full discussion on how to do a pretext and the Division of Licensing clue on pretexts in Chapter 9) on the man's father and learned that the diver was flying out the following day to Grand Cayman to work on a dive job down there. We hurriedly consulted with the client, who approved the trip, and I was off to Grand Cayman the next day. Ah, the life of a PI.

Alternate Light Source

If you only learn one thing about surveillance, learn this: the key to obtaining successful surveillance video is to get as far away from the subject as your video equipment will allow and still get good quality video. The client, and possibly a jury, has to be able to recognize the claimant's face in the video. If you get too close, you'll get burned every time. Amateurs always begin a surveillance too near to their subject. You can always move closer, but once you've been burned, the gig is up. Explain to a client how he paid for a round-trip plane fare to Grand Cayman, only to have you get burned on the first day—and not sunburned, either. That requires a different explanation. At any rate, stay as far away from your surveillance subject as possible.

We weren't sure what job he was working on, except that it was some sort of underwater pipe construction. The job could have been on land as well as in the ocean. The water table there is pretty high; you can dig a hole six feet deep and hit water, so a diver might be needed even if the pipeline was on land. After settling in, I stowed my camera equipment in the rental car and went looking. There was construction along Seven Mile Road and it looked like they were laying some type of pipe in a ditch alongside the road before repaving. It didn't take very long to spot the subject dressed in his dive gear, dropping into a hole filled with water. I guessed he was probably securing the pipe connections.

It was impossible to sit in the car anywhere close to the construction site and get good video. Construction vehicles blocked the view from the other side of the road and any attempt at setting up a surveillance from the rental car would certainly have resulted in being burned. ("Getting burned" has the same meaning as "being made"—the subject has become aware of the surveillance.)

In a situation like this where surveillance seems impossible, as we discussed in Chapter 1, you have to think outside the box. You have to step back, look around, and search for other alternatives. A PI cannot be successful and have tunnel vision. Be creative.

I studied the surrounding area and noticed a two-story hotel directly across the street from the construction site. It looked promising, so then I explored around the inside of the hotel and figured out which room numbers would give me the view I needed. I rented the room, explaining I wanted the roadside view instead of the ocean side because it was less expensive. In a few minutes, I had the camera set up on the tripod and was rolling tape. Two days later, the pipeline had moved further down the road and so did I, into another hotel. After four days of watching our diver working 10-hour days, I consulted with the client, and we decided we had enough. I took the next day off to do some diving (after all, it was Grand Cayman) and headed home with the goodies.

The diver's attorney dropped the lawsuit just as soon as he saw some of the videotape.

If you can get a fixed-surveillance site, do it. Sitting in an air-conditioned room is so much better than sitting in a car, suffering from heat exhaustion in the summer and hypothermia in the winter. And room service is a lot better than trying to use your cell phone to persuade a pizza place to deliver to some guy under a bush behind a lamppost.

The Division of Licensing

One caution on fixed-surveillance sites: if you're using a hotel room or other facility that has regular cleaning people, you have to hide the surveillance equipment before the cleaning people enter. The maids or the cleaning folks will report unusual equipment, like your long-range video lenses, to the management, who will in turn report it to the local authorities. There is no better way to get burned than to have a squad of police cars come roaring into the parking lot and storming your room to see what you're up to. Spending a night in a foreign jail, for working without a permit, is no fun either. If you don't believe it, ask me about the three days I spent in a Bahamian jail.

A fixed-surveillance site does not have to be a hotel room or rented apartment. In my firm, we've even climbed trees and sat in them all day long to obtain videotape of allegedly injured people. I have hidden under bushes in the rain at 4 A.M. to document a newspaper delivery person unloading, folding, and bagging stacks of newspapers. My guys have hidden behind sea oats at the beach to catch surfers who could surf standing on their heads, but couldn't work because of neck injuries. All of these—trees, bushes, and sea oats—constitute fixed-surveillance sites, because if the subject moves, you can't take the site with you.

Fixed-Mobile Surveillance

Private investigators universally use fixed-mobile surveillances for workmen's compensation, slip and falls, automobile accident claims, and other types of surveillances where obtaining video tape of the subject's physical abilities and range of motion are important. Not surprisingly, the most commonly used method is the surveillance van. However, we find that pickup trucks with a cab over the bed work just as well if the investigator can squeeze through the small window that separates the inside of the truck and the truck bed.

Surveillance vans come in all configurations. We always constructed our own from a bare, two-seated delivery van. Customizing your own surveillance van is fairly straightforward. The windows, except for the windshield, should be tinted. We always have this done professionally because too often, the do-it-yourself tinting leaves bubbles in the window that tend to distort the video, which is hard to explain to the client.

The exterior of the van should be painted white or blue. There are more white and blue work vans on the streets than any other color. If the PI ends up following the subject, then her white van will look just like all the others in the subject's rearview mirror.

If the van is a little beat up, all the better. It should not be a total junker, though, or you may find yourself being towed away after a call from an irate neighbor.

One more consideration with surveillance vans is the communication factor. The PI will have to evaluate his needs in his own locale. If all of the surveillance is done in downtown or major metropolitan areas, then perhaps a cell phone with push-to-talk, which combines cell phone and two-way radio communication, would be the best bet, if it's available.

Relying strictly on cell phones for communication between surveillance team members has two drawbacks. First, it can be very expensive. Second, you can only talk to one person at a time. Frequently, fixed surveillances turn mobile and end up with two, three, or up to five persons on the street at the same time. The best solution is to have handheld walkie-talkies that share a common channel as backups to whatever primary communication device you use. Why? Things do go wrong. Your subject may lead you out of a coverage area for cell phones. We've worked a lot of surveillances in rural areas where there was no cell coverage. In fact I can't even get cell coverage at my residence. A backup is always a good idea.

When setting up the surveillance van, try to think like your subject for a minute. If he sees a van pull up nearby, park, and no one gets out, he's likely to be suspicious. In fact, many subjects have been warned by their attorneys that insurance companies often use surveillance people.

To overcome this, have your video investigator safely out of sight in the back of the surveillance van while another investigator drives the van into the subject's neighborhood. The driver parks the van on the subject's street, with a clear view of the subject's residence. The driver then exits the van and walks to where she parked her car, a block away, out of the subject's line of site. If the subject is observing any of this from his house, hopefully he will assume that the van is now unoccupied and not be suspicious of it. The driver could raise the hood and fool around in the engine compartment, giving the impression the vehicle has broken down.

After the driver walks away, it's not unusual for us to see the subject come out of his house and inspect the van to assure himself that it is unoccupied. Of course it isn't, but if done properly, he can't tell. Be sure and have the camera running, because your client will have a good chuckle when he sees the videotape of the subject walking, unaided, to check out the van. But when you videotape him going to the doctor, he is limping heavily and using a cane, or crutches, or even a wheelchair.

Setting Up the Cover

In a typical insurance claim, the surveillance van is placed in a strategic location close to the subject's house, but not too close. Stay as far away as your video equipment will allow. If the subject starts mowing his yard, roofing his house, cutting down trees, or working on his car, the woman in the van can get the video. It's not unusual to use a surveillance van in conjunction with another chase vehicle.

In the event the subject leaves the house, the investigator in the van radios to the chase vehicle that the subject is leaving, giving a good description of what the subject is wearing, which vehicle he is leaving in, and in which direction he is headed. The chase car, which should have been parked with a clear view of where the subject would most likely leave the subdivision, picks up the surveillance. The van sits quietly until the subject is well out of sight. The van then follows behind as the second vehicle in a two-man surveillance team.

The PI should purchase several sets of magnetic business signs to place on both sides of the van. A safe telephone number that can be answered by the business name should be on the signs. South East Survey and Oasis Carpet Company were two names that we employed for a long time.

Sometimes it may be necessary to park the van directly in front of the subject's residence. Try to avoid this at all costs. Look for alternatives. If there is a vacant lot across the street and the undergrowth is thick, perhaps you can hide in the bushes instead.

As a last resort, if the subject is outside of the house and you must get the video, then put survey signs on the sides of the van and park directly across the street. This time, instead of the driver leaving the area, have him set up a surveyor's tripod and go about the business of appearing to survey the street, or a ditch, or the vacant lot. Wear the typical orange safety vest and take strings and stakes and spend a few hours tromping around.

Another good cover is to do the other type of survey. Take a clipboard and walk around the neighborhood, knocking on doors, filling out a questionnaire while the man in the back of the van is getting the video.

The Division of Licensing

Be careful about talking directly with the subject of an investigation, even if it is to do a phony questionnaire-type survey. Most claimants in insurance investigations are represented by attorneys. It is unethical for a PI to have direct contact with that claimant unless his attorney is present. This includes any casual conversation or any contact whatsoever, unless the contact is initiated by the claimant himself. In Chapter 15 we'll show you one way to get a subject out of the house without violating that rule.

Pesky Neighbors

If the PI specializes in insurance fraud, workmen's compensation, and slip-and-fall defense cases, then most of his surveillance will take place during daylight hours. Success here requires videotaping the claimants in some activity that they have previously sworn they can't perform. This type of activity usually takes place outdoors, and most people don't mow their lawn at night. This is an advantage to the investigator, because more than half of the neighbors will be at work and their houses are unoccupied. That means fewer people to become suspicious.

If the man in the chase car has to park on a residential street, you can be guaranteed that at least one neighbor will wonder what he is doing there. Wouldn't you, if you saw some stranger sitting in his parked car in front of your house for several hours?

What's the best way to handle that without blowing the surveillance? When the PI notices a resident peeking out the window at her, she should leave the car and approach the neighbor in a nonthreatening manner. She shouldn't hustle to the person's door just so she can get back immediately to her car. That'll just scare the daylights out of the poor folks. Instead, she should walk up to the front door, in a professional manner, with her identification displayed in her hand. Then she can explain to the inquiring fellow that she is a private investigator conducting a surveillance. The surveillance is not on anybody in this block, but she is just waiting for the subject to leave the subdivision.

Now, the inquisitive neighbor usually gets excited and will ask the PI who she is watching. Obviously, she can't tell him that. The PI needs to be careful here. You never know who knows whom in the subdivision. It is possible that this person and the subject are friends or even relatives.

Alternate Light Source

The best way to get nosy neighbors off your back is to tell them something. I suggest that if your female PI is working a potential insurance fraud case, she should tell the nosy guy that she is just working on a divorce matter. If she's working a divorce case, she should tell him she's working an insurance fraud case. Reverse the cases and the sexes. If the subject is a male, tell him you are watching some wayward wife. If the subject is female, tell him you are watching some cheating husband. Of course, that will make about 75 percent of the men in the neighborhood more paranoid about their own activities, but that's okay, too.

Many times, I've had women who are out for a late afternoon walk stop at my vehicle and ask me why I was parked on their street. If it's a woman asking, I always tell them that I'm trying to catch a wayward husband. They almost always say, "I hope you nail the son of a bitch" and then go on with their power walk.

Sometimes, despite all of your precautions, somebody walking by the van will realize that you are inside. They may have seen the van rock slightly as you changed positions. Or they may have heard you talking, or your two-way radio *breaking squelch*. Once they're sure you're inside, they will pound on the side of the van, or knock on the door and even call to you. This is not good. You're busted big time. All you can hope is that your subject does not become aware of this commotion. If you're parked far enough away from the subject's house, chances are he'll never know you were there.

The question then becomes, how do you get out of this situation? The easiest solution is to lay the camera down and cover it with a towel. Then open the side door, exit the van, and shut the door immediately so nobody can peer in to see what's inside. Confront the people knocking on the van and tell them you had problems with some equipment "back there," and had to stop and make adjustments. It took a little longer than you thought it would, but it's fixed now, and you'll be on your way. Proceed to the driver's side door, get in, and leave.

def•i•ni•tion

Breaking squelch is not related to bodily functions. It refers to the sensitivity adjustment on a radio receiver. The squelch is the point where the receiver is tuned to its most sensitive setting. If tuned beyond this point, the radio makes a loud, piercing sound similar to a screeching parrot.

PIs sometimes find themselves in confrontational situations. This can happen if you've been made by the subject and he's not happy about it, or if you're conducting an investigation in a high-crime neighborhood and the residents make you for a cop. Maybe you're knocking on a door to do an interview and a crime has just been committed inside and you don't know it. Whatever the reason for the confrontation, don't let it escalate. Don't let your ego, your right to be there, or anything else exacerbate an already potentially dangerous conflict. Just leave. Don't get argumentative. Don't answer any questions. Just turn around and leave. Leaving the area always defuses any situation you might get yourself into. This technique will save you grief and might save you from being physically harmed.

Rousted by the Cops

There is going to come a time in every PI's life when he is sitting on a surveillance and a neighbor calls the police about this suspicious man parked in front of her house. Most of the time this can be avoided if the PI approaches the neighbor as we discussed in the preceding section. This aborts the call to the police. If that's not done, the call is made and the police will respond.

Another method to keep this from happening is for the PI to actually advise the police himself that he will be doing a surveillance. The PI should call the police department from his cell phone as soon as he sets up, then ask the dispatcher to alert the patrol units in the area that a licensed PI is working on a surveillance on such and such street. He gives them a description of his car and the dispatcher passes the word to the police cars in that zone. However, you can count on at least one patrol car coming by just to see what is going on. Wave at them as they pass. Some of the less-clever patrolmen will stop to chitchat, which does wonders for your cover.

The Division of Licensing

If you're not a licensed PI and you are rousted by the police, then you have a problem. The best you can do is explain to the police why you're out there, trying to catch your husband with his girlfriend or whatever, and hope you've found a sympathetic ear. Remember, there is no law that says you can't be sitting in a parked car. However, if the police ask you to move, then you must obey a lawful order. If you don't, you risk spending the night in the pokey, and it's really hard to do any surveillance from there.

Only once, in 20 years, have I ever had a problem with a beat cop. In that case, the cop asked me to move on. I was sitting in the only place possible, several blocks from my subject's residence, where the subdivision exited onto a main thoroughfare. I told him I was on a public street, I was licensed by the state to be there doing what I was doing, and had just as much right to be on that public street as the neighbor who complained had a right to park her car on that same street. He relented, but said if he received any more complaints, she'd make me move. I told him that was fine, I would move then, but before he asked me to move again, he should check with his sergeant. I didn't see him the rest of the day.

Don't Ask and Don't Tell

If the pesky neighbor situation is not diffused, or goes unnoticed by the private investigator, the police will arrive. The PI now has a little bit of a problem. In a second, the blue lights will flash and the cop will bleat her siren once to let the PI, and the entire neighborhood, know that she's there. All the residents in the vicinity will come out to watch and then the cop will ask him to put his hands out the window where she can see them. In the midst of all that, there are two very important points the PI must keep foremost in his mind:

1. Attitude: Don't have one. Don't panic. And definitely be polite. Make this a conversation, one professional to another. Remember, the state has given you, the PI, a license to do what you are doing and to be where you are. Explain that calmly to the police. Don't fall into the TV cliché of the PI hustling the cop.

2. Despite the cop's repeated questioning, the PI is not compelled to reveal the identity of the subject, nor his client. In most states that license PIs, it's a violation of state law for a PI to reveal anything about the case he is working on, even to law enforcement, unless there are exigent circumstances. But know your own state's law. It may be different.

3. In this situation, again, use the reverse-sex, reverse-case-type fib. Tell the police-man that, as she knows, you can't really give her any details of the case ... but if she promises not to tell anybody, you're just watching some woman who is a claimant in a workmen's compensation case (when you're really watching a man in a divorce case). I don't recommend lying to the police, but the officer shouldn't be asking, anyway. This will satisfy her curiosity and she'll go away and leave you alone.

Why fib? You can bet that the officer will go right out and relay to the rest of her squad what type of case you're working on. Why would she do this? A beat or patrol cop just doesn't come into contact with private investigators all that often. A PI is something of a novelty to her. Also, many cops are already thinking that when they retire they might try their hand at being a PI. So when she's talking shop, taking a break with the other cops in that zone, she'll tell them where you are and what you're working on. So let her talk—just not about your case.

Eternal Vigilance

Working a stationary surveillance leaves little time for reading, daydreaming, or taking care of bodily functions. As soon as you pick up that book because nothing is happen-ing, the subject will come out of the house carrying a load of bricks and you will miss it. You can't read and do an effective job at the same time. You may think you can, but you can't. Nobody can. And that includes reading this book on surveillance. Put me down now and focus on the surveillance.

It's not unusual to only have one chance of obtaining videotape on some crucial activity. The activity may only last 15 or 20 seconds. By the time you put the book down and get the camera rolling, the important stuff will be over. You might have taped the 20 seconds of case-winning video had you not been reading. It might be the one time all day that the claimant comes out of his house, and you just missed it. The line between being a jerk and an outstanding investigator is very thin. About 20 seconds thin.

Plan the surveillance. Know in advance how long you're going to be in the back of that van, or in front of the window at the hotel, or under the bushes, or in the tree. Take food and drink with you. Have a large-mouthed cup to pee into, and don't forget the lid. Be sure and pour it out later and not leave it to ferment in the van. Forgetting to take it with you won't make you very popular with the other investigators on your surveillance team. And for heaven's sake, don't spill it in the van. This is the advice I give both my male and female investigators. If you're going to be a successful surveillance PI, you have to do it. So think twice before slurping down that 64-ounce iced tea.

Stationary surveillance may not be quite as much of an art as a moving surveillance, but it requires patience, planning, fortitude, determination, and good luck to be successful. The use of a fixed-surveillance van is much more physically demanding than a moving surveillance. Give me an air-conditioned car traveling 70 m.p.h. down the highway anytime over the 150° sweltering heat inside a stationary van during a summer surveillance.

The Least You Need to Know

◆ There are two types of stationary surveillances: fixed and fixed-mobile. Both are designed to obtain information from one specific point. The fixed-mobile may be a van that can be brought in and out as needed, but the surveillance should be conducted from as far away as possible while still capturing good-quality video or photographs—good enough to recognize faces.

◆ One method for setting up a surveillance in a residential neighborhood is to have the driver pretend the van is broken down and walk away, leaving a second PI in the back to get the video.

◆ Pesky neighbors are best dealt with directly. Introducing yourself and showing them your PI license will avoid a run-in with the police.

◆ If you are busted, make an excuse and leave the area immediately. Being rousted by the cops requires that you maintain your demeanor and speak to them as a professional. You must maintain your statutory obligations and not reveal, even to the police, the identity of your subject or the nature of the surveillance.

◆ Success in a stationary surveillance requires a constant alert status. The surveillance investigator cannot read a book, watch television, or leave the site. Have appropriate food and drink available and use a wide-mouth jar or cup with a lid to pee into.

Moving Surveillance

In This Chapter

- Five tricks to a one-man surveillance
- Learning the principles of foot surveillance
- Preparation techniques that ensure success
- Using additional manpower to maximum advantage
- Winning and losing with traffic lights

Coordinating and running a successful mobile surveillance requires experience, luck, and a sense, almost a mental gift, of knowing what your subject will do. Famous FBI criminal profilers talk about putting themselves in the criminal's head. Likewise, a good surveillance man will have the gift of putting himself or herself in the subject's head. There is no rational explanation of how that is done. Hopefully, this chapter will put on paper the esoteric sense of surveillance that a private investigator develops with enough time and practice.

Not all private investigators are good at surveillance. Just as some people have a talent for playing the piano by ear, others have a natural talent for sensing how people are going to drive their cars or stop at yellow lights or run the red ones. It's an art, but every art—be it painting, musical composition, or novel writing—has its craft that must be learned and is perfected through practice.

Going It Alone

Unfortunately for private investigators, most clients will not foot the bill for more than one man on a surveillance. Thankfully, there are a few who will. A few months ago we were looking for a runaway teenager. We had six men on surveillance in multiple locations around the city, staking out this spoiled kid's haunts. The father had the checking account to cover that heavy an expense. Usually, you're lucky if you get a client who will pay for a two-man surveillance team, not to mention six.

So how do you run a one-man moving surveillance? Well, it's not easy. The sections that follow describe five tricks you can use that will make it go a little more smoothly.

Know in Advance Where the Subject Is Going

So now you're supposed to be clairvoyant? Not really. If this is a domestic case, your client may know where and when his spouse is meeting with her lover. Men in particular are adept at tapping their own telephones. We'll talk about the nuts and bolts of tapping phones in Chapter 19. In most states, tapping calls on your home telephone, if you're not one of the parties involved in the call, is illegal. I never suggest to a client that he tap his wife's phone calls. But if it comes up, I do let him know that he can go to Radio Shack and for less than $85 he can get the proper equipment and they'll tell him how to do it. It's very simple.

> **The Division of Licensing** _____
>
> Learn the wiretap laws in your state. Never suggest to a client that he break the law. If you do, your client may take the suggestion, tap his own phone, and later tell his wife what he's done. She'll go to her attorney and tell him you suggested it. The next thing you know, the state will be prosecuting you or taking away your license. They might not prosecute the client, because he didn't know any better, but you're the professional—you're supposed to know the law.

If it's your husband that is cheating on you, a tap on your own phone line may save you thousands of dollars in PI expense. Of course, if your husband doesn't use the phone to talk to his lover, then it won't do you any good. But you really don't know if he does or not until you check. If he's using his cell phone, read Chapter 16, for tips and tricks about using a cell phone.

If you're following an insurance claimant, talk to the claim adjuster and find out when the claimant's next doctor's visit is scheduled. Scout the location of the doctor's office before the day of the visit. If you lose him on the way to the doctor's visit, no sweat. It's not good to lose him, but at least you know where to find him again and at what time. Claimants frequently run other errands en route to and from the doctor's office. It always makes for good theater in the courtroom when the claimant can climb ladders, cut the grass, or pump the gas without help until he gets to the doctor's office. Then, when he arrives, he can't even walk without assistance. And what an amazing cure rate these doctors have! The poor fellow limps on his crutches to his truck as he leaves, but at his next stop on his way home, he seems just fine again.

Follow the Yellow Brick Road

We call this the Yellow Brick Road Technique. Usually, the client will know who the other woman is. She's been told by friends or the husband has said flattering things about this woman at work or has tipped his hand somehow. If you've tried to follow the husband and he has a lead foot, runs yellow lights, pushes the red ones, and makes lots of U-turns, he might not be a good candidate for a one-man surveillance. So don't follow him. Follow the other woman instead. She won't be suspicious. She won't be looking over her shoulder, and nothing is going to happen until the two of them get together anyway.

We worked a domestic case recently in which the husband was a doctor. He was difficult to follow, so we followed the girlfriend. It wasn't long before he showed up at her place. She had him out in her yard doing chores, taking down shutters after a hurricane scare, and raking the yard. We had a good laugh at that. He could have done chores at home and it wouldn't have cost him a divorce.

Plan Your Exit

Working alone means working smarter, because you don't have the luxury of being able to cover an entire residential subdivision or company parking lot. If this is a domestic matter, talk to your client. She'll know which exit her husband usually takes. She can advise on which way out of the neighborhood from his house he always travels. The easiest time to lose the subject is when he's leaving a location. If the husband is at home, have the wife call you on your cell phone the minute he leaves the house.

If you've followed your subject and he stops at a business location and leaves his car, use the time to survey your situation. How many exits are there? Which way is he likely to go? Is there a median in the street so he can only exit one way or could he come out and turn right or left? Plan your exit. You don't want to be right on his bumper when he leaves. That's the best way to get made. You don't want to be too far behind him, either. That's the best way to lose him, because the car in front of you won't hustle out into the traffic and your subject will have made the next turn and be gone while you're still stuck in the parking lot.

You have to anticipate his exit strategy and put yourself in the best possible position to see him coming out (without him seeing you) and to be able to resume the surveillance. If there is only one way out and he can only turn one direction, go down the block and wait for him.

Don't Play Follow the Leader

Your subject has just made a left turn into a service station or a fast-food restaurant. What do you do?

Do not follow him into the restaurant parking lot. You continue traveling past the restaurant he turned into. Keep your eyes on the rearview mirror in the event he is making a U-turn. When you're sure he's parking and going to enter the establishment, just reposition yourself and figure out his most likely exit and direction of travel. Take into account the traffic flow. When the subject exits, can he make a left across the traffic or does he have to make a right and continue in your direction?

This is the nuts and bolts of a one-man surveillance. Watching the traffic and antici- pating what the subject's next move will be based on traffic flow, concrete medians, stopped buses, and one-way streets. Be prepared for any harebrained moves he might make. Don't lull yourself into thinking he's going to do what you would do. Count on his actions being something entirely different from what any reasonable person might attempt. When he exits the drive-through with his hamburger in one hand and a chocolate shake in the other, he is concentrating on not spilling his lunch all over his pants before he gets to his honey. Be ready for sudden illogical driving patterns. After all, do you think he's got his mind on traffic, or something else?

Do Play Follow the Leader

Now you're two cars behind your subject (good, you've put some cover between him and you) and he's signaling a right-hand turn into a large regional shopping mall. What action do you take?

You follow him in. I know we just said don't follow him into a business lot. That's true. But with a large mall lot, there are four reasons why you'd want to follow him right on in:

♦ It is very easy to lose the subject in a large mall lot. Don't be fooled into thinking you can cruise the lot later and find his car. It probably won't happen.

♦ He may just be cutting through the lot to get to the highway exit on the other side.

♦ The subject may be meeting his girlfriend in the lot and could leave in her car. If she's on time (I know, not likely), he'd be gone before you ever found him. If you do find his car and they left in hers, you will have missed the big show. Or they may meet in the lot and leave in separate cars headed toward the motel. She didn't want to be sitting in front of a motel waiting for him, and since he's going to pay for the room, they arranged to meet in the mall lot first.

♦ He may be meeting his girlfriend inside, where she works at one of the stores. You may find his car, but you probably won't find him in the mall.

Watch which aisle he takes in the parking lot. Once he's pulled into a space, park in a different aisle where you can see his car. You have to hurry here. Don't lose him now. You'll want to follow him into the mall and continue the surveillance inside, on foot. Any purchases he makes may be significant. Whom he meets may also be of importance to your client.

The Effective Foot Surveillance

Following a subject on foot is fraught with difficulties. You must stay close enough to see whom he comes in contact with, but remain discreet and unobtrusive so the subject is unaware of your presence. Easier said than done. Holding a newspaper up to your face when the subject looks your way is overdone in the movies. How many people do you see walking through a mall reading the paper? Okay, no newspaper—so how do you do it?

Here are three basic principles of conducting moving surveillances that apply to all forms, whether you're on foot, in a car, or have multiple people working the surveillance with you:

1. You should always keep something between you and the subject. In a mall, that means stay behind other people who are walking in the same direction. We're going to harp on this idea of having cover throughout this chapter. It's a very

important principle, but don't overdo it. No lurking behind pillars and tiptoeing between kiosks type of stuff. Most malls have pretty good surveillance security cameras hidden throughout, and if you make a spectacle of yourself, the next thing you know, two security guys will be hauling you down to their office to ask you a few questions.

2. Change your appearance. A good surveillance person always has a couple of extra hats and jackets in the car with him. When you follow your man into the mall, grab a hat and coat, even if it's during the summertime in Florida. By varying those two articles of clothing, you can look like four different people. If you're a female, keep a scarf in the coat pocket and now you can add five additional appearances for a total of nine. And don't forget the sunglasses or regular glasses. Use anything you can to change the way you appear to the subject. (Anything except streaking. It might call too much attention to yourself.)

3. Don't get in front of the subject. This third principle is particularly important if you are working by yourself. If you're with a partner, it's still a good idea to adhere to this, but you can make an exception if the situation demands it. If you're driving and he's behind you, he's looking at your tag, any bumper stickers you have, and how you part your hair. If you accidentally get in front of him again, he'll remember all of those things and will become suspicious. If you're on foot and you're in front of him, he'll notice how you're dressed and how you walk. If he sees you again, you're dead meat.

The preceding three principles of moving surveillance, if put into practice, will go a long way toward making your surveillance successful and keep you from getting burned.

A Bird in the Hand

All clients want photographs. The wife who wants to catch her husband cheating can read your report. She already knows in her heart that her husband is unfaithful to her. None of that makes any difference. Remember, her husband will come up with some logical explanation of why he went to the mall, bought that watch, gave it to some lady, and followed her to a hotel.

The explanation? The lady was a client, the watch was a gift for her because she can get him a big account, and the two of them had a business lunch at the hotel. If the PI she hired says they went into a hotel room, he must be mistaken or he's lying to justify his bill. PIs are a sleazy lot anyway, and …. Now he gets mad at his wife for having doubts about him and wasting the mortgage money on a keyhole peeper. That's what he'll say to his wife.

Get the photograph of him and the other woman kissing, holding hands, walking through the mall arm in arm. Your client needs to be able to throw it down on the coffee table in front of her husband when he comes up with excuses and gets defensive. "There, buster," she'll say, tossing the photograph at him. "Let me see you explain that."

The problem here for most investigators is they're not properly prepared for that unexpected moment. When the good stuff happens, a kiss between lovers, or an insurance claimant going into a handstand to impress his 4-year-old child, the PI must be ready, camera in hand, to grab that shot. Sometimes it's the only shot she'll get, and she'll miss it if she's not ready. The lovers won't kiss again until they're behind closed doors and the claimant's wife will remind him he's out on disability and he'd better stop with the gymnastics. You've got to get the first piece of incriminating evidence, because that might be all you'll see.

Two's Company

Say your client's a big spender, not some adjuster working for a tightwad insurance company, and he wants you to catch his philandering wife. If it takes two men to follow her, no problem, use whatever resources you need. He doesn't care what it costs, just get the job done. Hmm, he doesn't care what it costs … that's music to any private investigator's ears.

Running a two-man surveillance requires skill and practice to know how to use the extra resource wisely. Remember, if you mess up the surveillance now and lose your client's wife with two men on her, you're going to have one unhappy client. There are three areas to focus on with a multiple person surveillance team: communication, positioning, and information. Each of these areas will be discussed in the sections that follow.

Communication

Obviously, if there is more than one person working the surveillance, there has to be good communication between all members of the team. That's why we previously suggested having multiple forms of radio communication and relying on cellular only as a backup. The equipment you have will depend greatly upon what is available in your geographic area. Keep in mind that a surveillance will sometimes take you to areas not covered by cell sites.

My firm previously used a primary and two backup types of communication. The primary was a radio that worked off a repeater. The backup was a handheld walkie-talkie. The third was the cell phone. Commercial repeater services have in many areas gone the way of the carrier pigeon. Most of their business trade was to service companies, plumbers, air conditioning, and the like. Those companies have all gone to the push-to-talk cell phones. So we're down to VHF radios, some larger 25-watt units in our vehicles, and 5-watt handheld walkie-talkies.

def•i•ni•tion

A **point man** on a surveillance is the investigator that actually has "the eyeball," or has physical sight of the subject.

Having the means to communicate and actually doing it are two different things. All the investigators on the surveillance must first be taught to talk. Seems simple, right? It's not. Talking means the *point man* must give a detailed running commentary on the subject's actions if he is on the move.

The running commentary means that the point man must alert the rest of the surveillance team when the subject moves, changes directions, turns a corner, stops at a red light, or runs a yellow light. It doesn't mean that he keeps his microphone keyed the entire time. He must be short and clear in his comments. As the point man indicates a change in direction or speed, the other surveillance units should acknowledge it so the man on point knows he's been heard. The radios are not devices for idle chatter, and the only communication during a moving surveillance should be pertinent to the surveillance itself.

Even with the best equipment and excellent organization, there will come a time during a moving surveillance that the lead vehicle will be separated from the rest of the surveillance team. The team might be stopped or slowed by traffic lights, crawling freight trains, automobile accidents, raised drawbridges, or the highway patrol. It doesn't take long for that distance to grow to half a dozen miles going down an interstate at 75 m.p.h.

When this occurs, the point man should continue the surveillance and should broadcast his position *in the blind* even though he can't hear the rest of the team. Just because he can't hear their radio traffic doesn't mean they can't hear him. Radio transmission and reception are dependent on a number of variable factors, such as height of antennae, inclement weather, and even sun spots. As the lead car climbs a hill or bridge, he should report to the other cars his position. The increased height in his location of broadcast may be sufficient enough to allow what he says to be heard by the other units, even though he cannot hear them respond.

def•i•ni•tion

Broadcasting **in the blind**—when the members of a surveillance team have been cut off from one another—is something that must be taught. It means that the broadcaster may not receive acknowledgment that his message was heard, but he's putting it out there anyway because it might be heard by his surveillance team members. It's a valuable technique used by those in law enforcement. Add it to your tool bag. Many a surveillance has been saved by an investigator smart enough to broadcast her position in the blind, thereby allowing the balance of the surveillance team to catch up to her and the subject.

Positioning

There are two purposes for having more than one man on a surveillance. First is the ability to cover more than one possible point of egress by the subject. In a subdivision or an apartment complex, there is frequently more than one exit, and the subject may some days use one and other days use another. Having two cars available helps eliminate the possibility of losing the subject before he's even left the immediate area.

The second main purpose for a surveillance team composed of two or more people is to "confuse the enemy." A good set of surveillance investigators will change off the lead so the subject is not seeing the same car in the rearview mirror for hours at a time. Likewise, if the subject makes a turn into a business, shopping mall, or another residential area, the lead car, which has been behind the subject for a while, can drive on past as the subject turns and the next car becomes the lead car and makes the turn following behind the subject. The former lead car makes a quick U-turn as soon as the subject is out of sight and plays catch-up.

The Division of Licensing

The subject lives in a subdivision with multiple entrances and exits. Also, it is impossible to park discreetly and have a clear view of the subject's residence. In this case, it is tempting to drive by the residence periodically to see what is happening and to make sure his car hasn't moved. Resist the urge. The same car passing by the subject's house multiple times may alert him, or, at the very least, make him suspicious.

If there are two cars available and you can't resist the urge, then alternate each time you make a drive-by. Keep the drive-bys to a maximum of one per hour. If there is only one car available, perform the drive-bys once every two hours, but you will probably be skunked anyway. According to Murphy's Law, if anything can go wrong, it will. And at the worst possible time. This has never been more true than on a moving surveillance.

If it is after dark and the house is not in a cul de sac, then indulge yourself all you want.

Information

My client, the wife, was handing her 3-year-old over to her soon-to-be ex-husband. The husband was supposed to bring the child back to the mother later that same night. The father had been taking the child to the new girlfriend's house and sleeping over. The mother didn't approve, thinking it set a bad example for her older children as well. She wanted proof, somebody who could testify to the judge, that yes, the husband was indeed cohabiting and had the child with him when he did it.

The handoff was to take place after dark. This was a fairly busy residential area with major hotels and shopping areas along the street just before the security gate. Due to the heavy foliage, the gate itself could not be seen from where I had to park. My client was supposed to call me from her cell phone as the husband approached so I could creep out of my parking space and follow in behind him.

She didn't call until after he'd left (lack of communication) and informed me he'd taken a turn through one of the shopping areas instead of driving past where I had parked. I scrambled to where he turned and saw his vehicle making the turn onto the main thoroughfare a quarter mile down the road. I broke more traffic laws than I care to enumerate, but eventually caught up and followed him the rest of the evening.

The key objective in this case was to follow the husband to the new girlfriend's apartment and get her identified. Once we had her name, we would run basic background checks to include criminal and civil records. As it turned out, he did not go to the girlfriend's, but instead returned to his own apartment after picking up pizza. He parked his car in the garage assigned to his apartment, but left the garage door open. Since it was dark, I waited about 30 minutes and drove by the apartment again. There was another car now parked directly behind his.

I wrote down the tag on this other car and ran it on my laptop computer equipped with a wireless modem. In a few minutes, I had our mysterious girlfriend identified. With just a few more minutes of database searching, I had her full name, her date of marriage, her Social Security number, date of birth, her maiden name, her current address, plus five or six previous addresses, the address of her soon-to-be ex-husband, and the fact that she held a professional license in the health-care field.

Alternate Light Source

A PI has to make his own luck. Getting into gated communities requires luck, talent, or knowing somebody who lives in the area who will give you a gate pass or the gate code. In the example about the father and the 3-year-old, the father lived in a gated community. There was no security guard at the gate, just either magnetic pass cards for residents or a combination keypad for visitors.

You can tailgate another car through the gate. Cars do it all the time, and if there's no security guard, it's nothing to worry about. The only problem is you can't always get in when you want to, because there may not be a car entering when you need to enter. If there is an exit separate from the entrance, I don't recommend entering through the exit as a car leaves, because that is a dead giveaway that you don't belong there.

In this instance, I was waiting for a car to enter so I could tailgate my way in, when I noticed a visitor trying to punch in the code at the visitors' gate. I drove right up behind her, got out of the car in the rain, and in my friendliest voice, said, "This damn electronic pad always does that when it rains. What combination did they give to you?" "Pound, one, two, three, four," she said, giving me the combination. I hit the star key a couple of times to clear the pad and put in the combination. The gate opened. Now it opens on command for me whenever I want it to. No more waiting to tailgate through. The lady thought I was doing her a favor but really she did one for me. A good PI is always on the lookout to improve his luck.

The father returned the child to my client on time and went back to his apartment where the girlfriend waited. Now that I knew who she was, I didn't have to stay out there late into the evening to attempt to follow her home. She probably stayed all night anyway. I saved my client the cost of five or six more hours of surveillance, and I could hightail it on home, all because I had information available to me when I needed it.

If you're a professional investigator and you're doing surveillance, you need to have the ability to run license tags and other online database searches while you're in the field. Either make sure somebody is at the office while you're out so you can call it in, or be able to run searches from your car.

The following are a couple of methods available that will allow an investigator to run tags and data searches from his vehicle.

◆ **Cell phones and personal digital assistants (PDA).** Cellular telephones can access wireless application protocol (WAP) websites. The line between PDAs and cell phones has blurred. Mobile wireless technology continues to improve in download speed. Treo, PalmPilot, Blackberry, and Motorola Q have their own browsers and should enable you to access the databases you need.

◆ **Laptop computer with a cellular or wireless modem.** Wireless cards with significant download speeds have finally arrived. If you can get cell coverage on your cell phone, then your wireless card can probably access your provider's broadband mobile signal. The service subscription rates are not real cheap, but they're giving away the PCMCIA cards for your laptop.

Alternate Light Source

Billing clients is also something of an art. A new laptop computer, wireless modem, and cigarette lighter adapter can run between $1,500 and $3,000 or more. I use a Sony Vaio with a Wireless modem. Total cost, including carrying case and sales tax, was not quite $3,500. Broadband wireless service runs about $50 a month. An investigator has to recoup those costs. The only way to do that is to pass it along to his clients. If he doesn't, he'll be closing his doors quickly. When the PI bills the client, he should bill the database charges at between two and three times what the database services charge him. For the wireless access, a smart PI will add an additional charge on the invoice. At our firm, we just call it "wireless database access charge." I've had clients question me about it but never complain. Do you think the mother we discussed in this chapter is going to complain about a $25 access charge when it saved her $420 in investigative time?

The importance of having the necessary information at your fingertips is magnified if there is more than one person conducting the surveillance. Had the preceding surveillance been a two-man gig, my client would have been paying twice the rate. Having the ability to run that tag and secure the database information saved her 10 man-hours.

Red Light, Green Light, Duck for Cover

This is the one tactic of running a moving surveillance that an investigator must learn. If you're going to follow your own spouse, or help somebody follow her spouse, read this section. If you don't learn anything else in these two chapters on surveillance, I hope you learn this.

There are two rules you have to follow in order to be successful in following someone and not being made. Each is described in the sections that follow.

Keep Cover Between the Subject and Yourself

Try your best to use two to four cars as a cover screen. If the subject keeps seeing the same car in his rearview mirror, you will get burned sooner or later, and probably sooner. If your cover turns off or passes the subject, leaving you naked, slow down until the guy behind passes you. If your subject changes lanes, don't change lanes with him unless you're sure he's going to make a turn. Even then, it's better not to make the turn with him. Let the rear surveillance unit make the turn and you come back from the other direction.

If the subject pulls into a grocery store parking lot, don't park out in the open where you have a clear view of him, because he'll have a clear view of you, too. It's best to put a light pole and a whole bunch of cars between you and his car. Also, don't back into a parking space in order to see better out the windshield and make a fast get-away. This is a common mistake made by inexperienced surveillance investigators. Don't do anything that will draw attention to the fact that you're sitting in your car. If you smoke, don't stand around in the middle of the parking lot next to your car and smoke. If you have to smoke, stay in your car, but it's best if you wait until you're moving. Why? Because if you're holding a cigarette, then you're not holding the camera ready to pounce on that unexpected meeting or that quick kiss. You don't know who he is going to walk out with or who he is buying groceries for.

Play the Lights

This is absolutely a must. If you don't learn this trick, you'll lose your subject every time. "Play the lights" means to evaluate not when the next light is going to turn from green to red—you should already know that—but to figure out what the one ahead of that is going to do. Why?

You have two cars as cover. You're approaching a traffic light that's been green for a while. It turns yellow and your subject guns it, racing through the intersection. The two cars you're using for cover stop for the red light. You can pull around them and try to run the red light (not advisable), but if you know that the next light up is going to turn red before your guy gets there, then there is no rush. Save your own life by sitting through the light and then moseying on up to where your subject is patiently waiting for his light to turn green. If you don't know what the next light is going to do and when, then you're up a creek. You should always, always be aware of what the traffic light situation is two or three blocks ahead if you can see that far. If the first light is going to turn yellow and the next one up is red now, you know it's going to be green when your guy arrives at that intersection. You'd better ditch the cover cars and hustle through with your subject, then lay back and get some more cover.

Playing the lights and keeping good cover are the two most important aspects of being successful with moving surveillances.

The Least You Need to Know

◆ Know in advance where your subject is going by talking to the client or finding out from the insurance adjuster when the subject will be visiting the doctor.

◆ If a husband is impossible to follow, then follow the other woman. She won't be looking for a surveillance.

◆ Plan how your subject is going to exit from wherever he is, whether it's a subdivision or a grocery store parking lot.

◆ Don't follow the subject into a small business parking lot, but do follow her into a major mall lot and the mall itself, if she goes in.

◆ To conduct an effective foot surveillance, always keep some cover between you and the subject. Alter your appearance by adding and removing clothing and glasses. Don't get in front of your subject.

◆ You may only have one chance to get the photograph you need, so always be prepared to take it. There are only 20 seconds separating a jerk investigator from a hero.

◆ Multiple-person surveillances require good communication, the ability to position the rest of the team to maximum advantage, and the capability of obtaining license tag information during the surveillance.

◆ The most important aspects of a moving surveillance are keeping cover between yourself and the subject, and evaluating the traffic lights ahead of the surveillance so proper decisions can be made when the subject runs red lights.

Chapter 14

Tricks and Treats: The Basics

In This Chapter

- Using the garbage to get the dirt
- Learning legal pretexts
- Enlisting an airline ticket agent's help
- Tricking the subject out of his house
- Getting forwarding addresses for 50 cents

Every profession has tricks of the trade. These tricks are shortcuts to help the professional achieve successful results more rapidly than "traditional methods" might allow. In the investigative business, the case is considered successful if the client is happy with the work performed and the investigator gets paid. That is not to say that the PI is not emotionally involved with some of his cases. He cannot, however, let his emotions dictate his actions or color his reporting. If he becomes biased and loses his objectivity, then he has lost the case, regardless of the legal outcome.

It's not really an accurate description to call the techniques presented in this chapter "tricks." Actually, they are advanced and sophisticated methods for obtaining information necessary for a successful resolution of a case, keeping in mind our definition of what constitutes "a successful resolution."

Trash Covers

If you really want to get to know a person up close and personal, collect his garbage. Collecting another person's trash is called a "trash cover." This is a perfectly legal method of digging up information about a person. The law is pretty well established in most states that once a person has set his garbage at the front of his property for collection, it is considered abandoned property and fair game for anybody who wants it.

The Division of Licensing

State laws on picking up garbage that belongs to a third party vary from state to state. Most state laws agree that it is abandoned property and, as long as you don't trespass, there is no problem in conducting a trash cover. In the past, a few states argued in court that until the trash was commingled with other trash, it was still the property of the original owner. Before conducting a trash cover, check your state's statutes. Most attorneys have a complete set of the statutes in their offices. If a client requests a trash cover, ask the client's attorney what the applicable statutes are in your state. If they don't know the answer, they'll look it up.

If your spouse is nagging you to take out your own garbage, why would you want to go digging through someone else's? Because it's ripe. Not just with smells, but with very detailed information, such as bank account information, bills, credit-card statements, and new and expired credit cards themselves. You'll know what kind of liquor the person drinks and how much. Rough drafts of letters written to friends, cards from lovers that he doesn't want his wife to see, payroll stubs, and empty prescription bottles will all be found in the garbage. You name it and you can find it by performing a trash cover.

There are several techniques utilized in trash covers. You'll have to evaluate your particular situation and decide for yourself which would work best. First, call the local sanitation company or the city, if it's city run, and find out what days of the week the garbage is collected at the particular address in question. Next, scout your subject's house and look at his or her garbage cans.

Most people set their garbage out the night before the collection. The most professional technique is to purchase garbage cans identical to your subject's cans. About 3:00 in the morning, drive to the subject's house in a van and swap cans. Be sure that there is garbage in the cans that you leave behind so nobody gets suspicious.

If you don't want to do that, the next easiest method is to drive to the residence in the early morning, take the garbage out of the cans, and place it in the back of a pickup truck or a van. I strongly suggest putting some plastic sheets on the floor of the van or truck, or repackaging the garbage into clean plastic bags as you collect it. In addition to the paper products, there will be a lot of rotten food, dead animals, dirty diapers, and messy stuff of undeterminable origin.

Elementary, My Dear Watson

Speaking of diapers .... When Khrushchev was the Soviet premier of Russia during the era of the Cold War, one of the Central Intelligence Agency's greatest coups was snagging one of Khrushchev's bowel movements. By analyzing it, the government had an inside view into the premier's health. And you thought it was just government waste.

Latex gloves are a must. A mask to breathe through is not a bad idea either. Murphy's Law applies to trash covers: the papers with the information of most value will be the soggiest. Be sure to have a large, well-ventilated room to lay out the trash and examine it. You will also need a drying rack or some way to spread out mushy paper so it will dry and hopefully be readable.

Trash covers are disgusting, but we've always found them to reliably produce important information. You might not get what you're looking for the first time out. For a trash cover to be productive, you should plan on grabbing the garbage regularly for several weeks. Follow the rules of evidence that we will discuss in the next chapter. You never know what you might have to produce in court. Hopefully, not the dirty diapers. It's probably safe to just toss them.

Trash covers work very well with smaller commercial establishments as well. Especially those that have their own dedicated dumpster. We've conducted trash covers on companies supposedly ready to file for bankruptcy and found shipping documents and notes on wire transfers out of the country. This is a very good tool if you have the time and the stomach for it.

The Pretext

News reports to the contrary, a *pretext* is not just designed to obtain a subject's long distance or cell phone bills. Basically, a pretext is a lie. It is not a mean-spirited lie designed to injure. It is a clever lie designed to scam a person into providing information, any type of information.

def•i•ni•tion

A **pretext** is a subterfuge or a ploy used by private investigators to encourage an individual to reveal information about himself or another party without being aware of the true reason for the conversation. In the course of responding to what appears to be a normal, everyday query, the individual unsuspectingly releases the information the investigator actually is seeking.

Surprisingly, the hardest skill for many private investigators to develop is the formulation of good pretexts. Being deceitful seems to come naturally to some people. For those who never lie, developing good pretext skills will be difficult … but not impossible.

The Division of Licensing

A well-designed and executed pretext is not illegal. In 2006 and 2007 there was much discussion in the news about pretexting the phone companies to obtain a subscriber's toll records or cell phone records. Some investigators were prosecuted for this. Both California and Florida made it illegal in 2006. Other states have followed. Never cross the line from legal to illegal.

Identifying the Subject

Suppose you, the private investigator, are trying to locate Steve Brown. You think you have him located, but you're not sure that you have the right Steve Brown. Whatever you do, you do not want him to know a private investigator is on his tail. Why? Because if he is the right one, you're going to begin surveillance and you don't want him to be watching for you.

You call him from a safe telephone or spoof your number (see the next chapter on how to do this) and ask if Steve Brown is there. Be sure and use both first and last names. If you just ask for Steve, you could get any old Steve. There might be more than one Steve at that phone number, or you might have dialed the wrong number. The person answering will either say yes or no. If he is there, ask to speak to him.

When he comes to the phone, you employ the pretext. Assuming you know the background on the right Steve Brown, ask him if this is the Steve Brown whose date of birth is such and such. Give him the right Steve Brown's date of birth. Normally, he'll answer yes or no. If he answers no, then you have the wrong Steve Brown, so keep searching. If the answer is yes, you must now give him a reason for the call that will not alert him. A good pretext to use in this case is to say that you are looking for the Steve Brown, born such and such, for a high school reunion. The Steve Brown you're looking for graduated from Coral Gables High School in 1965. He'll say no, you've got the wrong Steve Brown, and hang up.

Now you know, in fact, you do have the right Steve Brown, and you also know where he is at this very moment. You can begin your surveillance whenever you please and be assured that you're on the right man. I know investigators who've spent days following the wrong person with the same name as their subject because they didn't do a simple pretext telephone call to verify they had the right guy.

Finding the Employment

Suppose you need to know a person's employer. This one works most of the time, but not always—no pretext works every time. This is one of those pretexts that sometimes works just as well if you're talking to a spouse instead of to the subject himself. Telephone the subject from a safe phone or spoof your caller ID. Tell him you are (make up a name) from (make up a bank name) and he has been preapproved for a credit card with the low introductory rate of 0 percent guaranteed for 12 months, no annual fee, and the preapproved credit limit is $9,500. Not everybody wants or needs a new credit card, but most of the people a PI deals with would kill for a card with a credit line of over $500.

Explain that you only need to have him verify a few items and he'll have his new card within two weeks. If he's gone with you this far, he'll go the rest of the way. Here is the important part of this pretext. You start giving him details about himself to make him feel comfortable that you are legitimate. Say, "Let's see. You were born on October 10, 1972, correct? You reside at" (give him his address) "and your telephone number is" (supply him the telephone number).

Now you have to get him to start giving you information. You say, "I'm going to give you the first part of your Social Security number, to verify that I'm actually talking to Steve Brown, then I need for you to verify the last digit for me." You give him the first eight digits of his Social Security number (so he knows you already know it) and he verifies the last one. Now he is starting to give you information. Next you ask him for his mother's maiden name to use as a code word for his account. Nobody ever balks at that question and he's still spitting out information you didn't have.

Next ask him how many cards he'll need, and does he want his wife's name on one of them? He is giving you even more information. It's not important information. It's not information you care one whit about, but he is growing accustomed to giving you information. Now you say to him, "The only thing left to verify is your employment. We're not interested in your salary, but we need to have in our records your current employer." He has time and emotion involved in the relationship with you and he wants that card. If he has an employer, and he's come this far, he'll give it to you. Get the employer's name, telephone number, and address. Bingo! You've got what you wanted.

The Division of Licensing

The Gramm-Leach-Bliley Act made it illegal to use pretexts to obtain another person's financial information by making false, fictitious, or fraudulent statements to a financial institution or to the financial institution's customer. The Federal Trade Commission regularly conducts sting operations on private investigators who advertise asset or bank account searches. Typically, those types of searches involve pretext calls to the banks and also the subjects. Be warned: don't do that. If you need financial information on a subject, try using a trash cover at both his residence and office, if appropriate.

Pretexting in general is getting an undeservedly bad rap. Pretexts used to encourage a subject to reveal information that is generally available, such as his employment, should be fine. His fellow employees know where he works. You could follow him to work. His employment is not private. You're not asking for financial information. Nevertheless, a wise investigator will stay on top of the current laws being passed. Stay on the right side of ethical.

If you've developed a friendly rapport with this subject on the phone, you can push this pretext a little further. If you're going to do surveillance on him, it might be helpful to know what his work hours are. Say something to him like, "Oh, that sounds like an interesting job. Do you like that?" Chat with him for a minute about his job and then slide in a question about his hours. Does he have to be to work very early or does he work a night shift? Ask whatever seems reasonable. If you're friendly with him and chatty, he'll volunteer his entire life story.

Where Is She Going?

A client wanted us to follow his soon-to-be ex-wife to Bermuda. I told him to twist my arm a little and maybe I'd take the case. He thought she would drive from Florida to Atlanta, their home, and leave from there. The client was flying into our local airport to pick up his 8-year-old and spend two weeks at the beach. We had to follow the wife from the moment she turned over the boy, because nobody really knew for sure where she was going. Bermuda was the client's best guess, and I was rooting for it, too.

He informed us that his wife had just undergone several different plastic surgeries, including a tummy tuck, liposuction on her thighs, and breast implants. He thought she probably had a lover, and in Georgia, at that time, adultery was not only grounds for divorce, it also figured big-time into alimony settlements or lack thereof, according to the proof that was given.

I told the client we would need a two-man surveillance team for this. He said fine; he didn't care what it cost. Got to love the sound of that. I chose one of my investigators to go with me. We had our carry-on luggage crammed with surveillance gear, radios, binoculars, and cameras.

The wife met our client at the airport and turned over the child. He left, and she got into her car, left the airport grounds, made a U-turn, and pulled back up to the curb of the terminal. She took two suitcases out of the trunk and gave them to a skycap. She then took her car to long-term parking.

I gave the skycap $10 and asked him where the lady with the bags was going. He took my $10 and then said he couldn't remember. Thanks a lot, bud. He did add she was flying out on Continental, but he wasn't sure which flight because she didn't have her ticket yet. He'd set her bags down near the Continental ticket counter.

Continental had two flights that left within 20 minutes of each other. One went to Los Angeles, the other to Houston. Nothing to Bermuda. Bummer. We needed to know where she was going so we could get on the same flight. Our only chance was to arrive with her and follow her from the airport. If we lost her here, or at the other end, we were out of luck and we'd never find her. The pressure was on.

When she came back into the terminal, I've got to admit, she looked like a million bucks. She was wearing a filmy silk dress and, it appeared, nothing else. As she got into the ticket line, I stepped in right behind her. I didn't want to talk to her because if she saw me in L.A. or Houston, I didn't want her to recognize me.

The line moved slowly, but eventually it was her turn to approach the counter. My only chance was to get to the same ticket agent she was talking to. Other agents became available and I pretended I was looking for my ticket in my carry-on luggage and let several people behind me go ahead. Eventually she bought her ticket. As she left the counter I hustled right up to the same agent, who happened to be a man. As my subject was walking away in her nearly see-through dress, I said to the ticket agent, "Man, what a fine-looking woman. Where is she going?"

He responded, "Houston."

"Well then," I said, "Give me two tickets to Houston."

He couldn't believe it. "Really, you want two tickets to Houston?"

"Yeah, really. I've got time. Maybe I'll get lucky," I said.

As he was printing the tickets, I inquired about seat assignments.

"Not to worry," he said. "I've put you right next to her."

What a nice guy.

I had him change the seats so that I was two rows behind her and my other investigator was a row in front of her.

What's the point to this story? Do you think that nice guy would've been as nice if I'd rushed up to him, pulled out my state-issued private investigator's license, and demanded to know where that woman was going? Not on your life. He would've started spouting company regulations about the privacy of their records and the need for a court order or a subpoena, and a supervisor would have appeared out of nowhere. I would've drawn attention to myself and been made. Instead, I got exactly what I wanted and had the agent on my team, giving me more help than I needed.

You can get information from almost anybody. You just have to find a reason for that person to give it to you. You cannot coerce it from people. You usually can't pry it out. And I've never had any luck buying it from anyone either. It has to slide out easily so they don't even know they gave you what you wanted. This trick can be used at any airport. Just adjust the facts to the particular case you're working on.

The Outhouse Routine

Your client is a workmen's compensation insurance company. Your assignment is to get some productive videotape of the subject who is currently not working due to an alleged injury on the job. The problem is the subject never seems to come out of his house when you have him under surveillance. How do you get him out of the house?

This little trick takes two people and a dog. The dog is optional. It can't be used on every case, but if the situation is right, adapt the facts to the neighborhood where your subject lives and go for it. One surveillance investigator is already set up with the video camera on and ready. The other, who needs to be a female, is walking her dog or jogging. She approaches the subject's front yard and gets down on her hands and knees on the lawn and begins searching carefully through the grass. This continues for as long as necessary until the subject can't stand it any longer and comes out of the house to see what is going on. The camera should be rolling.

The female explains that she was walking her dog and her $6,500 engagement ring, which her boyfriend just gave her last night, slipped off her finger and is somewhere on your subject's front lawn. She tells your subject she was going to get it resized today but hadn't gone to the jewelry store yet (it helps to mention a local, high-priced store) to have it done. What is she going to do? Her fiancé will kill her if she can't find the ring. By now, if she's a good actress, she'll be in tears.

One of two things will happen. Your subject may get down on his hands and knees and begin combing through the grass to help her. This makes excellent video for a workmen's compensation case. Or he won't. She can look all she wants by herself. If the subject retreats to the house again, she should look for a while longer and then approach the door, ring the bell, and give the subject a name and phone number, asking him to call her if he finds the ring.

The Division of Licensing

There are some things you cannot do to your subject under surveillance. Some investigators will flatten a subject's tire in order to videotape the subject changing the tire. Not only is this not fair, it's malicious mischief and against the law. The worst part is how you, the professional PI, are going to respond when the subject's attorney asks you in court if you have any knowledge of how the tire became flattened. Are you going to lie and thereby be guilty of perjury?

So you lie. Then the attorney produces the subject's neighbor, who saw you let the air out of the tire. Now you've ruined your client's case and run afoul with the court, all at the same time. Good move, huh? That story will spread so fast, you'll never get another case from an insurance company or any local attorney again. Play smart, play fair, and don't break the law.

After she's been gone for a while, the subject will come out of the house and begin combing through the grass by himself, with no intention of telling her he found the ring.

If the subject doesn't come out of the house at the beginning of the pretext, he might not be able to see your female investigator from where he is in the house. After a few minutes, she should ring the bell and tell him what has happened to her ring, to get the plot moving along.

This little maneuver usually works really well. At worst, you'll get a little video of the subject and know what he looks like. It's not unusual to get a lot of video of your subject and his wife and everybody else in the house, out on the front lawn looking for that $6,500 ring after the girl and the dog have left.

The Division of Licensing

> If this is an insurance case and you employ this pretext, or any other, to get your subject out of the house, remember, if he's represented by an attorney, then you can not initiate any contact with him. The subject must initiate the contact. It's unethical for one attorney to have direct contact with another attorney's client. While you're not the attorney, you're most probably acting as an agent for the attorney of the insurance company. Do not initiate the contact.

Proving the Hotel Stay

Working domestic cases has lots of entertainment value. There are some PIs that turn up their noses at domestic cases. We've always made them one of our specialties, for several reasons. One, we collect a retainer up front and put the money in the bank before we start the case. We don't have to wait for some insurance company to pay us in three or four months, or whenever they get around to it. The other reason is that these cases can be a lot of fun.

PIs often get asked to prove that a client's spouse stayed in a particular hotel during a certain time frame. This is kind of like the ticket agent in the earlier section in this chapter, "Where Is She Going?" If the PI asks the hotel directly for a copy of a bill, the hotel will steadfastly refuse. Before I worked out this little trick, I even tried to bribe a hotel clerk, offering her $1,000 for a duplicate bill. She refused. I developed this trick I'm about to reveal to you here and got the invoice anyway. The next day, she was kicking herself for not taking the $1,000. She told me herself how stupid it was for her not to take the money, since I "tricked" them out of the bill.

Let's make up two names, call them Gary Fielding and Sheila Smith. Sheila Smith is the wife of my client and had a fling with Fielding at a certain hotel on May 5. My client wants the bill for two purposes. He's hoping the invoice will show there were two occupants to the room. He also wants any long-distance calls charged to the room as additional proof that his wife was there. Here's how you can get it.

This works even if you're on the case several months after the hotel rendezvous. Call the toll-free number for the hotel chain and make a reservation for the next day. Tell the operator there will be two of you in the room. Give the reservation clerk the name of Gary Fielding as the primary name and include your own name, Steve Brown, as accompanying Fielding, and use Brown's credit card to guarantee the room.

The next day, check into the hotel. Use your own name, Steve Brown, to check in, and tell them Fielding hasn't arrived yet. This is important: make sure the registration says Fielding on it.

An hour or so after you've checked in, ring down to accounting and identify yourself as Gary Fielding. You're in room such and such. You stayed here last month on May 5 but seemed to have lost your copy of the statement and you need it to attach to your expense report. Ask them to drop another copy by your room. They can just slip it under the door sometime today, if that's not inconvenient. In a few hours, you'll have delivered into your hot little hands exactly what your client wants, and it'll only cost you (or your client) the price of the room, plus your fee, of course.

If your client really wants to nail Mrs. Smith, there's more you can do while you're there. Once you get the statement, you'll know she and Fielding occupied, say, room 502. Call the front desk and tell them you'd like to move to room 502 if possible, if not today, then tomorrow, when it becomes free. In your spare time, snap some pictures of the door to room 502. Make sure the room number shows in the photos. When you get the room reassigned to you, unmake the bed. Toss some bathroom towels around on the floor and make the room look recently used. Take lots of pictures of the unmade bed and the room and bathroom. Forward the pictures, with your report and generous invoice, to your client.

At a pretrial hearing, your client can toss a copy of the room bill across the table to his wife's attorney. Next, he flips copies of the photos, one by one, (very dramatic moment here) to the attorney, saying the pictures were taken of the room Mrs. Smith and Mr. Fielding shared after they checked out of the hotel. That's a true statement. It just so happens they were taken way after they checked out … like a couple of weeks after.

Sounds sneaky, you say? Not as sneaky as committing adultery and then trying to wring your spouse's wallet for all it's worth.

That combination works very well and has saved my clients hundreds of thousands of dollars in alimony payments.

The Least You Need to Know

◆ Pretext telephone calls can be used to prove identity and obtain a subject's employment.

◆ While attempting to obtain flight information on a subject under surveillance, a PI can enlist a ticket agent's help without revealing his status or real intentions in the case.

◆ A good method to encourage a subject under surveillance to leave his residence is to make him believe something valuable has been lost on his front lawn.

◆ Proving an overnight stay in a hotel can be obtained by registering at the hotel, on a later date, under the name of the subject and then requesting a copy of the previous bill. Accounting will provide it with no questions asked.

Tricks and Treats: Advanced Techniques

In This Chapter

- ◆ Bypassing caller ID
- ◆ Prepaid cell phones as a tool
- ◆ Spoofing caller ID
- ◆ Using GPS to track the subject
- ◆ Obtaining the elusive hotel statement

In the previous chapter, we talked about some tricks of the trade. Mostly those dealt with being clever and resourceful. A competent private investigator must be more clever and more resourceful than his subject, or witness, or client. As we stated in Chapter 1, we are in the information business. In this chapter, we're going to explore some techniques that aid us in retrieving information that is available. It's just not readily available, and the reason you get paid the big bucks is because you'll know how to get it and your client won't.

Laws change. Some state laws allow you, a party to a conversation to record those conversations without notice to anyone. Other states do not allow that. Some states allow you to put a tracking device on a subject's vehicle. Others do not. Know your state law. If some of these techniques we talk about in this chapter are illegal in your state, then don't use them. Never commit an illegal act. I don't care how much your client is willing to pay you. It will backfire on you because if your client is ruthless enough to pay for something illegal, do you think he'll honor his "commitment" to keep it a secret? Not if it is in his best interest to let the secret out. You can take that to the bank.

Fooling Caller ID

Caller ID has invaded North America. For the private investigator, it can be a blessing. More often, though, caller ID is a curse to the PI. It's a curse because the telephone is one of the greatest tools in our toolbox and sometimes it's better to keep the tool a secret.

For example, one of my assistants, Gretchen, was given the job to track down a potential witness in a case that we needed to interview. She ran this witness's name through all the different databases we've discussed. All she had was a name and a former address. In just a matter of minutes, Gretchen had identified the woman and obtained her Social Security number, date of birth, Florida driver's license number, and several former addresses, but no current address or telephone number. Databases are great, but they don't necessarily answer every question about a person that a PI might need answered, especially important ones such as where is this person right *now*.

In reviewing the information that the databases spewed out, I noticed an active phone listing at one of her former addresses that was listed to another person with the same last name. Figuring it was probably a relative, I picked up our best tool, the telephone, and called. It was the witness's brother. He wouldn't give me her phone number, but did give me her father's number. I called the father in another state and he promised to have his daughter call me. She did shortly thereafter. I could have spent hours searching directory information in the various states trying to locate her and might never have found her. But after just two phone calls, I had her interviewed and got the information my client needed. You can't beat a PI who is talented with a telephone. Maybe all those hours your teen spends on the phone will train her for PI work.

This past month I was given the assignment by an attorney to track down a passenger in a vehicle accident. I called the young man's family and they said he no longer lived there but they would pass along my message. No return phone call. A few days passed and I called the family again. Once more they said they'd pass my request to the witness. No return phone call. I called the family again, and this time got the father, who when I asked, without hesitation gave me the young man's cell phone number. The lesson there is if you don't ask, you won't receive.

I called the cell phone and left a message. No return phone call. I called the cell phone again and left a message. Yep, you guessed it, no return phone call. Okay, maybe I'm a little slow, but I finally figured out the kid didn't want to talk to me.

I called the little *&@#$ one more time, but this time I used a technique we're going to talk about in just a minute. Spoofing. I spoofed my caller ID. I could have blocked it by dialing #67 first, but it would show up on his cell phone as either "restricted" or "private." I didn't want that. So I *spoofed* it. Now before I decided to spoof my caller ID data, think for a moment. What number did I want to insert as a substitute that would show up on his cell phone instead of my real number? I wanted a number that he would see and be sure and answer.

def•i•ni•tion

Spoofing a caller ID is a technique where numbers are substituted in the caller ID data stream so that the "real" originating number is not shown, but "fake" numbers appear, or seem to appear, on the caller ID screen.

I had his family's home number. Right. I spoofed my number to look like the old homestead was calling him. Mom, telling him to come over, the meatloaf would be ready soon. And guess what? He answered the phone and I had him. In my mind's eye I could see him sitting there scratching his head wondering why his cell phone said it was his mom calling but instead it was me, but he never thought to ask. I set an appointment to meet him the next day and took a recorded statement from him. It wouldn't have happened if I hadn't be able to spoof my caller ID.

Part of being a clever and successful PI includes knowing how to keep your subject from knowing that your call originates from a private investigative office. It's a growing challenge, since caller ID comes standard on almost all cellular telephones, and many, many residential telephones are equipped with it as well. An astute investigator has to assume that every telephone number he dials is going to show the recipient the calling telephone number, and probably the name also. It's a fact of life the private investigator has to deal with and be prepared to circumvent when necessary.

How to Get Around Caller ID

Here are six ways to circumvent caller ID.

Use a Pay Telephone

When you use a pay telephone, the caller ID might display the words "pay phone." In making a pretext call, it'd be difficult to pretend you're doing a survey, when the caller ID reads "pay phone." The advantage to using a pay phone is that there is no way the call will be traced back to you. It can be traced back to your location (see Chapter 18). And there might be witnesses to the fact that you made a call from that pay phone. Remember, everything electronic leaves a footprint somewhere.

The Division of Licensing

A word of caution about pay phones. They are not usually tapped by the government, but they can be with a court order, just like any other telephone. Likewise, if you're using the same pay phone repeatedly, there will be witnesses to that fact. We put an employee of a major cellular company in jail for making repeated bomb threats to her employer from a pay phone located just down the street from her house. We tracked the location of the pay phone and developed witnesses who saw her making calls from that phone at the approximate time the bomb threats were received. Be aware that pay phones can be compromised.

Dial *67 Prior to Dialing the Phone Number

Most Regional Bell Operating Companies allow a person to dial *67 prior to dialing the phone number. Dialing *67 blocks the transmission of the Caller ID information to most telephone numbers. A *67 blocked call will be reported to the receiving party's caller ID as a "private call." There is usually no additional charge for this service if it's available within your area.

Another service provided by the phone companies is Automatic Number Identification (ANI). Some telephone companies call it Automatic Identification Number (AIN) instead of ANI. ANI is typically used with toll-free numbers, 911 emergency operations, and large companies, but anybody willing to foot the expense can have the service. ANI is sending different data over different lines than caller ID and cannot be blocked by dialing *67 first. However, with spoofing technology, you can spoof a toll-free number if the spoofing service allows it. Technically, it can be done.

If you call any subscriber to the ANI service, he or she will be able to see your number. Not all ANI subscribers have "real-time ANI," which gives the recipient the caller's phone number at the time of the call; 911 relies on real-time ANI to locate callers. Toll-free subscribers usually get their list of callers at the end of the month, along with their bill. Although, if they have caller ID service on their lines, your phone number will appear on their caller ID screen at the time you make the call. ANI service is usually combined with more-sophisticated telephone equipment and lines like a T-1 line. Expect to pay over $1,000 a month to get it started.

*67 does work from your cell phone. As you begin to enter the phone number you want to call on your cell, begin with *67 and then enter the normal number. It will show up on the caller ID as a Private or Blocked number. But do this while calling a toll-free number and your own number appears on the caller ID screen. ANI data is different data than caller ID data.

When someone phones our agency and refuses to identify himself, or we see some other need to know who a particular caller was, we write down the date and time of the call. When the toll-free bill comes, we compare it to our list of suspect calls by date and time, and usually are able to identify the caller. If the unknown call is particularly important, we can wait one day before calling our toll-free provider, who can then provide us with the phone number for the call. Remember, calling a toll-free number and blocking the Caller ID by using *67 doesn't work for ANI subscribers. You'll end up as naked as the emperor in his new clothes. You can run, but you can't hide.

Use a Prepaid Calling Card

If you're regularly making phone calls and you don't want your number to show on caller ID, then you might try using a prepaid calling card. In dialing the 800-number to access the prepaid calling card's call center, the caller ID information is passed to the call center, but is often not passed through to the final recipient.

This is not true of all prepaid calling cards. We find that some cards pass the caller ID information right on along. The best way to check is to purchase a card and try it by calling your cell phone or other phone with caller ID. If the incoming call shows "out of area," you're probably alright. If you have a need to make discreet calls to Texas, I'd find a friend there and try it first.

Use a T-1 Line for Phone Service

You can install a T-1 line in your office. Usually the installing company can have the phone equipment report as caller ID data whatever you desire. We had a T-1 line in our office for a number of years and it reported the phone number for the switch where the T-1 line connected to the rest of the phone company. It was a number that could not be called back.

Use a Spoofing Service

Telephone number spoofing may not be legal for collection agencies and telemarketers, but other than that, I know of no law that requires the calling party to provide to the receiving party the calling party's phone number.

Spoofing a phone number has gotten easier in the last couple of years. If you search the web, you can find details on how to make a device that will send a false number over your phone line to the receiving caller ID equipment. It doesn't eliminate your number on the receiving equipment, but what it can do is shove your number down the call list and puts the spoofed number in its place. If the receiving party goes back and reviews the calls they've received, your original number will be on their call received list.

The Division of Licensing

The Fair Debt Collection Practices Act prohibits "The use of any false representation or deceptive means to collect or attempt to collect any debt ...." Which means that debt collection personnel cannot spoof their telephone numbers.

However, there are now several companies that will allow you to buy time from their computers and dialers. You call the toll-free number they give you, enter your PIN, enter the number you want to show up on the receiving party's caller ID, and then enter the destination number. Bingo, the false number you entered is passed along as the caller ID data and the destination number never knows who called them.

Where do you find these spoofing services? Before we get to specific companies, remember that these "fringe" companies might be here today and disappear into the ether tomorrow.

I've had experience with one spoofing company, www.Spoofcom.net. Frankly, their product worked so well I was totally excited about it. It's one of the coolest new technologies in our PI toolbox to come along in a long, long, time. It's very cool.

Spoofcom.net sells you time on their system. The basic rate at this time is 100 minutes for $25,200 minutes for $40, and the rate decreases with volume from there. They have even cheaper member rates, but you can go to their website and see for yourself. Other companies sell the service for even less.

The Division of Licensing

The Truth in Caller ID Act of 2006 is a federal bill. It passed the House in the spring/summer of 2006 and went before the Senate where it was read and referred to committee. By the time you're reading this it might be law. It might not. However, its major provision is to make it illegal "to cause any caller identification service to transmit misleading or inaccurate caller identification information, with the intent to defraud or cause harm." Take note and only use caller ID spoofing for legitimate purposes, or you might find yourself before a federal judge.

You cannot dial 911 through their system. Some toll-free numbers might be blocked, and they can block whatever numbers they feel are appropriate. They also won't tolerate "misuse of their system." The spoofing works in North America and Canada, but it probably won't work in Hawaii because of the long-distance rates or any place where you have to dial a country code first.

Who do they sell their service to? Well, their website currently says, "Public Consumers, Commercial and Investigative services, Private Investigators, Law Enforcement, Skip Tracers, Debt Collection Agencies, Insurance Agencies and Lawyers."

There are a number of other companies that sell spoofing services. To find them, conduct your basic Internet search by using the search term "caller ID spoofing" and you'll find links to a number of different vendors.

Are there other ways to get around caller ID? Sure, several more; but I'll only mention one more. You can use a *Voice Over IP* phone system and designate whatever number you want to show up on the recipient's caller ID display. Although your VOIP provider may not allow this, technically, it is feasible.

def•i•ni•tion

Voice Over IP is a popular and cost-effective method of making telephone calls. IP stands for Internet Protocol and VOIP utilizes your broadband Internet connection to transmit your voice and make your phone calls rather than normal RBOC telephone wires.

The Myth of the Untraceable Prepaid Cell Phone

You can walk into almost any stop-and-shop market, or a discount store like Wal-Mart, and for less than $30 buy a prepaid cellular telephone with 10 minutes of airtime on it. You can buy time to add to your cell phone at the same store for less than 20 cents per minute. Using the "throw-away" cell phone is a favorite ploy of mystery writers. The kidnappers use them for ransom demands because they are "untraceable." Right? Well, yes, no, maybe, maybe not.

To understand if these phones are "untraceable," you'll have to define your definition of "untraceable." Let's look at some of these cell phones' qualities.

You can purchase them with cash and not reveal any personal identifying data. So in a sense, you can make anonymous calls on them and only the cell phone number assigned to your phone will show on the receiving party's caller ID.

If you make some illegal or threatening call, can law enforcement trace that call back to you? Think like an investigator. First assume that whoever you called will have the phone number of the prepaid phone. That's a given. If they happen to be the only person in the city without caller ID, then law enforcement (LE) can get the numbers that called that person's phone and your cell phone number will be there.

Now how is law enforcement going to trace the phone back to you? These phones are sold by various companies in numerous stores. But each phone has an *Electronic Serial Number (ESN)* programmed into it. The prepaid cell phone company certainly keeps track of which phones went to which retailer. So it's not too difficult to see how, once law enforcement has your particular cell phone identified, they can trace it to the retail outlet that sold the phone. The phones require activation at the time of sale so the exact time of the sale is recorded.

def•i•ni•tion

> **ESN** is the acronym for **Electronic Serial Number** which is the unique number that identifies a single particular cell phone. It is this number that is continuously broadcast to the cellular network from the phone which lets the network know where you are when your cell phone is turned on and which cell towers to utilize to transmit your calls.

When you're buying a prepaid cell phone, look around. Do you see yourself on a video monitor somewhere? Bingo. Now they not only have your phone identified, they have a photograph of you buying the phone. Now that they have your photograph, how far away do you think you are from being identified?

Also, since your ESN is now known, every time you switch that phone from off to on, it is possible that law enforcement will know which cell tower you're close to. If the phone is GPS-equipped you'll be located to within a few yards. If not, then to the nearest cell tower.

Not to give away all of law enforcement's secrets, but if the stakes are high, they'll have a list of all of the phone numbers you called using that cell phone. If you called your mom, she'll identify you from the photo they show her.

So are those prepaid cell phones untraceable? Well, you decide. However, if you want to use one just to side-step caller ID, I think they're a pretty good product for that.

Using GPS for Surveillance

Private investigators are quick to put technology to use in the field. Surveillance is a large part of the PI industry so, naturally, following a subject just got easier. Maybe. Check your state law on the use of tracking devices before investing. If allowable in your state, buy the equipment and rent it to your client. About two rentals will pay the cost of the equipment.

There are three basic methods of using *GPS* technology to track your subject. They all involve attaching a device to the subject's vehicle that will report the vehicle's location. It's in the reporting where the devices differ most.

def•i•ni•tion

GPS stands for Global Positioning System. It is a system of about 24 satellites that orbit the earth and send out very closely timed signals. The GPS receivers on the earth receive the timed signals from multiple satellites and can calculate the receiver's latitude, longitude, and altitude.

- A GPS receiver that records the travels of the vehicle. The receiver can be removed and the subject's itinerary may be downloaded and viewed. This is useful if you don't have to have real time reporting, but wish to show that your subject travels a certain route or stops at a certain hotel for a specified period of time.

- A GPS receiver that reports real time. These devices use what is known as "code division multiple access" (CDMA) wireless cellular technology. This requires that the vehicle be in an area where CDMA is available. Normally you have to subscribe to the CDMA account for 12 months at a time whether you use it or not. These devices can either be "hardwired" or battery-powered. Some devices claim a battery life as long as 20 days. The larger the battery, the longer it will broadcast. Larger batteries mean that it is more likely to be discovered.

The unit itself is about the size of a pack of playing cards. You can view the vehicle as it moves about the streets of your city. Pretty nifty. Cost for the hardware? Less than $1,000.

◆ A short-term device is a GPS-enabled telephone. Again, you'll need an account with the provider. You can even duct-tape the phone discreetly to some part of the vehicle and retrieve it when the surveillance is over. Some providers allow you to view in almost real-time where the phone is located at any given moment. Check your cell providers. They will be coming online with this feature if they're not there already.

In all three of the above situations the antenna needs to have a clear view of the sky. This makes mounting the receiver difficult and vulnerable to being discovered. You might be able to mount the device in a plastic bumper area where the weak GPS signal might penetrate. A good rule is to always try the installation on a similar make and model car before actually mounting it to your subject's vehicle.

Remember, this might not be legal in your state. Many states have flat-out legislated against the civilian use of vehicle tracking devices without the driver's permission. Notice the word "driver." Ownership of the vehicle might not make any difference. It depends upon your state law. Don't lose your license or worse by installing a tracking device where it is not legal to do so.

Where do you buy these devices and which ones are best? Do your homework. Ask other investigators which one worked best for them. You're the investigator. Investigate.

The Least You Need to Know

◆ Caller ID can be bypassed by dialing *67 before the number, utilizing a pay telephone, or using a prepaid calling card.

◆ Prepaid cell phones can be used to bypass caller ID, but may not necessarily be "untraceable."

◆ Caller ID spoofing can be an effective tool if used for legitimate purposes. It might be illegal to use it to defraud or with intent to cause harm.

◆ GPS technology can be used in surveillance cases if the law in your state allows. You can use itinerary recording devices, real-time devices, and even a GPS-enabled cell phone.

Part 4

In the Field

Okay, you've done your homework and you're ready to hit the street. What's your first case? This part takes you to the places where the PI works, and we'll teach you how to get the job done.

You'll learn professional tricks including how to locate telephone taps and install hidden video cameras and Nanny Cams. You're taught, in fascinating detail, how to track down a runaway teenager and find pay phone locations. Sifting for clues of an unfaithful spouse and everything you want to know about electronic surveillance are also part of a PI's caseload. After studying these chapters, you'll be up for all the challenges.

16

Clues to Infidelity

In This Chapter

◆ Diagnosing infidelity

◆ The most common symptoms

◆ Gathering the evidence

◆ Presenting the facts

You have a runny nose, a cough, your sinuses are congested, and you feel feverish all over. What do you have? Probably the flu, right? Almost every human condition has signs or symptoms associated with it, whether it's illness, well-being, depression, or joy.

Likewise, the unfaithfulness of a spouse or partner is manifested by a number of symptoms or clues. A good private investigator is aware of these signs. In this chapter we spell out clues that point toward cheating in a relationship.

Just as a runny nose by itself may not signal the onset of the flu, any of these clues, with the exception of the last one in this chapter, might have another explanation. But add enough of them together and you should be able to make a diagnosis.

Trust Your Gut

Two weeks before Halloween, a new client, Becky, came into my office. She'd called because she "had a feeling" something was wrong in her marriage and perhaps her husband was having an affair. She couldn't put her finger on why she felt that way; she just knew something was out of line.

It'd be impossible for me to count how many Becky stories I've heard. Some were longer, some shorter. Some involved lots of money, sometimes money never came up. Some included children. Others focused on drugs, alcohol, and physical abuse. Each one is different, but if you cut to the core, they all have the same basic genetic makeup.

Some call it instinct, others might say it's intuition that brought Becky to the realization something was wrong. But it really wasn't instinct or intuition. It wasn't magic, either. She hadn't had her palms read or her fortune told.

Alternate Light Source

Private investigators don't discriminate against persons afflicted with paranoia. They'll sometimes be your best clients. "Just because you're paranoid doesn't mean that there is nobody following you" is one favorite axiom of private investigators.

Becky came to see me because her subconscious recognized the symptoms of a foundering relationship, even though she couldn't consciously identify them herself.

Just like a doctor, it's a private investigator's job to be knowledgeable of these symptoms and make a correct diagnosis.

If you screen out the paranoid schizophrenics that frequent my office, only twice in 20 years and hundreds upon hundreds of cases has a client's gut feeling been wrong.

If you think about it, having lived with another partner for 1 year, 5 years, maybe 20, you know that person, his or her habits, quirks, and agenda. Your clients may not know how it is they're aware their partner is cheating, but they can feel it in their gut. It's your job to analyze the situation and point out the clues. If they "feel" their spouse is cheating, 99 percent of the time they'll be right.

Next you have to prove it to them, their family members, their spouse (who will deny it to the end), and perhaps to an attorney and a judge.

Behavioral Changes

Your client has lived with the same man for 15 years. All of a sudden the husband joins a gym and starts lifting weights, stops eating ice cream and French fries. His biceps are getting some definition. The abs aren't washboards yet, but the waistline is trimming down. He's going to live longer and his cholesterol, triglycerides, and blood-sugar levels are into a steep decline. Great. She should be pleased, right? But she still feels something's amiss. He's not paying much attention to her, so who is getting the benefit of all that exercise?

Almost all women and most men make an effort at improving their body image when a new love interest enters their life. They start—and this time stick to—a diet. The pounds melt away and new clothes appear in the closet.

A man's behavior changes in more obvious ways than a woman's. Besides getting more fit, he's working later, wearing cologne every day when before he hadn't worn it … well, since being single, anyway. He's more aloof and less affectionate with his partner.

A woman is frequently happier because now someone is paying attention to her, telling her how attractive she is and making her feel desirable again. She is more pleased with herself because she is trimming up and has a better self-image of her body.

Both men and women involved in extramarital affairs will have blank spots in their days or evenings, periods when they don't answer the cell phone or return the page. If they do communicate during those times, they will be short and curt with their speech and evasive as to their current whereabouts.

None of these behavioral changes necessarily signals a cheating partner. But keep a scorecard. Let's see what other clues we might look for.

Hang-Up Telephone Calls

Everybody receives hang-up calls. Why? Some might be rude misdialers who just hang up when they realize their mistake without apologizing to the person on the other end. But there's also a technological reason. Telemarketing and collection firms use computers to dial your home. When you answer the telephone, the computer connects your call to the next salesperson in line. If there is no salesperson available at that moment, then the computer hangs up on you. Presto, a hang-up call.

Naturally then, hang-up calls or numerous out-of-area calls are not necessarily indicative of any nefarious doings on the part of your client or your client's spouse. However, as with every other symptom, they might be.

Kathy's husband taught history at the university. When the calls first started, a female always asked for the professor. It seemed to Kathy that it was always the same student, the same voice. After she mentioned it to her husband, the student calls stopped but the hang-up calls began.

Alternate Light Source

In most telephone areas, it's easy for the caller to block his or her number from appearing on your caller ID. The person at the originating phone simply dials *67 and then the number. Your caller ID will then show "Private Call."

Hang-up calls will frequently show up on your caller ID as "Out of the Area" or "Unidentified," "Unknown," or "Private."

This does not indicate that the person calling you blocked the call. One reason the call may read "Unknown," etc., is that it is a long-distance call and coming from an area or phone system that does not yet support the caller ID function. The second, more-common reason is that many telemarketing and collection companies use T-1 lines instead of standard phone lines. T-1 lines don't have to transmit the caller identification information as do Bell Company lines.

Kathy rarely received hang-ups during the day when her husband was at the university. Usually she only received them in the evenings or the weekends, when he might have reasonably been expected to be home. Sometimes, immediately after a hang-up her husband would go into his study or run down to the corner store on some errand. Which brings us to our next symptom, the need for privacy.

The Division of Licensing

Many clients will ask you to tap their telephones for them. It sounds like easy money, but don't do it. It is illegal in every jurisdiction for you, a professional private investigator, to do this and you would be prosecuted, even though the client probably would not. You would also lose your license. It's not worth it for a few hundred or even a few thousand dollars.

Need a Little Privacy?

Everybody needs a little alone time, but the desire for privacy may indicate a problem. The key here is the change in the behavior, not necessarily the behavior itself.

Samantha awoke at 2 A.M. and realized her husband was not by her side. They had two phone lines in their home and she noticed that one line was being used. She assumed her son had failed to disconnect the upstairs computer from their Internet service. As she climbed the steps, she heard her husband talking in the spare bedroom. When she got to the top of the stairs, he hung up the phone.

Brian went shopping with his live-in girlfriend at the mall. They separated, each searching for something in different stores. He needed some advice from her and went back to the store where he'd left her. She was talking on her cell phone. As soon as she spotted him walking toward her she ducked behind a rack of clothes, quickly finished her conversation, disconnected, and stuffed the phone into her coat pocket. You can bet she wasn't getting advice from her mother on choosing between the pink or the blue dress.

Sarah's husband began to take long walks alone. He'd be gone for two or three hours at a time. "I just need to be alone. Time to think some things through," he'd tell her. Actually, he was hoofing it over to a girlfriend's apartment.

If your spouse hangs up the phone when you walk into the room or goes to another room to take a call, or waits until you've hung up the extension before she starts talking, or wants more time alone, you may want to see if she exhibits any of the other indicators in this chapter.

Reviewing the Bills

There are two major sources of bills that provide dead giveaway clues to infidelity: credit card charges and cellular telephone statements.

Credit Card Charges

Gretchen had a nagging feeling that just wouldn't go away. Her husband, Rod, a physician, attended a medical convention in Denver for a few days and then came home. Gretchen, following her suspicions, wanted to check the credit-card charges but didn't want to wait until the bill's usual arrival near the first of the next month.

She called me while her husband tended to patients at his office. After some discussion, I suggested she boot up his computer at home and bring up his credit-card statement online. Rod used *Internet Explorer* as his web browser and had the *AutoComplete* feature turned on.

def•i•ni•tion

Microsoft **Internet Explorer** is a web browser that comes standard with the Microsoft Windows operating system. **AutoComplete** is a function that can be turned off or on in Internet Explorer. As a user enters a secure website, he or she is prompted for a user ID and a password. Once the computer user has entered that ID and password the first time, AutoComplete will remember the ID and password as long as it's on. The next time you visit that website and begin to enter your user ID, AutoComplete will recognize where you are on the web and enter the ID and password for you if you want. Utilizing AutoComplete means you don't have to type in your user ID and password at every visit. AutoComplete is handy, but not very secure.

The AutoComplete option is found in MS Internet Explorer by clicking on Tools, then Internet Options. Under Internet Options click on Content. The third listing under Content is Personal Information. There you'll see the AutoComplete button. Click the AutoComplete button and make sure "User names and passwords on forms" is checked.

Gretchen had an idea what his user name might be and typed in the first letter at the prompt. The rest of the name popped up and the password, which she wasn't certain about at all, automatically inserted itself at the appropriate blank.

A few more clicks of the mouse and there on the computer screen lay all of her husband's charges for the previous week at the Colorado medical convention. There were several charges in the $60 and $80 range from the hotel gift shop, and another from a national lingerie chain. The only gifts she received when he had come home were some free pens bearing pharmaceutical company logos and two refrigerator magnets. There was no $80 item from the gift shop and certainly no lingerie.

In searching through credit-card charges, look for lingerie shops, sport shops, jewelry store charges, and the hotel gift shop. Large, unexplained dinner invoices or bar tabs are clues as well.

Cellular Telephone Calls

Many people use cell phones as their primary means of communication and don't even have a regular phone line to their home. That number is growing every day.

Most cell phone-bill printouts reveal the phone numbers of dialed, completed calls, and the duration of each call. These bills previously reported the phone number of incoming calls as well, but I don't know of any that do that currently, although the records are in the cell phone company's system and retrievable. How long they keep them is anybody's guess, but you'll need a subpoena to get them.

If the spouse suspected of cheating has his own cell phone, I'll guarantee you that calls have been made to the alleged girlfriend or boyfriend, if there is one.

Vicki's husband was always on the cell phone. He never turned it off and it was always at his side. I suggested she bring in his bill, which she had access to because he kept it at home, and we went over it together. The last month's bill showed calls of 30, 40, and up to 90 minutes in length, at all times of the day and night, to a number which Vicki didn't know. The bill also included a mix of shorter calls to other numbers.

We ran a reverse search on the telephone number of the lengthy calls and discovered the number went to the residence of an office assistant he'd hired six months earlier.

You can run a reverse search on phone numbers yourself. To learn how to run a reverse search, you can use one of the free white-pages reverse searches we detailed in Chapter 5, but remember that this data is old and you might end up knocking on the wrong person's door. Use one of the pay 411 sites I mention in Chapter 6.

If you try the telephone break methods outlined in Chapter 10 and can't come up with subscriber information, then it is probably not a listed home telephone number but likely another cellular number, a pager, or a nonpublished number. Check at www.phonevalidator.com and find out. That's a free search.

At the time of this printing, the wholesale price of cellular subscriber information (cell phone number break) is running about $55. This price only includes the name of the subscriber to a particular cell phone and the billing address. It does not include the phone calls made from that number. Most professional investigators will double that price and charge the client from $110 to $125. That is a reasonable, common practice.

Remember, it's now illegal for PIs to obtain copies of the cell phone bills or the calling history, without a subpoena. If you have one offer that service to you, don't do it. You both might find yourself with a long-term-roommate you'd rather not have.

Missing in Action

It's not unusual for persons engaged in the romance of an affair to have unaccounted time or to not be where they've told their spouse they were going to be.

Philandering doctors, male or female, frequently use the excuse of being called out on an emergency or making rounds at the hospital. They might be making the rounds, but not the kind their spouse expects. Just like doctors, nearly every profession has emergencies or provides its own brand of excused absences. Even private investigators are out late working surveillance or doing a *drive-by*.

def•i•ni•tion

A **drive-by** is performed by private investigators to make a casual check of a subject's residence to see if he or she is home, or to observe what activities are taking place at a particular location during a specific time.

Amy fulfilled her obligation to her country one weekend a month in the Naval Reserves. This required her to fly from Florida to a Midwest location. Her normal flight would leave on a Friday evening. Amy, being enamored with her old boyfriend, told her husband the flight left on Thursday so she could spend the night with the boyfriend before she left town.

One Thursday evening, a couple of punks broke into her van, which she'd parked on the street, and stole the stereo out of it. A passerby noticed the break-in and the police responded. They checked the vehicle's ownership and called her home.

Imagine her husband's surprise when the police told him their van, instead of being parked in long-term parking at the airport, had been broken into on the other side of town in front of Amy's "old" boyfriend's home. Busted.

Listen Up

An anonymous caller rings you up and informs you that your spouse is having an affair with his wife. Do you believe him?

You ask your spouse directly and he says, "No, of course not." Which one do you believe? Here are some other examples:

♦ Your friend tells you that your husband is cheating. Then someone from your church says she thought you had the right to know that your spouse was seen coming out of another woman's house.

- You're at your husband's office and his secretary pulls you aside and says, "We need to talk sometime."

- Your best friend, or your sister, says your husband came on to her or kissed her.

- You have a party at your house and your 3-year-old asks why daddy was kissing that lady in the hallway.

Do you believe them even though your spouse denies it? You'd better. Without exception, every one of my clients who'd been told something like that had an unfaithful spouse.

Nine out of ten times, family, friends, or co-workers will know about it before you do. Unfortunately, most of the time they "don't want to get in the middle," "don't want to see you hurt," "don't want to be responsible for breaking up your family," and on and on and on.

If they finally pull up the courage to tell you about your spouse's illicit behavior, check it against the other indicators in this chapter. What they've told you is probably true. Listen. Sooner or later, you'll have to.

Alternate Light Source

Most clients still require proof, even after friends and family inform them of spousal infidelity. Their spouse will frequently deny it until the bitter end. This is the opportunity for the professional investigator to suggest surveillance be placed on the spouse. It increases revenues, and with satisfactory photographic evidence, puts your client in an emotionally superior position. Depending upon the state where the divorce proceeding is filed, it may make a substantial difference in any monetary settlement.

Reasonable Right to Privacy

We've talked about the "reasonable right to expectation of privacy" in other chapters. I have good legal opinion that in the marital relationship, because it is so close, there is no "expectation of privacy" between spouses. One spouse is free to open the other spouse's mail, cruise through his computer, or listen in on the extension from the kitchen. Several state courts and appellate courts have ruled concerning access to a spouse's computer. If it's password-protected, the line becomes slightly fuzzier. The court ruled as follows:

"And, using a Fourth Amendment analysis for purposes of analogy, one's expectation of privacy must be objectively reasonable; a person's expectation of privacy to a room used for storage and to which others have keys and access is not reasonable, and a subjective belief that the room was private is irrelevant.

"One who intentionally intrudes, physically or otherwise, upon the solitude or seclusion of another or his private affairs or concerns, is subject to liability to the other for the invasion of his privacy, if the intrusion would be highly offensive to a reasonable person.

"That turns on one's reasonable expectation of privacy. A 'reasonable person' cannot conclude that an intrusion is 'highly offensive' when the actor intrudes into an area in which one has either a limited or no expectation of privacy.

"The Appellate Division overruled the trial court's suppression of this evidence. Is rummaging through files in a computer hard drive any different than rummaging through files in an unlocked file cabinet? Not really."

A good PI site that has a number of different court rulings on this matter is www. dalmaninvestigations.com/id7.html. There are many fine points in the law, so you might want to have your attorney give his legal advice before attempting this. But if it's legal in your state, searching your spouse's computer can be a very good tool.

Diseases of the Body and the Heart

Infidelity in a relationship breaks the heart. Your client may know intellectually that his or her partner is unfaithful, but finds it difficult to accept it in the heart.

Alternate Light Source

As a private investigator, your clients will be discussing with you the most intimate parts of their lives. The tales are sometimes bizarre and wild. Treat them with respect and sympathy and they will refer you to their friends and associates and help you build your business. And try not to snicker.

There is one sure sign of an unfaithful partner, short of laying the photographs on the table in front of him or her as we discussed in Chapter 14. That sign is a sexually transmitted disease (STD). Even when confronted with having acquired an STD, some clients attempt to make excuses for their spouses.

Joe had a casual affair without his wife knowing. After the affair ended, Joe began to experience symptoms of gonorrhea. He visited a urologist, was treated, and the disease left—or so he thought.

Ten days later, the symptoms reappeared. The urologist informed Joe he'd caught it again. Although he'd been treated and cured, he'd apparently infected his wife, and then she'd reinfected him. Serves him right, huh?

He dragged his wife down to the doctor's office with a story of an infected prostate. The doctor treated them both and the symptoms were gone for good. That time.

Did she believe his story? She wanted to believe, so she did. Believing Joe was easier than facing his unfaithfulness and its consequences.

Her refusal to see all of the symptoms didn't change the facts. Joe and his wife are still together. Joe still cheats on her.

 The Division of Licensing

Medical records are considered confidential and it is not advisable to call the doctor, pretending to be the patient, to obtain the spouse's records. Having those confidential records might backfire in court at a later time. Once a divorce action has been filed, your client's attorney can subpoena the records if necessary.

If your client has developed an STD and has been monogamous in a long-term relationship, then the client's spouse is unfaithful. And it's probably not the first time. Ask your client if he or she has been suspicious on earlier occasions and the answer is almost always yes.

This is a plain and simple fact, but one that is often ignored or passed off as some other benign type of infection.

Counseling the Client

With domestic relation cases such as we've discussed in this chapter, you have an obligation to your clients (or to yourself, if you're the client) to help them put together a plan of action.

The diagnosis of an illness has no value if you can't help with a cure. Likewise, in relationships, as a professional, once you point out the symptoms and identify the illness, you must solve the problem.

Ask clients direct questions. If you ask something general, such as what they want to accomplish, they won't have a clue. You have to guide them. Be specific: if you prove that their spouse is involved in an affair, will they divorce him? Some will say yes. Others will say no. Some will say they don't know.

The Division of Licensing

The divorce laws of the United States vary from state to state. Many states are no-fault divorce states. In these states fault is not assigned to the divorcing parties and the rules for property settlements and child support are set by statute. In other states, blame is laid to the party committing adultery and generally, property settlements and alimony can be greatly affected if proof of adultery is submitted in court. Even in no-fault divorce states, some judges are more generous with alimony if adultery was shown to occur before a marital separation.

Children, and the upheaval of their lives, have to be taken into account. The financial repercussions of a divorce or separation are usually monumental. I counsel clients not to make a decision either way until they have all the available facts at their command.

Not to be forgotten are health considerations. We touched on those lightly in the previous section, but as we all know, there are life-threatening and life-altering diseases spread through promiscuous behavior. Your client has to know and has a right to know the facts of their partner's secret life, if there is one.

Alternate Light Source

A professional investigator gives a full accounting to his client of the work performed. This accounting should be in a written report prepared in a professional manner. Clients who perhaps originally don't want to pursue legal remedies later change their minds. If your investigative work is done in a legal and professional manner, then you will be prepared to testify in court or be subpoenaed for a deposition.

At this point, explain to her that she needs to know what the real facts are before she can make a decision. This is a momentous occasion in most relationships.

Most partners will not admit to their infidelity. The next step is to gather enough irrefutable proof so that the partner can no longer deny his actions, and gather it in such a way that it is admissible in a court of law, even if at this time your client does not intend on to pursue any legal remedies.

Follow the techniques in Chapter 14 and you should get the proof your client needs.

The Least You Need to Know

- ◆ Infidelity has certain identifiable symptoms. These symptoms include changes in personal behavior.

- ◆ There are two major sources of bills that provide dead giveaway clues to infidelity: credit-card charges and cellular telephone statements.

- ◆ Tangible evidence of infidelity can be obtained by examining credit-card charges, cellular telephone bills, e-mails, and surveillance photography.

- ◆ Once the symptoms have been identified and supporting evidence gathered, a plan for resolving the problem should be formulated.

Chapter 17

Watching the Home Front

In This Chapter

- ◆ Making your own spy camera
- ◆ Nanny cams and covert installations
- ◆ Tapping your own phone line
- ◆ Legalities and technicalities of phone taps

Private investigators are routinely asked about using some sort of surveillance equipment in private homes. Frequently, it pertains to the need to know what is going on in a teenager's life. The teenager is coming home late, skipping school, and spending a lot of time with friends who don't have the standards the parent would hope they'd have.

Or perhaps you've employed a new babysitter, and you can't shake that nagging feeling that all is not right when you're not there.

It might be simple paranoia, but it's not unusual for a female client to request a camera in the home because an ex-boyfriend, who claims he's returned her keys, enters the home when the client is not there. He denies that he comes in, but she thinks items are moved around while she's at work.

A tenant might want to catch a nosy landlord. Also, we've had cases where the rental apartment's handyman made unwarranted entries into a client's apartment to snoop around and steal our client's underwear. There are many good reasons why a person may want some sort of surveillance set up within his or her own home.

Cameras in the Home

There are three approaches to using hidden or disguised cameras in your own home. We call them the Camera in a Bag, the Nanny Cam, and finally, the Installed Camera. They each have their advantages and disadvantages. We'll talk about wireless cameras later in this chapter, but using a wireless camera or transmitter and receiver is an option to consider with all three of these camera installations.

Camera in a Bag

This is a fairly simple technique that works very well for a constant time frame of about two hours, and it's mobile, so you can move it from room to room. It's portable, is easily constructed at home, and good for the do-it-yourself PI.

To make a camera in a bag, you'll need:

1. A battery-operated video camera.

2. A gym bag.

3. A small piece of fine, thin, black see-through material.

Cut a hole in the end of the gym bag and remove a square patch of material. A gym bag that is ventilated on both ends works best; if you can get one, just remove one of the ventilated screens.

Replace the material you've removed with the black see-through material. This material can be purchased at any fabric store. Before purchasing the material, hold it up to a light at the store or to the front window during daylight. You should be able to see through it fairly easily. Stitch this material onto the bag where you've removed the ventilated strip or cut the patch.

Place the video camera in the gym bag. Make sure the battery is fully charged. You might want to buy a longer-life battery, depending upon your individual needs. Use the longest-play tape that will fit in your camera.

Pad the camera with a towel or some clothes to keep it from shifting. When placing the camera in the bag, be sure to turn off the auto-focus feature. Some cameras, with auto-focus on, will focus only on the black cloth screen you've sewn into the bag and that's all you'll get in your picture. Other cameras that can't focus on something that close to the lens will continuously, unsuccessfully, adjust the focus because the screen is so close to the lens and nothing will be in focus at all. Turn the auto focus off and focus it yourself.

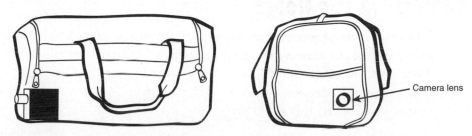

Camera lens

A camera in a bag is easily made at home.

Set the bag wherever you expect the action to take place. Turn it on just before leaving. Remember, the camera will only run until the tape ends or the battery is depleted. I recommend adjusting the camera settings so that it does not automatically rewind when the tape ends, because the rewinding would make some noise that could cause your subject to wonder why your gym bag is purring. You'll need to read your instruction manual about this feature, since each camera is a little different.

After you've made the bag, try it out a few times before setting it up to catch whatever it is you expect to happen. Make sure you have the focus where you want and the zoom on the lens adjusted to get the coverage of the area that you want.

We use this setup frequently when we're trying to catch action indoors and the bag would not raise any suspicions. We nailed an aerobics instructor once with this camera trick. We sent one of our investigators to take her class. He turned on the camera, set the bag down, and we got an hour tape of her and my investigator doing aerobics. She was claiming she couldn't work because of injuries sustained in an automobile accident. She not only was teaching aerobics and dance classes, but also had taken out a new business license for a dance studio she was planning on opening with the money from the insurance settlement. We hated to rain on her parade but, hey, that's what we get paid for.

The camera in a bag would work fine to check up on a babysitter if you're going to the movies or just out for a while. If you have more than one video camera, you could make several units and place them throughout the house. If you do that, you should probably use different styles of bags.

Nanny Cams

You can go to any search engine on the Internet and type in "Nanny Cam." You'll find hundreds of websites that talk about Nanny Cams, and dozens that actually sell them. If you're a little bit electronically oriented, you can make your own.

Here are three sites where you'll find equipment, but shop around. Prices for identical equipment vary tremendously from site to site: check out PI Gear, which is run by PI Magazine, at www.pigear.com, or try www.pimall.com. Also, you might look at www.superciruits.com. All three sites are run by reputable people who have been in the industry for a long time.

A Nanny Cam basically is a covert, or hidden, camera. Typically, the camera is hidden behind a "smoked glass" plate or plastic faceplate of a clock radio or a boom box. You can put this covert camera in any room, and usually the radio will still function as it should, in case the nanny decides to turn it on.

The boom box has an advantage in that it can run off of batteries if there is no convenient electrical outlet. The problem with Nanny Cams is they do not include a video-cassette recorder (VCR). In order to use it, you must either connect a transmitter to the video output of the camera, or run a cable from the video output of the camera to a VCR. If you can't hide a cable, then you'll have to use a wireless transmitter. However, you might look at mini digital video recorders (DVR). Some are the size of a pack of cigarettes, are battery-operated, and save the video to a removable media card like an SD card.

You can buy these Nanny Cams on the web for less than $300. Of course, cameras can be placed and camouflaged in almost any household item that you might desire, and you'll find them hidden in motion and smoke detectors as well as wall clocks, VCRs, and videocassettes themselves.

If you do run a cable to a regular household VCR or use a wireless transmitter, then you are limited to six hours of record time, as long as you set your VCR to the longest play time available. Some VCRs are labeled differently from others, but usually the setting for the longest play time will read "super long play" and be abbreviated SLP or "extended long play" (ELP) on the front of your VCR. Instead of buying and using normal 120-minute tapes, you can purchase the 160-minute tapes. Using those on the SLP setting will provide eight hours of recording time.

Technology just keeps moving along, so take a good look at the DVRs. They're coming with longer and longer record time, mainly dependent upon the size of the memory cards.

The Installed Camera

Some private investigators install covert cameras for their clients on a temporary basis. The typical installation will include a *pinhole-lens* camera and a time-lapse VCR. An advantage of utilizing a time-lapse VCR is you can record from 2 to 24 hours, up to multiple days of activity, on one videocassette.

def•i•ni•tion

A **pinhole lens** is literally a lens for a camera that is about the size of the tip of a ball-point pen. Not literally "pin" size, but close, it can be concealed quite easily, particularly in dropped ceilings, where the ceiling tiles have a rough texture. This size lens is also popular in Nanny Cams, where the hole for the lens can be concealed behind a small piece of plastic, such as you might find on radios or many other appliances. Pin-hole lenses are frequently used when installing a camera in an air-conditioning vent.

Typically, when a time-lapse recorder is used, the images are recorded from about four images every second to one image per second, depending upon the length of recording time needed. Even with one image every second, it is unlikely that a person can enter a room and pass through it without his entry being recorded.

A problem with all installations is that somebody needs to review the tapes. Whether you're using a camera in the bag or a professionally installed camera with a time-lapse recorder, you will have two hours of tape to review. Using a professional quality VCR that has *jog and shuttle* capability can shorten the reviewing time. These features allow the viewer to fast-forward through the tape, stop the tape when action is observed, and run the tape forward or backward, one frame at a time. Nevertheless, it still takes a keen eye to catch the action.

The Division of Licensing

With the demise of standard videocassettes, now being replaced by digital video recorders, you can find good deals on used videocassette time-lapse recorders. Many of these have been used for thousands of hours and the recording heads will be dirty or worn down, so buyer, beware.

def•i•ni•tion

Jog and shuttle are two functions of a videocassette recorder that allow an operator to play the tape backward and forward, one frame at a time, or in multiple-frame increments that are determined by the user. Generally, the jog-shuttle control is a wheel device on the VCR that the operator rotates forward or backward causing the VCR motors to rotate in sync with it forward and reverse, faster and slower.

Another way to minimize how much tape you have to sort through every day is to set up the installed camera so that it records only when activated by a motion sensor. Most professional time-lapse recorders can be activated by passive, infrared motion sensors or, if a monitor is left on, video motion on the monitor can trigger the recorder.

The Digital Video Recorders often come with a zone feature. You can set the camera and recorder up and mark zones on the image so that if there is movement in that zone, the recorder will begin recording. When the movement stops, the recorder returns to standby. On covert installations utilizing battery power, this extends the period between required battery changes. And it reduces your playback review time to only those times when there was movement in the area of interest. It's a great feature, and you should consider paying a little extra for it if you're buying a new recorder.

Information obtained from hidden surveillance cameras can be used in a variety of places, including the courtroom, as long as ethical and legal standards are followed.

The basic rule of thumb for the placing of covert or hidden cameras is: when does a person have a reasonable expectation of privacy? My firm will not place cameras in bedrooms or bathrooms where persons other than the client himself might be caught on tape. Obviously, if we're going to catch an underwear thief, then the camera will have to be in the bedroom. But the camera will not be turned on while that client is home. Again, in commercial buildings, we won't place cameras in restrooms. Somebody else might, but we won't, because most people would have an expectation of privacy there.

Elementary, My Dear Watson

The U.S. Postal Inspectors used to have cameras and peepholes in the employee restrooms at the Post Offices. Postal employees would sometimes steal items from the mail, retreat to the employee restrooms where they could close the door, open the package in secret (they thought), remove the valuables and hide them on their own person before returning to work. At least, that was the alleged reason why the Postal Inspectors said they needed to see what happened in the restrooms. Finally, the inspectors were forced to close the peepholes and remove the cameras to insure privacy in the restrooms.

Suzanne was facing a divorce. Her husband was the son of a prominent businessman. The husband's family owned a professional sports franchise in the western United States, and her husband helped manage the business. The soon-to-be ex-husband smoked marijuana heavily. This habit wore on the marriage until, finally, Suzanne had had enough of it. Obviously, his drug usage could prove embarrassing to the family because the team's management subjects the players to regular drug testing. It wouldn't look good for management to be hypocritical in the area of zero drug tolerance.

Proving her husband's drug usage would be difficult in court without some corroborating evidence. Otherwise, it would just be her testimony against his. Obviously, she expected him to deny the drug allegations. Who wouldn't? She didn't really want to create problems for him and the family, and she recognized that it was also in her best interest if the sports franchise continued to thrive. After all, her future alimony payments would depend upon it. Basically, she wanted to extract a fair settlement from the husband without damaging his reputation and the business.

Suzanne showed me her husband's stash of marijuana. He really had quite a bit. Multiple mason jars of it were hidden in different places throughout the house and in the garage. He certainly had more than enough to be arrested for possession with intent to distribute. That usually only takes more than 20 grams. She swore that he did not sell it, but only had it for his personal use.

This presented me with an ethical quandary. Private investigators frequently find themselves in situations that make them privy to what might be illegal activity. To some, it may appear black and white. There is marijuana in the house. It is illegal. Call the police.

On the other hand, the very key to the nature of private investigations is the fact that it is *private*. PIs are not officers of the court. Nor are they sworn law enforcement personnel. Clients usually call on private investigators because the issues involved are civil in nature as opposed to criminal. Or, if it is a borderline civil/criminal issue, the client doesn't want to involve law enforcement. Just as often, the local law enforcement officials refuse to become involved, even though they've been invited into the case (such as runaway teenagers, parental kidnappings, a partner in a business who's violating his noncompete agreement, or an employee who's sleeping with a competitor and giving away company secrets, or members of a firm who are stealing company products). Banks, law firms, and high profile local companies are particularly hesitant to involve law enforcement and hence, the media, in embezzlements or other high-ranking employee dishonesty matters where the institution's reputation might be tarnished. They'd much rather prove to their own satisfaction that the transgression has taken place and quietly have the guilty party leave the company.

Each private investigator has to address this type of situation with his own conscience, subject to his own standards, and draw the line where he will. A good private investigator uses discretion, tact, and an experienced hand. In Suzanne's case, we agreed to help her without involving any law enforcement.

We placed a pinhole-lens camera in an air duct located in the study where her husband smoked his marijuana. He usually smoked when she was not in the house because he knew she disapproved. We transmitted the video signal to a time-lapse recorder concealed in an attic crawl space. We set the VCR close to the opening where Suzanne could change the tapes daily.

Suzanne brought us the tapes every two or three days and one of my investigator interns reviewed them. At the end of a two-week period, we had a dozen instances of the husband rolling, lighting, and smoking joints while seated in his favorite chair. We made a composite videotape with all of the smoking sequences on it. Our client received a generous alimony settlement shortly thereafter.

Some people might say that Suzanne blackmailed or extorted her soon-to-be ex-husband. This might sound cold, but I've worked this business too long not to know. The reality of divorce is that it involves emotional blackmail, extortion, exposure of illicit acts, and the fostering of guilt on the part of both parties. In this case, we just documented the facts. That is our job as private investigators. How the documented truths of a person's actions are later used in negotiations is beyond the control of the private investigator.

You've read this before in this book and you'll read it at least one more time before you turn the last page: the private investigator's job is to get the facts and reveal the truth to her client. Then she has to let the chips fall where they may.

Tapping Your Own Phone

It's Saturday morning and you're pushing the lawnmower around the yard, trying to get the grass cut before the temperature rises to 100°. The screen from your 14-year-old daughter's bedroom window is off the window and leaning against the house. That's funny. This makes the second time in a week you've put it back on.

An hour later, you've finished the grass and go to speak to your daughter. The door to her bedroom is locked, as usual. Well, girls need their privacy, right? Eventually, your daughter opens the door. You ask her about the screen and she shrugs her shoulders. What do girls know about windows and screens? It's a dad's job to keep those things fixed.

Now it's midweek. You're up late, say 2 in the morning, working on a project. You step outside to get a breath of fresh air and clear your head. You walk around the house, admiring your begonias and there, darn it, is the screen standing against the house again. Then it hits you. If the screen were just falling off, it would be flat on the ground, not leaning against the house. Either your daughter has been climbing out or, worse, somebody unknown to you has been climbing in.

Knocking on your daughter's door brings no response. You find the little key that unlocks interior doors and go into her bedroom. It's empty. Where is she, what is she doing, and who is she with?

Three hours later, she finally comes home. You're thankful she's home safe, but this kind of behavior can't be tolerated. You threaten to ground her for life. She shrugs her shoulders, says fine, and still she refuses to tell you where she's been or with whom. She's not going to talk about it. At least, not to you.

Teenagers, especially teenage girls, will talk at great length with their friends about exploits, problems with parents, and the general unfairness of life. There is probably no better way to find out what is happening in your teenager's life than to listen to her telephone conversations with her friends.

That being said, eavesdropping does have its downsides. It's an invasion of privacy. Some parents can't keep a secret and will have to pull the superior tone, telling the child that they know what she's up to. Once you let on to your child that you're listening in on her conversations, you can kiss that technique good-bye. She'll be much more guarded in her conversations on the telephone for quite a while. In addition, she'll claim no forgiveness for you in this life, or the next. The teenager may get really mad, and have to act out in some way to show you that you can't control her. The acting-out behavior could actually be worse than the sneaking out. And lastly, listening in on someone's phone conversations might be illegal in your state.

Legalities

The recording of telephone conversations is covered in most state statutes under the interception of wire communications. To record or intercept a telephone call without breaking the law, under federal statutes, one party to the conversation has to be aware of the fact that the telephonic conversation is being recorded. This means that under the federal law, I can record a telephone conversation I'm having with another person and not advise them that the call is being recorded. Why should I have to advise them? If I took shorthand, I could record the call on paper just as easily. This is called the one-party rule.

Some states have a narrower view of recording telephonic conversations than the federal government. These states insist that all parties to the telephone conversation be aware that the call is being recorded. This is called the two-party rule, or a two-party state. See Appendix B for a list of one-party and two-party states. Note, two-party actually means all parties in the conversation. The laws do change, so keep abreast of the relevant laws in your own state. Also, you should note that California (an all-party state), considers it illegal to record conversations as long as one party to the conversation is in California even if the recording is taking place in another state which is maybe a one-party state.

Elementary, My Dear Watson

Remember Linda Tripp and her recording of her telephone conversations with Monica Lewinsky? After the President Clinton-Lewinsky fiasco, the state of Maryland brought charges against Linda Tripp for the illegal recording of those telephone calls. Why? Because Tripp was in Maryland, which is an all-party state, meaning that all parties are supposed to be notified that the phone conversation is being recorded. Lewinsky was in Washington, D.C., which is a one-party jurisdiction. Tripp didn't tell Lewinsky she was recording the phone calls, so she was in violation of Maryland's interception of wire communication law, but not Washington's. Eventually, the charges were dropped against Tripp, but it took awhile and probably some big-dollar attorney fees.

So how can you legally record your daughter's phone calls? Obviously, you don't want her, or her friends, to know that her calls are being recorded. If you live in a one-party state and your child is a minor, then basically, as her adult guardian, you can give consent for her to record her telephone calls. If she's over 18, however, that won't work.

I've had many clients complain that they're paying for the phone line, so they should be able to record the calls on it if they want to. Let's talk real life here. The likelihood of a local district attorney prosecuting parents for listening to their own child's phone conversations is nil. The legal research hasn't been done in each state, but certainly, at someplace, at sometime, some parent has been prosecuted for recording his kid's calls. Just as certainly, there were some other exacerbating facts that warranted the prosecution. Perhaps there was parental abusive behavior or some other action on the part of the parent that required prosecution.

If my teenage daughter were sneaking out at night, you can bet that I'd be listening to the conversations between her and her friends, and I live in a two-party state. Traditionally, the courts give wide latitude to parents in how they raise and control their youth.

Technicalities

The simplest way to record a telephone conversation within your own home, without letting your teenager know about it, is to purchase a Smart-Phone Recording Control from Radio Shack. The product number is 43-2208. You can search the Radio Shack website at www.radioshack.com. Put that number in the search field, and you can read the specifications on the device. The normal retail price is $29.99, but it sometimes is on sale.

Decide in advance where you want to locate the recording equipment. It should not be in your child's room. I suggest in your own bedroom or some room that your teenager doesn't normally use. You can put it in the garage if you have a phone extension out there.

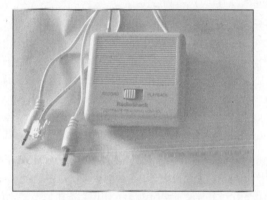

The easiest method to record telephone calls within your house.

In conjunction with the recording control device, you're going to need a cassette or digital voice recorder with a remote switch input jack and a microphone jack. The recording control device has a telephone modular plug that will plug into a spare phone jack. If you don't have a spare phone jack, then also buy a modular duplex jack (Radio Shack catalog number 279-357) for $6.99. This will allow you to plug both your phone and the control device into your phone line at the same time.

Plug the microphone jack into the microphone input on the recorder. Insert the remote switch plug into the remote switch jack on the recorder. Put a tape in the recorder. Set the cassette recorder's control Record/Playback switch to Record. Push down the Play and Record button on the tape recorder. Now take any phone on that line in the house off the hook, lifting up the telephone receiver. As soon as you do that, the recorder will start recording.

The duplex jack lets you plug a phone recording control and your telephone into one phone jack.

Anytime someone makes or receives a telephone call on that phone line, anywhere in the house, from any extension, it will be recorded, as long as there is a blank tape in the recorder and the recorder has power. It doesn't make any difference if the phone call is on a hardwired phone or a portable phone. It works just as well either way. It's that simple. The instructions that come with the device are very clear, and the help at Radio Shack is very good. You just have to hope that the guy who's helping you at the store isn't the one your daughter's sneaking out to see in the middle of the night.

The last step is to hide the recording equipment. Usually, shoving it under the bed and covering it with a towel will work. The devices make no noise and generate no heat, so they are pretty innocuous, as long as your kid doesn't stumble across it.

One problem that does occur is that teenagers sometimes spend hours on the phone. You may find that you need to record more than one 90-minute tape will allow. If that's likely to be the case, find an electronics specialty shop on the Internet and buy a cassette recorder that's been designed to slow down such that a 90-minute tape will last 12 to 24 hours. These recorders aren't that expensive—a couple hundred dollars at most.

Alternate Light Source

Remember that 90-minute tapes are usually 45 minutes per side. Take a serious look at Digital Voice Recorders instead of cassette recorders. Depending upon the memory installed, you can get upward of 300 hours of record time. You can download the audio files to your computer in Windows Media Audio (WMA) format. Wow, 300 hours of listening to your teenager on the phone. Wouldn't that be fun?

You'll have to spend some time listening to the tapes to find out what your daughter is up to, but this technique never fails for getting the facts. One recommendation is to be sure to get all of the facts before you confront the teenager. Don't jump to conclusions based on one phone call. Take your time, settle down, work out a game plan with your spouse that you both agree to, and then speak to your child. Remember, teenagers don't think of themselves as children. To put the whole situation into perspective, it might help to remember what antics you pulled as a teenager, including the ones where you never got caught. Now that's scary, isn't it? How you handle the situation after that is beyond the scope of this book, but tar and feathering would probably get you in trouble with the law, and Radio Shack doesn't carry those supplies, anyway.

The Least You Need to Know

- Placing a hidden camera in the home can catch abusive babysitters, uninvited visitors, and illegal behavior by spouses or friends.

- Techniques for using hidden cameras include the camera in a gag, Nanny Cams, and installed cameras, which usually utilize pinhole lenses.

- Tapping your own phone is a valuable technique for obtaining information about family members.

- Tapping your own phone may be illegal in all-party states, or if the persons being recorded are not aware of the recording. In one-party states, you may give consent for your minor child's conversations to be recorded, making recording in those instances legal.

- Tapping your own phone is easily accomplished by purchasing equipment at Radio Shack.

- Wireless camera advertisements are frequently seen on the Internet. Shop around before purchasing, as prices vary greatly for the same piece of equipment.

Catching the Runaway Teenager

In This Chapter

- Making a to-do list
- Dealing with the police department
- Tracking the runaway down
- Determining if the ex-spouse is harboring
- Making other parents your ally
- Sending photos around the country
- Using the "credit" in credit and debit cards
- Taking advantage of cellular technology

The wall clock reads 2 in the morning, and your 15-year-old daughter, Billie, is not home. Acid churns in your stomach. One moment you're mad as hell at her for not being there, the next instant you're close to tears worrying about your baby girl.

You're afraid to call the parents of any of her friends because you don't want to wake them up at such an awful time in the morning, plus you're feeling a little ashamed. As a parent, you should have better control over your teenagers, shouldn't you? Boy, are you ever going to give it to her when she gets home. No dating until she's 21. No telephone for two years, and she can forget about ever, ever having a car.

You've dozed off in the chair for a little while. The first light of the day is creeping through the blinds. The clock reads 5 A.M. Now you know for certain that the reason she's not home is more than just a flat tire or an empty gas tank. In Billie's room, you notice her makeup bag is gone. But she carries that in her purse, no big deal. You can't tell if any clothes are missing, since she and her girlfriends trade clothes back and forth like they own a consignment clothing store. You don't know how they keep track of who bought what.

At 6 A.M. the phone rings. You and your husband both look and then simultaneously lunge for it. You get to it first. It's Missy, a good friend of Billie's. Missy is calling to relay a message. Billie just called her and asked her to tell you that she was all right and not to worry. Don't call the police because she was old enough to be on her own. Billie doesn't want to live at home anymore. She's tired of you making her go to school. She doesn't like school and school doesn't like her. She'll call you when she gets settled down someplace. She has a few dollars and she'll be okay. Not to worry. Yeah, right.

Evaluating the Situation

If the evidence is clear that your or your client's teenager has run away and has not been abducted, then the next step is to collect the facts at hand and make some hard decisions. Find out from your client why she ran away. Be probative in your questions and observant of your surroundings. You're not going to get the real answer at the beginning. Down the road, when you've located the missing girl and are ready to have her picked up, you have to be convinced that her home environment is better than whatever alternatives exist. While your contractual obligation is to your client, your moral obligation is to the child.

Is this the first time she has run away? When I get calls from clients about their runaway teenager, almost invariably it's not the first time the child has left for parts unknown. It's just the first time the parents haven't been able to find her.

Here are 10 things to accomplish that will get you started and help move the investigation along. For the questions, write the answers down on a piece of paper. Gather the other materials together. If you are the parent, you'll want to have this information handy when you go to the police or to a private investigator. If you're the investigator, you'll see how we'll use it later in the chapter.

- Find the most recent picture you have of her.

- What was she wearing when she left? Runaways don't change clothes very often, and she'll probably be wearing the same thing for several days.

- Does she have any tattoos, piercings, or other identifying marks?

- Where did she run to before?

- Is the same boy or friend involved? Get his or her address and phone number.

- How did she make her escape? Chances are somebody drove a car and waited for her down the street. If you find the driver, you'll find the teenager.

- If she has a car and it is gone, write down a description of the car and the license plate number.

- Does she have a cellular telephone or a pager? What are the numbers? Did she take them with her? Get the last month's bill for her cell phone.

- Does she have credit cards or ATM cards with her? What banks do they draw on? Write down the account numbers.

- Make a list of all her friends, even if there are 50. Include their names, telephone numbers, and addresses. If you don't know their addresses and complete names, write down their first names and who else might know the rest of the name and how to contact them.

Next, if you don't have caller ID on your telephone lines, then call the telephone company and have it installed immediately. Usually, it only takes 30 minutes for the telephone company to add it to your service. Send somebody down to the store to buy a caller ID unit. It's probable that when she calls home, she'll block the call, but if she knows you don't have it she may not think to block it. You could get calls from her friends who might not think to block their calls.

Handling the Police Department

I always recommend reporting the runaway to your local police or sheriff's office as a runaway/missing person. The reality is that thousands and thousands of teenagers run away from home every year. Unless there is some sign of physical abduction, your local police department has bigger fish to fry than to look for your wayward daughter, so don't expect much help from them until you've done the legwork and have her located. There are several other reasons why you want to report her missing, though.

Elementary, My Dear Watson

If your teenager is a good kid and a reasonable student, and gets involved in some illegal activity, I never recommend calling the police unless you absolutely have to. Having your child arrested and subjected to our criminal justice system is one of the worst things you can do to your teenager. I know that goes counter to what some say, but having been involved in this business for 20-some years, trust me. I'd do everything necessary to keep my child out of our jails and court system.

Some well-intentioned fathers will say that a night in jail will be good for the kid. Wrong. Once you put a child in that system, your control of the situation is lost. You've abdicated your rights as parents and turned those rights and responsibilities over to society. The jails are nothing more than a school where delinquents can learn to be better delinquents. They'll learn how to steal, do drugs, and become con and scam artists. When they are released, they'll be heroes among their peer group, and you don't want their illegal actions to be glorified in that manner.

The only time I'd consider having my child arrested would be if a jail were a safer place than where he is now. If your child is endangering himself or others, then give up your rights as a parent and have him arrested. Otherwise, handle the problem yourself.

With runaways, we're not talking about arresting your child—just having her picked up and transported home. The police can, and you need to insist that they do, put your child's name, date of birth, and description into the NCIC (National Crime Information Center) as a runaway or missing person. Be sure to include any tattoos or other identifying marks. When kids are picked up, they'll deny their own identity. A good description of a tattoo, especially one with a name or word on it, is very helpful to the patrolman on the street if he thinks he has a runaway.

Reporting her missing to the police accomplishes three things:

♦ When the kid is picked up someplace for loitering or is stopped for whatever reason and she is identified, the agency that stopped her will hold her, usually in a juvenile facility if it's in another city, until you can make arrangements to retrieve her.

◆ A timely reporting of the disappearance of the child shows that you are a caring and concerned parent. You'll have a lot less trouble with the police and the juvenile authorities if you've reported the child missing right away. If you wait three days before reporting it and she is finally picked up, you might have some explaining to do to the state family services department before they let her come home.

◆ While your child will huff and puff and pretend to be incensed that you've involved the police, she will secretly be pleased that you wanted her back. Imagine how she will feel if she finds out she was gone for three whole days before you finally got around to reporting her missing. You think she'll want to stick around after that?

The Division of Licensing

Police departments and juvenile workers will interview a runaway teenager prior to releasing her to the custody of her parents or guardian. They have a responsibility to assure themselves that they are not returning the child into a harmful environment. If she makes allegations of physical or sexual abuse from her parents, stepparents, or another person in the home, even though totally false, then a whole can of worms is opened that you may not want to open. It's not unusual for a teenage girl to make false accusations against her parents. Be prepared for it. This is her defense mechanism and a way to hurt those parents. And it works very well.

Unless you live in a small community, the police probably will not come to your residence to take a runaway child report. They may assign the case to one of their officers who handles juvenile offender cases. Find out who this person is and write her name and contact numbers down. If they don't have an officer who works juveniles, then ask whom you can talk to in the future. You will want to make additional contact with this person if the child is not found within 48 hours.

Most runaway teenagers either return by their own choice or, if entered into the NCIC, are picked up and returned to their parents (or reach some sort of accommodation with their parents) within 48 hours.

The bottom line with police departments in mid-size to large cities: don't expect any real investigation to happen based simply on the runaway report. If you know where the child is located at a given moment, you can call the police, and they will send a squad car to pick her up and return her to your home. Other than that, you're basically on your own, as far as tracking her down is concerned. That's another good reason to keep this book handy. It'll help when the cops can't.

Tracking 'Em Down

In the rest of this chapter, we're going to get into the nuts and bolts of actually "running to ground" a missing teenager. I'm going to assume that you have unlimited financial resources. I know you don't, but I'm going to lay out here all the things you can do. Most of them don't require much in the way of money, anyway. Some will. You can pick and choose what you can afford to do, and decide for yourself where the action might fall on the cost-benefit curve.

People are creatures of habit, even teenagers. If she's run away before, she might use the same support apparatus that she used last time. How did she make her escape last time? Contact whoever drove her away before, or whomever she stayed with before. That's the first place to look. If she used a boy before and he is long out of the picture, don't discount him. Even if he hasn't had any contact with her for a while, if he's in the area, he'll know whom your daughter has the "hots" for and who has the "hots" for her. It could be a boy that she doesn't even like, but she'll use him as a vehicle to get away. The old boyfriend will likely know whom that would be.

If she was missing overnight before, who put her up? She stayed somewhere with somebody, and she just might be there again. You have to be a little sneaky here. I wouldn't just call and ask for her. Even teenagers have more street smarts than to fall for that. If there are some parents there that you trust, you might call them at work. Keep in mind that your daughter might be hiding in the house and the adults might not even know it. Teenagers stick up for each other, so those parents might ask their children, who in turn will lie to "protect" your daughter.

There are two options in this case: ask the parents to search their home after work and look for any signs that your daughter may have been there. Or set up surveillance on the house or apartment and see if she shows up.

My client Ralph finally called me after his son, Jimmy, had been gone for three days. This was the second time I'd worked this runaway, the other being the year before. He's the same boy we talked about in Chapter 9 in the pay phone section. You'll meet Jimmy again later in this chapter. Jimmy was a big 14-year-old. He was bigger than his father and as tall as I was, and he's kept me pretty busy.

I had his father make the list as we talked about earlier in this chapter. In going over the list of friends, we evaluated the lifestyle in each kid's home. Remember, kids will hide each other and protect each other from their own parents. In a runaway situation, all adults are the enemy. One friend popped out. This friend figured prominently in the previous escape. He lived in an apartment complex with his single mother. The mother worked during the day, so the kids were free to come and go as they pleased.

We thought this living arrangement might provide an opportunity for Jimmy to have a place to hide out during the day without any adult supervision. We had listed Jimmy as a runaway with the local sheriff's office and we confirmed that his name had been placed into the NCIC.

I tried to make contact with the *courtesy officer* at the apartments, but he was working on duty at the moment. I didn't want to contact the management of the apartments and create any grief for the friend's mother. Single working mothers have it hard enough, and my intention is almost always to try to calm situations down, not inflame them.

def•i•ni•tion

> A **courtesy officer** is usually a local police patrol person or sheriff's deputy that is given some sort of discount in his rent at an apartment complex in exchange for parking a marked patrol unit on the grounds and handling disturbance complaints at the complex when he is present. This is usually considered a good deal for the apartment management and the law enforcement department, as it reduces crime and does not increase law enforcement costs.
>
> In working surveillance at an apartment complex, it is normally a good idea to make contact with the courtesy officer, if there is one. Because apartment complexes have so many people coming and going, you can hide for several hours and usually the tenants won't be concerned over your presence when they do see you in the parking lot. However, employees of the apartment complex will notice you and will contact the courtesy officer to have you checked out. If you've already spoken with him, then you head off a confrontation, and he'll tell the management that you're okay.

We set up surveillance on the apartment where the friend lived. There were a number of kids coming and going, and I felt it would be beneficial to have another investigator on site so we could follow some of these other kids, as they might lead us to Jimmy. The client approved the second surveillance man. Just a few minutes after my second man arrived, a green Volvo showed up at the apartment. Jimmy hopped out of the back seat and ran into the building. In a few moments he was back and into the Volvo. It left the complex and we followed.

Jimmy's father had told me that Jimmy was using marijuana, and he hoped that when we had Jimmy picked up, we would find marijuana on him, because he wanted him to spend a week or two in a juvenile detoxification center.

We followed the Volvo around the beach area until it finally returned to the apartment. The car left a few minutes later, but Jimmy remained in the apartment. At that point, since we had Jimmy located and he was not on the move, we contacted the local sheriff's office. About this same time, the friend's mother came home from work. In a while, the courtesy officer showed up, and we explained what was happening.

We followed the courtesy officer to the apartment where we found Jimmy hiding underneath a bed. The mother didn't know he was there. Jimmy didn't have any marijuana in his possession, so the sheriff's office would not transport him to the detox center. The clients arrived and, with them in the front seat and myself and my other investigator on either side of Jimmy in the back seat, we took him to the detox center, where he spent the next two weeks.

The Division of Licensing

A word of warning here. Never pick up a runaway teenager yourself. Remember, PIs are not law enforcement and generally don't have the right to use force except as an ordinary citizen would in defense of himself or others. Also, unless you have a contract with the client/guardian that gives you temporary guardianship rights, you don't have parental rights either. You don't want the client suing you later when the teenager, especially a female, alleges that you hurt or abused her. The runaway is not going to be happy about being found, and she will lie about your actions as a form of revenge if she can. It is best to ensure that she is listed as a runaway in the NCIC, and then have the local police department pick her up.

If I were the parent of a runaway, I wouldn't pick up my own child, either. Suppose I go to a house where I know she is staying, and three 20-year-old males greet me at the front door holding baseball bats as they inform me she's not coming home. What do I do? It's best to have the police make the actual pick-up and avoid any confrontations yourself.

Checking Out the Ex

Some divorces are friendly and some are not. With child custody thrown into the mix, divorces can get downright nasty. If your client has custody of the runaway and there is an ex-spouse in the picture, take a good look at the relationship. If the ex is talking and being helpful with your client, then the kid is probably not there. But if there is animosity between the two parents, it's not unheard of for the ex-spouse to hide the child from the custodial parent.

Remember, all the ex is hearing is the nasty stuff coming from the teenager, detailing the mistreatment and unfairness of living with the custodial parent. The ex, perhaps, doesn't have the true picture, or if he does, he maybe can use this as a method of causing some grief for your client. Childish, I know, but so is most of the bickering that goes on during and after divorces. Makes you wonder who the adults really are in this world.

In Jimmy's case, the third time he ran away he was 16. That time he hid out at his mom's place for a while. The dad, meanwhile, was spending big bucks with my firm trying to find him. Making her ex (my client) spend money unnecessarily was part of her retribution plan.

We actually never found Jimmy at the ex's place, even though we did stake it out that time. We talked to the maid who worked there and she told us the ex was expecting Jimmy to show up. She'd left instructions with the maid to let him use the guest bedroom when he arrived.

Be sure to consider that a runaway teenager might try to get to the ex's residence. If it is out of state or some distance away, that makes it even more attractive to the kid. In her mind, the more distance she can put between herself and "the problem," the better.

Likewise, if your client has a troubled relationship with any other of his own children, especially older siblings of the runaway who are already living independently, be sure to consider them as possible hosts for the teenager. The siblings may harbor the runaway and not tell their parents for a while. It all depends upon the fundamentals involved in the relationships.

Rely on Other Parents

With all of the missing/runaway teenage cases I've worked, I've almost always gotten good cooperation talking to parents of other children. Parents seem to stick together in this type of case. Parents of teenagers seem to have this "us against them" mentality, just like their offspring.

When Jimmy was 17 he ran off for the fourth time. This time we thought he'd taken off with a bunch of other kids his age for a skateboarding tournament on the west coast of Florida. The young men and women who worked at a local surf shop verified he'd been in there earlier in the day, identified his picture, and told us how the boys were talking about who got the bed in the motel room and who had to sleep on the floor.

We tracked down the mother of a member of that group of boys. She worked as an early-morning waitress in a local breakfast eatery. I called on her at work the next morning, and she confirmed that her sons were headed to St. Petersburg, Florida, to participate in the tournament. She didn't know where they were staying but the kids had promised to call her when they found a room. She, in turn, promised to call us when she found out the motel and room number. That is just an example of the kind of cooperation you can expect from other parents.

As it happened, our client flew myself and another of my investigators down that same day to St. Petersburg to try and intercept Jimmy at the skateboard rink. Again, we received very good cooperation from the management at the arena, after we promised them there would be no trouble. Jimmy's friend, who was actually entered in the tournament, wasn't scheduled to skate until late afternoon.

When we arrived in St. Petersburg, I coordinated with the local sheriff's office, and they confirmed that Jimmy was listed in the NCIC as a runaway. They agreed to pick him up once we had him located and identified. See the value of making sure the child is listed in the NCIC? Wherever you go after he's in the NCIC, you will, to some degree at least, get local cooperation.

Identifying him was a problem. A lot of skaters maintain similar appearances. Even though I'd run him to ground twice in the past, I hadn't seen him for nearly a year. Fortunately, by this time, he'd tattooed his name on his shoulder, so once we got a look at his shoulder, we'd know if we had the right kid or not.

While we were waiting for Jimmy and his friends to make an appearance, the Daytona Beach Police Department called and said they'd picked him up in Daytona. Apparently, he wasn't in St. Petersburg at all. He'd had a change of heart, and instead of going to the skateboarding championship, he'd decided to catch a ride to Daytona with another friend.

My investigator and I hopped back on the plane and flew across the state to Daytona. Eventually, the Daytona authorities released him to us, and we returned him to his parents. How long do you think he stayed at home that time? Less than a week. I wasn't uncomfortable taking custody of him because there were two of us, a male and a female. It was unlikely he'd try to accuse us of anything in that situation.

The waitress mom, true to her word, called me later that evening and told me which motel the kids were staying in. Parents of other teenagers are usually willing to help in runaway cases. Don't hesitate to be honest with them and inform them about the case you're working on. You might get unexpected assistance from them. And, who knows, as a PI, you might end up getting a new customer, too, when it's her turn to deal with a runaway child.

Plaster the Country with Photographs

The fifth time Jimmy ran off, he was still 17 and not too far away from his 18th birthday. We didn't know for sure whether he had headed north or south. We did know that he was traveling with a guy who was about 22 years old, whom we were able to identify. He was from a town in New Jersey, and had been involved in selling marijuana in the beaches area of northern Florida.

I prepared a one-page report on Jimmy, including his description, tattoos, the fact that he was a juvenile, and the name of the person we thought he was traveling with. I included five copies of Jimmy's picture plus a disk with his picture on it in *JPEG* and *GIF* format. I first called the police department in the New Jersey town where the parents of Jimmy's friend lived. I asked for the name of the officer who worked juvenile and runaway matters. I then directed the letter and photographs to his attention.

def•i•ni•tion

JPEG (pronounced *J-peg*) and **GIF** (pronounced the way it looks) are two common digital formats for graphic files such as photographs. If photographs are going to be transmitted to a police agency or another investigator electronically or via a computer disk, it is best to save them in either JPEG or GIF format, because most computer photo programs can open and work with those formats. Other formats are not as common, and the police department might not be able to open and print the photograph.

I did the same thing when we heard rumors that he was in Daytona and then again in West Palm Beach, Florida. It's amazing the different levels of cooperation I received.

In New Jersey, where I expected the least amount of cooperation, the police staked out the residence of the friend for a week and kept a close eye on the neighborhood for a long time after that. They'd call me every few days with an update.

In Daytona, they shrugged their shoulders and basically said, "So what?"

In West Palm Beach, we had a list of pay phones that his girlfriend was calling. Jimmy would call her from a pay phone, give her the number he was calling from, and she would turn around and call him right back at that pay phone, using her cellular phone.

Since the girlfriend had the pay phone numbers Jimmy was calling from, it wasn't too difficult for us to get them.

We tracked down the location of the pay phones he was using and marked each one on a map. They were all within a three-block radius. See Chapter 9 for a discussion of how to find the location of pay phones in this type of case.

With the letter and photographs, I also sent to the West Palm Beach Police Department the list of pay phones he was using and their locations. They agreed to keep an eye out on the phones for us. If our client had really wanted the boy back, we could have staked out the phones ourselves, and in a few days we would have found him and had him picked up.

I think our client was about ready to give up trying to force his son to stay in school or to lead a productive life. If the police found him, fine. Otherwise, he'd just let him turn 18, and then there was nothing he could do anyway. And that's exactly what happened. Interestingly, after he turned 18, Jimmy came home all by himself. It figures, huh? I was half expecting to get a call from Jimmy, saying that the day after he'd come home, his dad had run away, and did I think I could find him.

Checking the Credit

If the runaway teen has a credit card or an ATM card that either belongs to the parents or for which the parents cosigned on the bank account with the teen, the parents should be able to have nearly immediate access to the usage information.

You can check the usage of most credit cards online. Most credit-card websites update daily. Depending upon how a transaction occurs, however, it might not post until several days after the transaction. You can try talking to the credit-card company to see if they can tell you when authorizations on the card are received. Usually those are all done electronically, and the company itself might not know where the authorization comes from until the charge actually posts. In serious kidnapping matters, it's a different story. The information is there, but getting it out of the credit-card company depends upon the stakes at hand.

ATM transactions, even on an ATM machine that is not part of the bank network, usually put a hold almost immediately on the account for the sum withdrawn and post the same night that the transaction takes place. The client's bank should be able to tell which machine was used for the transaction as soon as the hold is placed. With that information in hand, you might only be hours away from the teen. Hours can transform into hundreds of miles, but then again, you might get a handle on the child's direction of travel. Many ATMs have video surveillance cameras. You should liaison with the bank-security folks to get photos from the surveillance tapes. You might also get lucky and obtain a photograph of whom the runaway is traveling with. That person might be easier to track than the runaway. I've had good luck getting the banks to make available photos from their surveillance cameras. If you don't ask, you won't get it.

The Division of Licensing

A word of warning: some parents are tempted to cancel the credit cards immediately, but unless it's a serious money factor, you should advise your client against that. Credit-card charges can provide good leads to finding the runaway. If the child is under the influence of someone much older, he'll probably max out the card pretty fast, the person of influence will take the cash or goods. If the card has a high credit limit you'll want to lower it ASAP. You have to balance the financial cost with the quality of the information you're receiving concerning your child's current whereabouts. There are no cut-and-dried answers on that one.

Tracking the Cell Phone

In the previous edition of this book, we talked about obtaining cellular phone records. The legality of this practice has come into question, so we don't acquire those any longer without the subscriber's permission. There is an aspect to cellular usage that is more immediate than the monthly statements. Each cell phone has its own electronic serial number (ESN). When a cell phone is in the "on" position, it periodically broadcasts this ESN. This is how the cellular company knows where to route a call when one is received for any particular cell phone customer. The company computers keep track of where all the active cell phones are at any given minute.

Under the right circumstances, a cellular company might be convinced to alert you when the teen's cell phone is turned on. Again, it will take some pressure, and perhaps even some law enforcement intervention, to get the cell company to do this, but it's worth it. Why? Because when the cell company picks up the ESN signal, its computers will know that it's coming from a specific cellular site. This would pinpoint the location down to an area of no more than a few square miles or, in a downtown area, to within a few blocks. Today almost all teens have cell phones. With GPS-enabled phones, parental cooperation, and law enforcement involvement, you should be able to pinpoint exactly where the teenager's phone is when it's turned on.

There might be no other case that carries with it so much emotion as a missing child or teenager. Some of us wish our teenagers were missing more often. (Just kidding.) More than one mother has said that she wouldn't sell her teenager for a million dollars, but some days she would flat out give her away.

Alternate Light Source _____

When a cell or telephone bill has dropped, it means that the billing cycle has ended, and the charges are en route to the consumer. Usually even the customer cannot access the list of phone charges until the bill has entered the billing system's computer. With enough pressure, in exigent circumstances like a runaway situation, you might get the cellular company to give you the calls daily as they're made.

Except for the mother in the preceding paragraph, usually the parent of the missing youth will have her emotions run the gamut from worry, to fear, to anger, to hurt, to frustration, to desperation, and finally, to resignation.

When dealing with these clients, be sensitive to their needs. Keep the welfare of the child uppermost. Don't make promises you can't keep. Be the calming influence, the face of reason, and the beacon of hope.

The Least You Need to Know

- Runaways should always be listed in the NCIC by informing the local police departments. The police should be informed of the missing child as soon as possible as a sign of good faith on the part of the parents.

- Consider surveillance of possible friends and ex-spouses' residences where the teen may be hiding. Always ask the police to pick up the runaway once he's been located. Don't do it yourself.

- Parents of other teenagers usually will cooperate in a runway case. Use them.

- Send photographs of the teen to police departments in cities where it is likely the teen might be.

- Charges on credit cards, as well as ATM withdrawals, can provide timely information as to where the teenager is located or her direction of travel.

- A cellular phone in the "on" position transmits its serial number to the cellular company. With enough pressure, the cell company might tell you the location of the cell site on which it is receiving the signal, or if the phone is GPS-enabled, you might get the latitude and longitude.

Chapter 19

The Ins and Outs of Electronic Surveillance

In This Chapter

- ◆ Learning the differences between bugs and taps
- ◆ Who done it? Cops or robbers?
- ◆ Tapping the line
- ◆ Gathering the tools
- ◆ Finding the inside taps
- ◆ Catching the neighbor

The second-most-common call received by a private investigative agency is a request for a countermeasure sweep. The caller doesn't use those words, but that's what she wants. Normally she'll say, "I think my phone is tapped." Or, "My husband and I are getting a divorce and I want to make sure he's not recording my telephone calls."

A countermeasure sweep is an active measure by an individual with the goal of finding or countering an aggressive action taken against him or her. Typically, the term is used in the sense of actively searching for and eliminating any electronic transmitters (bugs) or wiretaps that are directed toward locations or facilities where the target of the measure would likely be heard. A variation of the term is also used with respect to surveillance. A counter-surveillance is a surveillance initiated by an individual to determine if he is under surveillance by an outside group. If properly conducted, a counter-surveillance will identify the entity conducting the surveillance. So you'll know who at the diner counter is watching you.

There are four aspects to conducting a complete countermeasure sweep:

- ◆ Evaluating the threat level
- ◆ Intercepting wire communications: telephone sweeps
- ◆ Intercepting oral communications: transmitters
- ◆ Locating hidden video equipment cameras

In this chapter, we're going to examine the first two. Hidden video cameras we've talked about to some degree in Chapter 17. Sweeping for concealed transmitters (bugs) is beyond the scope of this book. If you have a situation that calls for this type of action, contact a reputable PI firm that specializes in countermeasure sweeps.

Before we go into details, though, we have to understand exactly what we're looking for.

Bugged or Tapped: It's Terminology

I frequently receive telephone calls where the new client says, "I think somebody has bugged my phones." Is that possible? Sure. Is it likely? Not unless we're dealing with a bug or a phone tap instituted by law enforcement under a legal warrant. Can somebody bug your house? Sure, it happens all the time. Can somebody other than law enforcement tap your phone line and record your conversations? Sure, we see it at least once a month. But bugging your phones is unlikely. Confused? That's because the general public doesn't make a distinction between a bug and a wiretap. It's a matter of terminology. To understand intercepts, we need to understand intercept technology and get the terms right.

What the caller probably means is that some privileged information that he told somebody on the telephone has leaked out. He didn't tell anybody else, and he's sure that other person didn't relate it to anybody either; hence, his phone must be tapped (not bugged).

A bug generally refers to a microphone-transmitter combination. The microphone picks up the conversation and the transmitter sends it out using radio frequency (RF) energy. There are other ways to get a conversation transmitted out of the room without using RF. A conversation can be picked up by a microphone and transmitted outside of the residence by using the power wires. A recorder can be connected to your power line outside the house and it can record the conversations overheard by the microphone. High tech, sure, but it can be done. If you hire somebody to "debug" your office and all they do is search for RF transmissions, they've only done half the job.

Bugs—let's call them transmitters—are used to capture a conversation between two or more people within the same room. We're all familiar with the bug disguised as an olive in a martini glass. In that case, the olive is the microphone-transmitter and the toothpick is the antenna.

Having your phones tapped generally means that, at some point on your *landline telephone line*, an interception has been made, and the interceptor most likely is recording the conversations that travel over your phone line.

Other forms of communication, such as cellular phones and portable handsets, can be compromised as well. If any conversation travels through the air, or through wires, it can be intercepted.

def•i•ni•tion

A **landline telephone line** refers to a normal telephone line that has a physical demarcation point at a residence, business, or pay telephone. The phone call at least begins and ends its transmission along a pair of wires, regardless of whether transmission of the call includes microwave or satellite in between both ends. This is in contrast to a cellular phone, or any type of radio communication, which is considered wireless communication—literally, not connected to the ground at some point with wires.

Evaluating the Threat

Paranoia runs rampant in our society. We like to say in our business, just because you're paranoid doesn't mean someone hasn't tapped your phone. (It's a variation of the old axiom, "Just because you're paranoid doesn't mean that there is nobody following you.") The real question you have to ask yourself, or the client, is whether there's anything you're saying on the phone that's so valuable to another person that they'd be willing to go to an awful lot of trouble and expense to listen to your conversations. It doesn't have to be illegal stuff. For example, is the client involved in big money deals? Then it might be worth the effort for the competition to listen in.

Is his wife fooling around on him and he wants to know for sure? Then he might consider tapping his own phone to listen to her conversations. Generally in most states, taping your home telephone to listen to your spouse's calls would be illegal. There are special circumstances that might make it legal to tap your own phone involving calls made by your minor children. Check Chapter 17 for the details on that.

If you're searching for a phone tap or a transmitter placed by your client's spouse, then chances are you can find it with the instructions from this chapter. Even if the spouse has big bucks, it's unlikely that he'll spend the tens of thousands of dollars it would take, assuming he knew the people who could do it, to tap the phone in such a way as to make detection impossible.

If you think the FBI or Homeland Security has tapped your phone and a PI offers to sweep the phone lines for $150, you have the wrong PI. When law enforcement executes a legal telephone tap, they basically have the phone company run an extension of your phone line into their offices. There is no physical connection made at your house or business. There is an electronic connection made at the telephone company's central switch to have your calls routed both to your phone at home and to the local FBI office. That puts a few chinks into some of those television movies, doesn't it?

There are some equipment manufacturers who claim their test equipment can alert the technician performing a countermeasure sweep that a legal tap is on the line. How? In a legal tap, the length of the telephone circuit has basically been extended to include the local FBI office. The manufacturer is selling you on the ability of their equipment to test for a change in the length of the circuit. If you really think your phone is tapped by law enforcement, that means it's been done with a warrant, and this chapter won't help you find it. And if that's what you're up against, don't buy the fancy testing equipment. Hire a good lawyer.

However, if you're thinking it's an illegal tap by a cowboy cop, then there is a good chance you'll find it. If the telephone tap threat is from your husband, next-door neighbor, or the guy who lives two floors below you in the same building, then $250 per line to check your phone lines is reasonable, because finding that sort of wiretap is not a high-tech search. Still, the person doing the sweeping has to know what he is looking for. Before this chapter is over, you'll be able to do it yourself.

Tapping telephones without the consent of the parties involved, or without having a warrant for the tap, is illegal in every state. That means you have to consider in advance what action you'll take if you discover that your telephone is tapped or your house is bugged.

Do you call the phone company? Call your lawyer? Call the police? The natural reaction is to want to nail the person responsible, but you need to stop and think it through. Do you really want the person responsible to go to jail? If the guilty party is a soon-to-be ex-husband, just remember that he won't be able to pay child support or alimony if he's in prison. You might have to go to court to testify, and that risks making everything part of the public record for anyone to read. Are you sure you want to do that? Think this through very carefully before you involve law enforcement, because once you start the legal system in motion, there's no turning back.

Know what you're going to do before you start looking, and then be prepared to photograph the tap for later evidence.

Tools of the Trade

Remember the old gangster movies of the 1940s? Neither do I, but I've seen a few remakes. In the old movies, when the guy wanted to tap a phone, he went down to the basement of the building and found the telephone junction box where all the phones in the building came together. Then he clipped on a couple of wires using alligator clips, ran those wires to another set of wires that went to an apartment in the same building, or maybe to a small room or closet in the basement. He could sit in the room with a headset on and listen to the phone calls all day. The PI would bring him coffee periodically throughout the day and ask if there was anything new. Ah, the good old days.

Well, surprise. The good old days are basically still here. Things haven't changed that much. You can find most local telephone taps with three tools: your eyes, a screwdriver, and a *butt set*.

def•i•ni•tion

A **butt set** is a handheld device that looks like a cordless phone, has a touchtone keypad, and is used by telephone and electronic service people to identify telephone lines. It will have a set of wires with alligator clips at the end. You can buy butt sets for less than $100 over the Internet or at Radio Shack.

Type "butt set" into any Internet search engine and you'll find lots of listings. You can spend over $1,000 if you want, or you can make your own for less than $20. Here are full instructions for making your own butt.

Take an old touchtone telephone or buy one from a local phone store. You don't need any special type of phone; the plainer the better. Buy a short phone extension cord (cost $3) and a couple of alligator clips (cost $2). Plug one end of the extension cord into the telephone. Cut off the other plug end from the cord. Strip the outside wire cover back about a foot. Strip the red and green inside wire covers back about two inches baring the copper wire. Assuming it's a two-pair extension cord, clip off the yellow and black wires because you won't need them. Attach the alligator clips to the red and green bare ends.

There you have it. A homemade butt set for the cost of a telephone and $5 in parts.

The Inside Job

The easiest way to access your phone lines is from within your residence or the property in question. If your spouse, partner, or some other person who has regular, daily access to your home wants to tap your telephone line, it's probably being accomplished as an "inside" job.

A butt set is a tool used to identify phone lines.

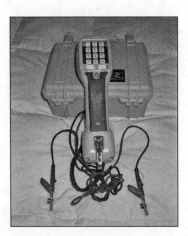

Look in Chapter 17 at the telephone recording control device from Radio Shack. That's what you're looking for. Search under every bed. Get a flashlight and look behind every piece of furniture. Using the light, search every wall in the house for a phone jack. If there are wires coming out of any phone jack, examine them to make sure they are only going to telephones and not to a control device or a tape recorder.

Physically run your hands along the wires from the phone jack and trace them back to the phones. Don't just eyeball it. A clever guy will splice the wires partway up the line and put the recorder and controls behind a piece of furniture. If you just look at the wall and at the phone, you'll say to yourself, "Okay, nothing there." So run your hand all the way down the line from the telephone to the wall jack.

Check under the beds and in your home office. Do you have a locked drawer or cabinet in your study? Are there any wires leading to that drawer or cabinet? Check the spare bedroom, too. You have to check every room, every wall, and every phone jack.

Still didn't find it, but you're sure it's there? Hit the garage. He's going to be sneaky, so you have to be as thorough as he is clever. Look in every closet. If your husband is the least bit technical, he can splice into the phone line in the attic and put the recorder up there. Or he can run a line from the splice in the attic to another location in or around the house.

Walk around the outside of the house. Are there any phone lines coming out of the crawl space that you can't identify? Most women, and men for that matter, won't know which lines are supposed to be on the outside of the house and which aren't. That's okay. Just follow them visually to see where they go. No need to run your hands on these wires. You might accidentally be following an electrical wire that is not grounded and fry yourself, so don't touch any wires outside the house. It'll be pretty obvious if they go into a box that your husband has made to hold the tape recorder.

Husbands frequently hide the recorder and controls in a box under the porch or under a wooden deck, so get a flashlight and look there. If you don't want to be poking under the porch yourself, then find a PI who advertises countermeasure sweeps and get him to do it. But you can save the $250 by spending an hour and doing it yourself, since you know what to look for.

The Outside Job

In most areas of the country, it is fairly easy to tap a neighbor's telephone. I say *neighbor* because tapping the phone is also going to require that you be able to listen to or record the conversations. The further away the listening post is, the more problematic the exercise becomes. A method to circumvent the distance problem is to tap the phone outside the house or at the *junction box*, and hide a recorder in the bushes somewhere close by. This happens all the time.

def•i•ni•tion

A **junction box** is a piece of telephone company equipment where several customers' telephone lines are housed and connected to a phone company cable. Typically, these junction boxes house from two to two dozen connections. There is normally one on every block, or one for every 10 to 12 subscribers.

To find an outside wiretap, you must have a basic understanding of how telephones work. Phones require two wires. These two wires are referred to as one pair, just as two shoes equals one pair. If you have two pairs of shoes and only one pair of feet, like most of us, then you have an extra pair of shoes. If you have two pairs of wires and only have one phone line (one active phone number, not to be confused with extensions with the same phone number), then you have an extra pair. Almost every house in America that is wired for phone service has at least two pairs of phone wires in the house. Many newly constructed houses will have three or four pairs of wires so you can have three or four different telephone numbers at the same location.

All of these pairs of wires run throughout your house and lead from your building to the telephone interface, and then to the junction box. Typically, the active pair of wires are the red and green wires, known as tip and ring. The other pair is usually yellow and black, but can be blue and blue/white, or orange and orange/white, or any other two colors.

Your telephone wires from the inside of your house will interface or connect with the phone company's wires. Do not confuse this telephone interface with the telephone junction box.

A typical Bell System junction box.

The telephone interface attached to your garage or outside your house is usually a gray box divided into two sections. Your side can be opened by a flat-bladed screwdriver. The other side belongs to the telephone company and normally requires a special tool to open it. You don't really need access to the telephone company side of the interface anyway.

A telephone interface joins the lines you own with the lines owned by the phone company.

Locating the Junction Box

Now you need to locate the junction box. How will you recognize one when you see it? The junction box is usually a 2½-foot-tall, cylindrical, green metal post or cabinet. It'll be located on the ground and you might find it in the middle or at the end of a block, or any logical place where phone lines come together.

Our client, Heidi, asked us to check her lines for taps. She was suspicious of a neighbor who lived across the alley from her. He'd been insinuating that he was listening to her telephone calls after she'd ended their relationship. He wasn't stalking her, but he clearly pined for her. He also had occasional access to her apartment, feeding her dogs for her when she was out of town. Consequently, we did the inside checks as we've talked about and then went outside. The figure of a typical junction box on the preceding page was actually Heidi's junction box exactly the way we found it. It is not unusual to find them falling open or with the covers askew. It certainly makes getting into them easier.

Cable television junction boxes are similar and frequently are shorter and more round. However, just to mix you up, some cable boxes are larger and more square. Walk up and down the street or around your subdivision and you'll see the phone junction box. It probably has a phone company logo or sticker on it, but sometimes it may be weathered off. The cable boxes usually say "cable TV" on them.

The junction box is easily opened by a flat-bladed screwdriver. Some phone companies have recently begun utilizing security screws, which require a special tool. Don't let that stop you. Most of those boxes are left unsecured by careless telephone serviceman anyway, as was Heidi's. Often, they've been run over by cars or backed over by trucks, and that usually leaves them open as well.

On the older models, the front cover will lift up and then slide forward. There should be no need to completely remove the cover. Newer editions are totally round and the cover lifts completely off.

Finding Your Phone Line

In order to tell if your phone line has been compromised, you have to find your terminals inside that junction box. When you open the junction box, it may look daunting, but it's really not that difficult. Sometimes the telephone numbers are written on paper or plastic tags attached to the wires. I hope you're one of the lucky ones, but don't count on it.

Inside a telephone junction box.

The inside of the junction box will look similar to the one in the previous figure. In this box, the serviceman had written one of the phone numbers and the address inside the box for us. I like that guy.

Telephone wires carry about 52 volts of direct current. That's why your phones still work even if the electricity to your house is shut off, unless you have only cordless phones, which require the base station to be plugged into the AC current. There is not enough amperage to really hurt you, but you can get shocked, so don't be messing around in the junction box in the rain. The trick here is to find your lines and make sure that nobody has jumpered them to another pair like we talked about with the old gangster movies. That's exactly what we're looking for.

So you open the junction box and none of the phone lines are tagged or labeled. How do you figure out which one is yours? You'll need your butt set, and something called an *ANAC* number that will work in your area.

Every telephone company has a local phone number you can dial that is hooked to a computer that will repeat back to you the number from which you are calling. You might try dialing 211 or 311 (or any number between 205 and 220). That works in a lot of areas. If that doesn't work, then the easi-

> **def•i•ni•tion**
>
> **Automatic Number Announcement Circuit (ANAC)** is a telephone number that, when dialed, will announce back to you the number you are calling from. These numbers vary within area codes and sometimes vary within switches in the same city.

est way to get this callback number is to ask a telephone service repairman. When you see one working on the street, just stop and ask him. You might have to ask two or three before you find one who will give it to you, if he knows it.

Surprisingly enough, many repairmen don't know it themselves. Some phone companies will give it to you if you ask for it. Try calling the repair department and asking.

Take your butt set, homemade or purchased, and attach the alligator clips to the first pair of terminals in the junction box. You should hear a dial tone. If you don't, it's not an active pair.

Disconnect the clips and move down to the next one. Make sure the clips don't touch each other while you do this. It's not dangerous, but you won't get a dial tone if the alligator clips are touching. At each dial tone, use the touchtone keypad on the butt set to dial the ANAC number, and it will tell you the telephone number for the phone line you are connected to. If you connect to a line and hear voices, you are listening in on your neighbor's conversation in progress. Simply disconnect and move to the next one, or else you will now be the one who is illegally tapping another's line. Even though it's accidental, it's still not nice. Sure, it could be interesting, but don't be nosy and certainly *don't talk*, because if you do they will hear you, just as if you had picked up an extension in their home.

Alternate Light Source

Here are some 800 numbers you can use that belong to MCI if you want to find out the phone number for the phone line you are using. You may have to navigate through a set of menus to get the number repeated back to you. Press option one and then one again. 1-800-444-4444, 1-800-444-3333, and 1-800-888-5622 will all give you that number. Now, rather than using an ANAC, it's just as easy to use your butt set, dial your own cell phone number and see what number comes up on your cell phone's display.

Eventually, you will find your phone line. Examine it closely. Is there anything out of the ordinary? Anything different from the other lines and terminals in the junction box? I suggest you mark the terminals with a felt marker so you'll be able to identify your lines in the future. If there is a set of jumpers from your line to another, then yes, your telephone is tapped. Mark both sets, photograph the inside of the junction box, and replace the cover.

If by the time you read this the 800 ANAC numbers given in this chapter do not work, and you don't have a cell phone with caller ID or you're out of range of your cell tower and you can't find ANAC numbers for your area, there is still another way to determine which pair of wires in the junction box belong to you.

Have a friend sit in your house and make a phone call to anybody. Have them continue talking while you're at the junction box, methodically plugging into one pair of wires and then the next, until you eventually hear your friends discussing your paranoia. Voilá.

As I mentioned earlier, if your line is tapped, you have to decide what action to take.

In Heidi's case, I checked the junction box. The cover was half off the box as you see in the photograph. I opened the junction box and easily found Heidi's phone lines. How? Because I could see that one set of terminals had a pair of wires running to another set of terminals further down the box. I checked the phone number for the first set of suspicious terminals by using my butt set and dialing the ANAC. These were Heidi's lines, all right.

I then went over to the telephone interface, the gray box where the phone lines entered the subject's apartment, and checked there. Yep, he'd basically run an extension of Heidi's phone to his place.

Heidi didn't want to involve the police. After photographing it, I disconnected the tap and closed the box. One of the investigators who works for me is about 6 feet 4 inches tall and 260 pounds. When I walk down dark alleys, he's the one I take with me. I usually let him lead the way. He and I went and had a little talk with the neighbor who'd tapped Heidi's phone. She hasn't had any trouble with him since.

Tapping a phone by jumpering wires has its dangers. It's possible that an alert phone company serviceman will discover the tap while he is in that junction box working on someone else's line. The phone company may then report it to the police.

I don't advocate tapping phones. I get asked to do it all the time but refuse to do so. It's illegal and I won't do anything illegal because it's not worth losing my license for a few thousand dollars. However, let me emphasize that it is not illegal to find out if your own phone line has been tapped.

The Least You Need to Know

- The term "bug" refers to a microphone-transmitter combination that transmits room conversations to another location. "Tap" refers to an interception of wire communications.

- The threat level must be assessed. If the suspected source of the bugging or tapping is the FBI, then more sophisticated equipment will be needed to determine if both the room and the phone lines are secure. If the threat is a soon-to-be ex-husband, other, less-sophisticated techniques are probably adequate.

- Tapping telephones without consent of the parties involved or without having a warrant for the tap is illegal in every state. Upon discovering an illegal tap, evaluate if you want to involve law enforcement. If the guilty party will be paying your alimony, you may not want him in jail.

- Most illegal telephone taps can be located with your eyes, a screwdriver, and a butt set. You can make a butt set at home or buy one for less than $100.

◆ Thoroughly check every phone jack and every conceivable hiding place in the house for a tape recorder and a telephone remote control device. Also check in the garage, the attic, and the bushes outside of the house.

◆ To find an outside telephone tap, locate the junction box and examine the appropriate pair of wires.

◆ When dialed, Automatic Number Announcement Circuits (ANAC) will announce the number calling them.

Chapter 20

Catching the Burglar

In This Chapter

- ◆ Learning the ropes of personal crime
- ◆ Finding help from unlikely sources
- ◆ Hot sheeting the stolen cars
- ◆ Solving the burglary
- ◆ Detailing the pawnshop detail
- ◆ Crime scenes and dumpster diving
- ◆ Owner-applied numbers and the NCIC

Crime in America is a fact of life. In the year 2005, the FBI Uniform Crime Report indicates there were over 2 million (2,154,126) reported burglaries in the United States. To help you put that number into perspective, it means that 1 person out of 137 was a victim of a burglary. Want to get personal? Boil it down to households, and it means about 1 in every 35 homes was burglarized. Makes you want to step outside and look up and down the street and count how many houses there are. It is the only property crime statistic that increased from the year before.

If you add burglary to other property crimes, including larceny-theft, theft of motor vehicles, and arson, the number of reported crimes for the year 2005 was over 10 million. That means that about 1 out of every 29 persons, or every seventh household, was a victim of property crime. Uh-oh. Better step outside and recount your street.

In this chapter, we're going to talk about what to do when you're at the shopping mall and your purse is snatched. Then you go out to the parking lot and your car has been stolen, and after a cab ride home, you find your house has been burglarized. That's going to be a bummer of a day, huh?

There's Never a Cop Around When You Want One

In many larger metropolitan areas, the police do not respond to smaller property crimes. They'll take the report over the telephone and give you a report number for insurance purposes, but you'll never see a detective and no investigation is ever done on the crime. Makes you wonder who's winning the war on crime.

Even though the police may not respond, there are other avenues. Private investigators don't often get called to investigate purse snatchings. The criminal and the evidence are both long gone before a PI could get to the scene. Don't give up. There are steps that you, a do-it-yourself PI, can take when something like that happens.

You're in the mall, walking through a store, and a lady bumps into you. She might actually apologize to you for her carelessness. Still, you'd better check your wallet, your watch, and your bracelet. Anytime you are jostled or bumped by another person, inventory the valuables you're carrying on your body and the contents of your purse, if you're carrying one. You might have been the victim of one of the most common pickpocketing techniques.

If your wallet is lifted while you're in a crowded place such as a mall or a large store, look around quickly. Whoever that person is, she will now be walking quickly away. Memorize what she looks like, what she's wearing, and, if she spoke, how she sounded. For example, did she have an accent? The pickpocket's next move is usually to hand the stolen item over to a third person. If you're quick, you can see her walk close and almost brush by her cohort, who will be approaching from another direction. If you think you see that, even if you're not sure, again, do your best to memorize what they are wearing.

The next step is the most important one, and you have to make a quick decision. There are three good options that follow. Each requires an action on your part. Choose one. The worst option is to do nothing.

- You can chase after the person who stole your wallet and confront her. Remember, it's likely she will no longer have the stolen goods, so even with a confrontation that brings the store security running, it's your word against hers. However, not all pickpocket and purse thieves work with an accomplice. If you don't see a handoff, and the thief hasn't had the opportunity to ditch the billfold anyplace, she might still have possession of it. Purse snatchers, in particular, seem to work by themselves and don't hand off the goods to a buddy. They'll just grab the purse and run. But are you up to a physical confrontation? If you haven't been running 30 miles a week, lifting weights, and keeping current on your karate lessons, I wouldn't recommend it. Confronting a thief is a personal decision and a decision you should probably analyze and make before the critical moment ever occurs.

- Make a scene. Call out that you've been robbed and point toward the person walking away from you. You might get immediate help from people around you. We'll talk more about this in a minute.

- If making a scene is too embarrassing for you, then at least immediately ask a salesperson to call the store security and mall security. Don't be polite about it. Don't wait until the salesperson finishes ringing up the sale she's working on. Tell her to stop what she's doing and make the call right now! Time is of the essence here. Major retailers have plainclothes security people on the sales floors during most of their open hours. There might be one right next to you and you wouldn't know it.

Regardless of which course of action you choose, a security person will eventually arrive. Tell him briefly what happened and give him the description of the thief. Shopping malls generally have very sophisticated closed-circuit television camera set-ups and can track any particular individual's movements throughout the building.

By acting fast and giving security a good description, there is a good chance the pickpocket and her cohort can be spotted and apprehended.

Several years ago, I was with the FBI, working in the downtown Loop area of Chicago just prior to Christmas. I witnessed a young man snatch a briefcase from an older gentleman. The snatcher took off running. I gave chase. He was younger than I was, a little bit faster on his feet, had a good head start, and certainly had more motivation to run than I did.

I chased him down the street where I spotted another FBI agent I knew. I yelled at him and he joined with me. We ran into the Palmer House Hotel, the thief just 15 yards ahead of us. We entered the hotel from one street and ran clear through and came out on another street. In the process, we passed two house detectives in the lobby of the hotel. They also gave chase.

The pursuit continued across the street and up the block, where the perpetrator entered what was then a Montgomery Ward department store. Being just before Christmas, the store was incredibly crowded. People and tables of sale items went flying in all directions. Two plainclothes store detectives heard the commotion, saw us coming, and tackled the thief. I was huffing and puffing, but at least the thief hadn't been able to increase his lead any, so I felt good about that.

The briefcase belonged to a jewelry repairman who was making his rounds. It was full of watches and jewelry.

On another occasion, in New York City, a would-be bank robber had a bad day. He was in a teller line, waiting until it was his turn so he could rob the bank. He didn't know it was payday and the local FBI office was just up the street. When it was finally his turn, he slipped a note to the teller, instructing her to put all of her money in the bag that he passed to her.

An alert FBI agent standing behind the robber noticed something strange was happening. The agent said, "What's going on here?"

"Nothing," the bank robber said, turning to the agent. "Mind your own business. I'm robbing this bank." He returned his attention to the business at hand.

At least, he did, until the agent drew his weapon, stuck the barrel to the back of the robber's head, and said, "Like hell you are."

Instead of getting a large cash withdrawal, the would-be robber got bagged and tagged as the evidence.

The point is that even though a uniformed policeman may not be standing by to assist you, there are many security and undercover police folks around. You might be standing next to one and not know it. When your purse is snatched or your wallet lifted, don't just bemoan your bad luck and go home. Take some immediate action and you might actually get your belongings back. Even if your property is lost forever, at least you've waged your own little war on crime.

Flag Me a Cab, My Car's Been Stolen

In the year 2005, there were over 1 million two hundred thousand (1,235,226) reported thefts or attempted *motor vehicle thefts* in the United States. There is no more bewildering experience than to come out of a store and not be able to find your car, only to eventually realize it's been stolen. I know; it's happened to me three times.

Again, time is the important factor here. If you can get the report made and have the reporting officer call it in so that the vehicle's description and tag number are reported over the air, there is a chance the car will be seen and recovered.

My car was stolen the first time in San Juan, Puerto Rico. We'd parked on a busy street late one evening after the office Christmas party and visited with some friends living in a condominium on the beach. We'd only been in their place about 45 minutes. When my wife and I returned to the street, the car was gone. Unbelievable.

We went back upstairs and called it in. Then, using my friend's car, we drove home, halfway to the east end of the island, an hour away. It was now about 2 in the morning. The telephone rang. It was the police of Puerto Rico. A patrolman had been driving down an unpaved road through the jungle, in a place about an hour west of San Juan. He saw a group of men stripping a car—my car. As he approached with his blue lights on, the men took a couple of shots at him and then fled.

When it was safe, he called a tow truck and had the car towed back to the police impound lot. They wanted me to come and get the car right then. I suggested we wait until daylight, but they insisted I retrieve it while it was still there. They couldn't guarantee it'd be there the next day.

Theoretically, the vehicle was drivable. All of the tires had been taken off but the tow truck operator put them back on. Everything in the interior had been taken out except for the steering wheel and pedals. The dash was removed, as were all of the seats, interior lights, everything. The patrolman and tow truck driver had gathered up all of the parts they could find and tossed them into what was the backseat area and the trunk. Only now it was just one large open cockpit.

The thieves had broken the ignition switch, but you could start the car with a screw-driver instead of a key. I drove it the two-hour drive back to my residence and spent the next week putting it back together. Every part was there, with the exception of a few screws. The only part I had to buy was a new ignition switch.

I was very lucky. The car wasn't insured and I would have eaten the entire loss. You never know when your stolen car might be spotted by the police. That's why it's best to get the report in as quickly as possible. Had I not reported it until the next day, it would have been too late. The police would have eventually found it, but the vehicle would have been totally stripped to its bones, and we would have needed the car's dental records to make a positive identification.

If your, or your client's, car is stolen, report it immediately. Police departments will usually broadcast the stolen report to the entire department on the chance that some-body might see it. Also, departments produce a *hot sheet* that is reviewed by each new shift. As the patrols prowl around the city streets, they are always on the lookout for any vehicle on the hot sheet.

def•i•ni•tion

A **hot sheet** is a current list of recently stolen vehicles. Police departments, of course, have hundreds of patrol cars driving around their jurisdiction all day long. Patrolmen are on the lookout for any car that is on the hot sheet. Many police department patrol cars are now in communication with their headquarters by computer, and they access the hot sheet list on the computer rather than a physical printed list, as in smaller departments.

Now, as a PI, you'll sometimes get calls about stolen vehicles. Usually, the victim will have some ideas or some clues as to who might have stolen it. We have recovered sto-len cars for clients that the police never got around to looking for. One client owned a franchise for a major tune-up shop. He had four locations in the city. He called me one day, frantic because a customer's car had been stolen from one of his shops. It had been missing three days and the police didn't appear to be actively looking for it. His customer wanted his car back, and he was running out of excuses. He'd lost other cars, and if he lost one more, his insurance company was going to cancel his policy. He was getting desperate.

His 25-year-old store manager, Robert, had taken the car home, along with the bag containing $3,000 of the day's receipts in credit-card charge slips and checks. During the evening, Robert partied at several bars and, while traveling to the next bar, picked up a hitchhiker named Jason. Robert's impaired driving ability didn't go unnoticed. Eventually, he was stopped and arrested for driving while under the influence. A search under the front seat of the car led to an additional charge of possession of cocaine. Robert passed the car keys to Jason, and that's the last anybody had seen of the vehicle. The police report did have the name and alleged address of Jason, the hitchhiker.

Robert's parents bailed him out of jail the next morning and whisked him away to a drug rehab facility. They would not tell me, or anybody else, where he was, and I had no way of locating him. Most drug and alcohol rehab facilities will not respond to any questions about whether a certain person is or is not a patient.

My next move was to attempt to locate the hitchhiker, Jason. I talked to the detective assigned to the case. He told me the address for Jason was fictitious. I went to the address given on the police report, 2872 Magnolia Circle South, anyway. The detective was correct, there was no such address, but there was a Magnolia Circle South. Just no 2872. Magnolia Circle was an unpaved, heavily rutted sand road that led back into the woods. The mailboxes were clustered together on the shoulder of the main paved highway.

I did what any good investigator would do, just as we discussed in Chapter 12; I started knocking on doors. At the third door, a neighbor told me which house Jason lived in.

As I approached the house, a kid, about 13, was fooling around in the street. I asked him if Jason lived where I'd been told he did. "Oh, yeah. He lives there. But he's not there right now. He's at work."

I knocked on the door anyway. Nobody answered.

"See, I told ya. I bet you're here about that car, ain't ya?"

That got my attention. The kid wanted $100 to show me where the car was. I negotiated him down to $40. In a few minutes, he'd led me down a sand trail about one fourth of a mile away.

He got his money and I called a tow truck to haul the car out of the sand, where it was stuck.

From start to finish, it took about four hours to locate the stolen car and have it towed back to my client's shop. I'd called the client to let him know it was on the way. With a spare set of keys from the owner, we opened the trunk, and the bag with the $3,000 in charge slips and checks was in it. The client thought I was a genius, and to this day he continues to refer business to me.

My genius abilities aside, the reality was that the police detective assigned to the case could have done the same thing, but he stopped at the first roadblock, the nonexistent address. Persistence and the neighborhood investigation are two of the best tools an investigator has. Don't forget to use them both.

The Home Burglary

Do you live in a suburban neighborhood? Drive around your block. Odds are that one of the houses on your block will be *burglarized* this year, and one was last year as well. If your house has been burglarized once, the odds of it being burglarized again are higher. Doesn't that just make your day? This chapter is not designed to talk about preventive measures, but you should know that simply having a burglar alarm system in the home will reduce your chances of being burglarized by 90 percent.

def•i•ni•tion

The Uniform Crime Report defines **burglary** as the unlawful entry of a structure to commit a felony or a theft. The use of force to gain entry is not required to classify an offense as a burglary.

You've had a long day. Your purse was snatched at the mall. Your car was stolen from the mall's parking lot. And now, as you enter your home, your place of sanctity where you can isolate yourself from the world, you realize that burglars have been hard at work while you were gone. The feeling of violation that occurs with the discovery of a burglary is tremendous. Strangers have been in your bedroom, pawed through your clothing, and taken your personal belongings.

Burglaries are particularly hard cases to solve. Nationally, the police solve just over 12 percent of cases involving forcible entry, whereas they solve nearly 50 percent of rapes and sometimes over 60 percent of aggravated assaults. But you can see why. With rapes and assaults, the victim has seen the perpetrator. With most burglaries, the perpetrators are never seen, so there are no eyewitnesses.

Typically, private investigators get calls to solve burglaries for two reasons:

1. The police don't investigate because the dollar amount of the loss is not sufficient enough to warrant the manpower.

2. The police responded but haven't solved it.

In either case, chances are you won't be called until several days after the fact. Any evidence that was there is now probably destroyed, with the exception of fingerprints. Remember, fingerprints can stay on surfaces for years.

The bottom line on a burglary is you're not going to solve it unless your neighborhood investigation turns up something or your client has a suspect already in mind. Most victims of burglaries know the burglar; they just don't realize it. Sure, some burglaries are committed at random. But usually, the burglar has been in the house before, either on a pretext, as a salesperson, or perhaps is a relative of the cleaning staff. Don't overlook friends of the victim's teenaged children. You'd be surprised how often property crimes are committed by teenagers who know the victims and who associate with their children.

Elementary, My Dear Watson

Contrary to popular belief, the crime scene unit (CSU) is not normally the first to respond to a burglary. Most police departments start by sending a patrol car to the site. Some departments have what's called a minimum-loss policy, where they won't send a CSU for a loss that's less than or equal to $5,000, for example. The responding officer will get an estimate of the loss from the victim. If that estimate exceeds the policy's minimum amount, he will call for the CSU to process the scene for fingerprints and other evidence. Other departments, however, don't have a minimum-loss policy, and leave the decision about involving the CSU to the discretion of the responding officer. As a consumer, you might want to find out what your local police force's policy is so you can be prepared to gather your own evidence, should your loss not qualify for a crime scene unit.

If you're a do-it-yourself PI, go over the list of people who might have committed the burglary. The perpetrators probably don't go to church with you, but consider who else has been in your home in the last 90 days. Delivery men, movers, installers, employees? House cleaners are almost always suspected, but I've found they're almost always innocent. However, their boyfriends certainly should be suspected. The house cleaner might not even know for sure, but she probably suspects her boyfriend and doesn't really want to know the truth, because then she'd have to choose between her boyfriend and her customer.

Hopefully, a neighbor will have a description of someone, or the perpetrator will have left some evidence behind—a cigarette butt, maybe. Thorough interviewing of your client and a careful neighborhood investigation will sometimes turn up the culprit.

Remember Chapter 11 when Luke Smith burglarized his parents' house, removing the safe and the $40,000 that it contained? The sheriff's office had come out and done a mediocre crime scene investigation. They had not done a neighborhood investigation, or a detailed interview of the parents. They even neglected to ask the parents if they had any suspicions about who was responsible.

In just a few hours, I had their money back and the crime solved. It can be done, but you have to be smarter than the criminal (usually not too difficult) and more motivated than the police department (again, usually not too difficult).

If it's a random burglary committed by a crackhead looking for some quick bucks for his next piece of rock cocaine, you're probably not going to solve it. However, the next two sections detail some other steps to take to cover all of the bases. Only by covering each possibility will you have any chance of recovering the stolen property and seeing the burglar in jail.

The Pawnshop Detail

Most local law enforcement agencies maintain some sort of a pawnshop detail. Pawnshops are required to inventory each item they purchase or take in on pawn. They send, sometimes weekly, sometimes daily, a ticket to the local police department with the description of the item received, including a serial number, if there is one.

This is usually not a voluntary system. In order to keep their licenses, the pawnshops have to comply. The police pawnshop detail will also make periodic, unannounced visits to each pawnshop, checking their inventory against the pawn tickets it's submitted.

Likewise, the detective or officer in charge of the pawnshop detail will check the pawn tickets against lists of stolen property already entered into the NCIC. Matching descriptions of jewelry or electronics sometimes will result in the pawnshop detail confiscating the stolen property from the pawnshop operator.

> **Elementary, My Dear Watson**
>
> Police departments that have moved into the twenty-first century require the pawnshops to upload this information daily in electronic form to the police department's computer server. In these departments, the paper tickets are a thing of the last century, but not all departments are so computerized.

Therefore, if your, or your client's, property is stolen, be sure that an accurate and detailed description is given to the police department. If it is an item that might show up at a pawnshop, request the description be given to the pawnshop detail unit. This doesn't always happen automatically. Usually, it is up to the investigating detective to compare the items stolen with the information provided by the pawnshops. There is nothing wrong with calling the pawnshop detail directly.

Working the Crime Scene

If a crime scene investigation was not performed by the responding police department, then do it yourself. If you can find the first edition of this book at a library, in Chapter 17 of that edition you'll find full instructions on how to conduct a crime scene investigation.

One aspect to crime scene investigation that we didn't talk about there is checking the dumpsters and trash cans in the local area. If your wallet is lifted, purse snatched, jewelry box stolen from your house, or briefcase and camera taken from the trunk of your car, search the dumpsters and trashcans in the immediate area.

The Division of Licensing

Most dumpsters are dived every day. If you want to dispose of something and you don't want anybody to ever find it, don't put it in a dumpster thinking it will be commingled with the other trash. In all likelihood, somebody will find it. Even if the garbage truck picks it up, there are people at the garbage dump going through the trash.

I have one investigator, Bob, who has worked for me for 15 years. Bob regularly dives dumpsters for fun and profit. He and another investigator were working a workmen's compensation surveillance and saw our subject throw something into a dumpster. Bob went diving. The subject was just discarding trash, but Bob also found a couple of purses that had been snatched, complete with driver's licenses and other identity cards. He turned them over to the local police department. He's found unopened envelopes with valid credit cards. Diving the dumpster behind the Internal Revenue Service office, he found boxes and boxes of unused, perfectly good red pens imprinted with "U.S. Government" on them. Now that's government waste. Maybe the bureaucrats thought that if they got rid of all the red ink, they'd get rid of the deficit. Don't I wish. Bob brought them into the office, and we didn't have to buy any red pens for years.

In the mall, look through the trashcans within 200 to 300 yards of where the crime occurred. Purse snatchers and pickpockets will rifle through the purse and billfolds they've lifted, remove the credit cards and cash, and then toss the stolen item into the nearest garbage can. Even though the money is gone, the driver's license and other identity cards may still be recoverable.

When burglars break into your home and only take small items like jewelry boxes and important papers, they'll toss the material that can't be converted into quick cash

Alternate Light Source

NCIC allows not only for manufacturers' serial numbers, but also for "owner applied numbers." If your client had the foresight to engrave his or her Social Security or driver's license number on items that were stolen, be sure to get them into the NCIC as well.

into a dumpster. They want as little incriminating evidence on themselves as possible, because they never know when they'll get stopped by the police. Individual pieces of jewelry are a lot easier to hide than the entire box.

Also, after a burglary, be sure to walk around the premises. If there is a wooded area nearby, search it. I can't tell you how many times we've recovered stolen items that were stashed close to the crime scene by the thieves for later retrieval. You just never know, so you have to cover all of the bases.

NCIC

We've mentioned the NCIC in Chapter 18. The National Crime Information Center is a huge computer database run by the FBI. Within this database, there is a stolen articles section. Stolen items that can be uniquely described or have unique serial numbers can be entered into this database.

The Division of Licensing

If you're a fugitive and warrants have been issued for your arrest, don't get your hopes up, thinking your name will be purged from the NCIC after four years as if you were a car or a boat. No such luck. Your name will remain there until you're caught, or until the charges are dropped.

The NCIC has different files, or sections, for different types of stolen property, such as vehicles, license plates, boats, guns, articles, and securities (stocks, bonds, and bills).

If your client has the serial numbers of any items that were stolen, be it a motor vehicle or television, be sure that this information is relayed to the police department. It, in turn, will have the items entered into the NCIC. ·

Stolen items remain in the NCIC computer for a certain length of time. Unrecovered stolen articles will be in the computer for the balance of the year they are entered, plus one additional year. If for any reason during that time an officer gets suspicious about a certain item, he can run it in the NCIC. If it's stolen, a match will be made, and eventually the item will be returned to you.

Unrecovered motor vehicles remain in the NCIC computer for the year of the theft plus four more, as do stolen boats.

The Least You Need to Know

- If random crime strikes, make a scene. Help is frequently available from undercover or plain-clothed security people.

- Stolen cars are located faster if the report of the theft is made quickly. Police departments have hot sheets that are reviewed by each shift.

- Victims of burglaries usually know the burglar. It is somebody they've met, or somebody who has been in their house recently.

- Police agencies have pawnshop details that compare items pawned with lists of stolen items.

- After a burglary or other property crime, the investigator or victim should always look in the nearby trashcans and dumpsters. Thieves dump billfolds and purses into the trash after removing the money.

- The NCIC maintains lists of stolen articles for up to two years from the date of theft. Stolen vehicles and boats can remain listed for up to five years. Wanted persons, missing persons, and fugitives are listed until found or removed by the listing agency.

Part 5

Advanced Techniques

Now that you've learned the basics, it's time for the heavy-duty cases. You should be up to the challenge; you've learned the techniques.

These chapters will show you how to catch a burglar. You'll learn how to check backgrounds and even get tips on starting your own background-screening company. Professional investigators will learn how to triple their billing rate. Handling the evidence and preparing your case for court is the next step. When the big moment finally arrives, you'll be ready to present your case in front of a judge and jury.

21

Background Investigations: Digging the Dirt

In This Chapter

- ◆ Tricks to uncovering personal identifiers
- ◆ Finding criminal records
- ◆ There is nothing civil about civil lawsuits
- ◆ Starting your own background company
- ◆ Understanding the FCRA
- ◆ Beat the competition by using a web-based client interface
- ◆ Verifying the degree of education

Every third inquiry for services a private investigator receives is a request for some type of a background investigation. Generally the new caller has no idea what she's looking for, only that she needs somebody checked out, doesn't have a clue on how to do it herself, and has no idea really of what is encompassed in a background investigation. The professional investigator first has to determine the actual need of the client and then educate her as to what is possible and what is not. Many of us have a vague notion of what a "background check" might include, but are not really clear as to the specifics. In this chapter, we're going to talk about two basic backgrounds. The Type-A do-it-yourself dig-up-the-dirt background and the Type-E (E for employment) employment background screening. These are two totally different backgrounds and are subject to different laws and requirements.

Let's look at some typical Type-A problems everyday people have:

♦ A father and former husband is concerned about the ex-wife's new boyfriend. The ex-wife has custody of the children, and the boyfriend appears to be a slime ball. If the father can prove his ex-wife is letting some degenerate hang around his kids, perhaps the father can get custody.

♦ A woman has her wedding planned and the date is soon, but some doubts linger in her mind about the soon-to-be husband. Some of the things he says just don't add up.

♦ Your new boyfriend claims to be a secret agent, or an ex-Navy SEAL, but his beer belly has you wondering. What else is he lying about?

Type E:

♦ A small business owner has a new employee and wants to make sure the person he just hired is honest, hardworking, and dependable.

♦ A mother and father are thinking about hiring a nanny full-time. They want to ensure the new nanny is not a child abuser, or worse, a molester.

♦ You have a new cleaning lady. You're going to be out of town on cleaning day. Do you give her a key to the house?

The preceding six points are real problems from real people. Their lives are tied in knots until they can get answers to their questions and resolve the doubt in their minds.

To find the answers to your questions, there are five ingredients that make up a good basic background or employment check:

♦ A criminal-arrest and/or conviction search (Type A and E)

♦ A civil-records search (Type A)

♦ Verifying and checking with previous employers (Type E)

♦ Interviewing personal references (Type E)

- ◆ A driving history, if applicable to your needs (Type A and E)
- ◆ Verifying credentials and education (Type A and E)
- ◆ Credit check (Type E)

This type of knowledge is power. In this chapter, I'm going to show you how to get that knowledge and some items to consider if you're thinking about setting up a pre-employment background-screening company.

Type-A Background: Obtaining the Basic Goods

Before beginning any background check, you must assess the level of detail and the depth of the check you desire. Regardless of what type of background investigation you intend to perform, you must have the first three items here, and the fourth is highly desirable: name, date of birth, Social Security number, and current address.

Finding the Name

If your purpose for the background is employment, you'll have all this information on the candidate's application. Other than employment, most of us don't start out with much information about the person. That's why we want a background check done.

You'd think that knowing the name of the person that you want to check out would be a simple, commonsense item, but you'd be surprised at how often that little detail is difficult to come by. I can't tell you how many times husbands have come to my office because their ex-wife is seeing some new boyfriend and they are concerned about who this guy is, what he does for a living, and whether he's had any run-ins with the law before. The trouble is, they don't know the new boyfriend's name.

A good father who does not have custody of his children *should* be concerned about another male who is living with his children or might have influence over them. The last thing you want is somebody who is abusive or with a history of child molestation living with your kids. If the client doesn't know the individual's name, how do you, the PI, find it? Here are four good methods that work:

- ◆ If you're on good terms with the ex, just ask her. Most of the time, however, our clients aren't on very good terms with the former spouses.

- ◆ If the kids are old enough, ask them. If they are young, they may only know a first name or the name by which the ex refers to him. If you can get a first name, that's a start.

Alternate Light Source _____

You need to be sure that the name the child gives you is, in fact, the first name. We have spent many useless hours and incurred countless database charges because our client told us the person's name was Scott, for instance, only to find out later that Scott, which is the name he goes by, is actually his middle name.

◆ If you are allowed regular access to the ex's house, perhaps when you're picking up the kids, check the caller ID on the telephone or the list of dialed and received calls on her cell phone if you can get your hands on it. Chances are the new friend has called and his telephone number and name might be right there. Even if his name isn't shown, his number might be recorded. Chapter 6 tells you how to do a reverse phone search. Even if you have a list of 30 numbers, spend 20 bucks at 555-1212.com to buy a hundred searches (the smallest package available) and run all 30 numbers.

◆ Jot down the license tag on the guy's car. This means you'll have to be there when he shows up. That might be easy, and it might not, depending on your situation. If you can't be there, perhaps there is a friendly neighbor who will do it for you. By running the license, you'll get the name, date of birth, Social Security number, and an address (a bases-loaded home run). As a professional, I always go right for the tag.

Finding the Date of Birth

In order to run a criminal record check, you need two things: the name and date of birth. A Social Security number is nice, but not necessary. Race and sex are also helpful as identifiers, and in running criminal records you usually have to include both items in the request. Race and sex should be easy for you, although these days, with spiked hair and baggy clothes, a person's sex might not be clear.

Once you have the person's name, you'll need the date of birth. Go down to your local voter's registration office and check the voter's records, which are usually considered public information and will include the name and date of birth. Different states have different rules concerning taking notes while reviewing the voter's registration records, but often they won't let you write anything down. That's to keep people from coming in and making marketing lists. You'll just have to remember the date of birth until you can step around the corner and write it down.

If the new boyfriend is not a registered voter, head for the clerk of the court's office and check for previous marriages and divorces. There you will find all the identifiers you need.

Excuse me, you say, but I've spent half a day running around the courthouse only to discover the new boyfriend is not a registered voter and was divorced in another state. Now what do you do? If you're absolutely determined to do it yourself and not pay a PI (who can tap into one of the subscription databases we discussed in Chapter 8, and have it for you in a matter of minutes), then you have to make a pretext call.

Before attempting this, see Chapter 14, for detailed instructions on how to perform pretext calls. The following pretext we've used quite successfully in the past to uncover the date of birth. It cannot be used on the subject himself. It is best used on a close relative like a parent or sister, or on a roommate. In either case the subject cannot be present when you make the call.

Call the phone number you got off the caller ID when you're sure the subject is not home. If you know anything about the subject's parents, call them instead. Be sure and use one of the tricks we discussed in Chapter 9 to block your phone number before calling.

When Mom answers, tell her you found her son's wallet in the parking lot of a nearby shopping center, referring to the store by name. (If the mom lives out of state, better still.) Explain you're not sure that you have the right family, but you'd like to get the wallet back to its owner. If Mom asks how you got her number, tell her it was in the wallet. If Mom will just confirm the date of birth you found in the wallet, you'll make arrangements to return the billfold. Tell her you'll need the person's current address to take the billfold to him. Now you've turned your base hit into a double (date of birth and address). We used to go for a triple asking for the SSN, but now with identity theft such a hot item I wouldn't push it. Be happy with the date of birth and the address if you can get it. I've never had this pretext fail.

The Local Sheriff's Office

This is very important. While you're at the courthouse, chances are your local sheriff's office or city police department is not far away.

Walk across the street to the police department and check their records. Why? Because they might have records of incidents that never went to court because nobody was ever charged. In some states you can get the arrest records, for a small search fee, typically about $5, right there while you wait.

Suppose the new boyfriend was beating up his live-in girlfriend. The next-door neighbor calls the police when she hears the girlfriend pleading for help. The police arrive, but there is no blood spread around, so they calm the couple down and leave. Before they leave the scene, they write up a domestic disturbance incident report. Nobody was arrested; no charges were filed. There will be nothing in any court file. But still, you'd like to know about that incident, wouldn't you?

Frequently, patrol officers will stop somebody who is acting suspiciously or loitering. When they do, they always ask for identification and usually run a computer check on the subject to see if there are any warrants on him or her. In most jurisdictions the officers will fill out what is known as a *Field Identification* (FI) card, or they might write an incident report if they were responding to a call. Those FI cards and incident reports contain a lot of information and should be reviewed.

def•i•ni•tion

A **Field Identification** card is a card used by patrol officers when questioning persons who might have been acting suspiciously. It will contain the subject's identifying data, the date and location of the incident, and a short synopsis of why the subject was questioned.

That's why, if possible, you should always check the local police jurisdiction's files in addition to the court records when performing a criminal background check. When you check the local police department they'll do the searching for you. Usually you write the name and other identifying information on a form and hand it to a record clerk who searches for the information while you wait. There is almost always a nominal, $3 to $15, charge for this search.

The Driving History

In Type-A backgrounds, you're looking for the dirt. The ex-spouse is dating some guy who, from time to time, has your kids in his car. You don't like the guy but you have no control over the situation. So run a driving history on him. If he has a DUI on his record, or a bunch of points for speeding or reckless driving charges, you can probably get a court order to prohibit your ex from letting your kids be in the car with him when he's behind the wheel. The court order may or may not actually have some effect on the situation, but there are two reasons to do this:

1. You'll feel better having taken some action.

2. You can hire me or another PI to catch the creep driving with the kids in the car and then go for permanent custody. These are your kids. You need to do all you can to insure they are in a safe environment. Do this; if it works, you'll thank me later.

Locating the Address

Keep in mind that the address is not usually required as an identifier except in searching civil court cases. Usually, in civil cases, a person's date of birth and SSN are not listed. A party in a civil case is identified by his name and address. Not a problem unless the name of the person you are searching is Steve Brown and there are twenty of them in the city. Then you have to have the address to differentiate between all of those Steve Browns.

If you've gotten the name and date of birth, the address is a cinch, and there are two quick ways to find it. The vehicle tag, of course, is by far the easiest and most direct approach. Sometimes, though, people change addresses and don't notify the DMV, so the vehicle registration might not always be current. The good news is, eight times out of ten, it is. The other easy method is by using the telephone records. Reverse search the number you got off the caller ID and, unless it's a cell phone or a nonpublished number, you'll have the address.

Sometimes, clients really want the address for other reasons. Maybe the client needs to see for himself what's really going on at the new boyfriend's house, or maybe the client needs to prove that his ex-spouse has moved in with a man. This can figure into alimony adjustments in a big way as we discussed in Chapter 7.

Here are two surefire ways to locate the address:

- If the person dating the ex is a reasonably mature person, of medium or higher means, and lives in a single-family residence, then check the local property records (real property tax rolls) at your property appraiser's office. If he's a younger person living in an apartment, that won't work.

- Follow the subject home. That always works. Be sure and read Chapter 13, before you attempt this. There are a lot of tricks of the trade that go into a successful surveillance, so study up. The last thing you want is for your ex to find out that you've tailed her new boyfriend to his apartment. And you don't want a confrontation. This is very important.

The Criminal in Our Background

In Chapter 7, we talked about getting records from both the clerk of the court and the state criminal record system. Now's your chance to put that knowledge to work. Yeah, it means you've got to spend a couple of hours driving to the courthouse and getting someone to help you. Actually, at most courthouses you'll spend more time looking for a parking space than you will inside looking for records. Twenty minutes, in and out, is all you should need if you're only checking criminal cases. Be sure and check both the upper and lower courts. In the lower courts you'll find the misdemeanors. Remember, a lot of misdemeanors began as felonies and were *pled down* to misdemeanors. So you want to review the file and examine the original charges.

def•i•ni•tion

To **plead down** means that the prosecuting attorney's office, in order to expedite the flow of cases, as well as lessen his load and the burden on the court, reduces charges from higher offenses to lesser offenses. He or she does this if the defendant agrees to plead guilty to the lesser offenses.

Even before you go to the courthouse, check and see if your county has their criminal records online. Call the clerk of the court and ask, or use a search engine and use the search term "clerk of the court your county your state. Like "clerk of the court Clay county Florida." If you happen to search Clay county, you'll see their criminal records are online and free.

The Sometimes Not-So-Civil Cases

Checking civil-court files in prenuptial investigations is important because divorce files contain some of the most bizarre allegations you'll ever see. Husbands and wives in the midst of a bitter divorce spill all the dirty secrets about each other, including drugs, sex, adultery, violence, anger, and perverted behavior. It's all right there in the divorce file, a public record in most but not all states, for anybody who cares to read about it. Certainly, were I to remarry, presuming my new wife-to-be had been previously divorced, I would want to review her divorce file before popping the question.

A while back, a female stockbroker called me, indicating she was going to be married in 10 days. She had some lingering doubts about her fiancé, who was from another state, and thought that before the big day came she should check a little into his background. "A little late," I thought, but we took the case.

I had my man in the western state that the gentleman was from start with the civil records and the local police department. Guess what? In the clerk of the courts office he found a marriage record but no divorce on file. True, he could have gotten divorced someplace else, so we kept on digging.

Across the street at the police department, guess what we found? Nope, not an arrest record, but a missing person report filed by his still-legal wife, nearly a year before.

Apparently the man just upped and left his family of 20 years and headed east, leaving behind his wife and three sons. They had no idea where he was, or if he was dead or alive, but they did know for sure that he hadn't been divorced. Well, what's a little bigamy between friends?

The kicker is, my female client decided she was still in love with the guy, postponed the wedding, and waited until the divorce was final from his first wife, and then married him anyway. At least she knew what she was getting into. After all that, do you still think doing a prenuptial background is silly?

Type E: Starting Your Own Background Company

You've been in the PI business for a long time and are tired of leaving home at 5 A.M. to follow some plaintiff with an early tee time to a golf course where he can swing a club but can't swing a paint brush. So you want to start an employment background screening company and not worry about keeping your camera dry when it rains. Good for you. Here are some tips.

Start a Brand New Company

First you'll need to incorporate a new entity that has nothing to do with your PI licensed firm. Remember when we talked about the credit bureaus? The bottom line is if your background company holds a PI license, the credit bureaus probably will not grant you access to their files. Many employers want a credit report run on their prospective employees. If you have no access or have to buy the credit report through a third party, your costs will go way up.

Whole books have been written on how to do background screenings, but we'll try and cover some of the basics in about six pages. This is not meant to be all-inclusive, but is intended to give you an idea of how to proceed. I wish I'd had this information when I began my background company. Just knowing about the client interface below would have saved me a year of wasted effort.

Learn the Fair Credit Reporting Act (FCRA)

There are provisions in the FCRA that affect your new company. The FCRA is cursed by many private investigators who don't understand it, but it really opens several doors for background companies. As a background-screening company, you are considered a consumer-reporting agency, just like the big credit bureaus and bound by the same rules. As a small employer, performing your own backgrounds before hiring, you are also bound by those rules. So let's have a look.

You can find the complete text of the FCRA at www.ftc.gov/os/statutes/031224fcra. pdf. It's 86 pages long; if you want to read it, knock yourself out. But instead of doing that, let's look at some of the provisions that will impact how you do business.

Section 603 defines consumer reports and includes reports made for employment purposes. Section 603 (k) includes as "Adverse Action", any denial of employment. Section 604 (b) allows a permissible purpose to access credit information for employment purposes.

Adverse Action

Section 604 also states that if "adverse action" is taken in whole or in part because of the consumer report, then the prospective employer must within 3 days communicate to the applicant that adverse action was taken and they should name your company as the consumer-reporting agency.

The prospective employee has a right to a copy of your report and if requested, you must send them a copy. Then they may dispute anything in your report that they believe is inaccurate. Wow, sounds like a mess, huh? If you're a small business, you might want to reconsider performing your own backgrounds and hire my company, or some other background-screening company to deal with all of this. But if you *are* the background company, you have to know the rules of the FCRA.

The Website

We haven't talked much about websites for private investigators. That's a whole book by itself. But we do need to spend a couple of minutes on your background-screening company's website. Why? Because most of your background work is going to be conducted from your office, and it doesn't make any difference if you're in Austin, Texas; Chicago, Illinois; or Boone, North Carolina. So your website should imply that your firm is national in scope. The big boys do that from just one location and you can, too. Your client doesn't need to know that the company is just you and one person running the data sources. You can have just as big a presence in Los Angeles as can some firm with 40 employees that is based in New York City.

In designing your website, pay attention to how your competition does theirs and make yours better. You'll understand why this is so important in the next section.

The Client Interface

Most progressive background-screening companies have gone to a web-based client interface where established clients can log in and enter the applicant's data. This data is saved on a server that you access from your office. This sounds like a lot of computer knowledge is needed. Not really. There are companies out there that provide this interface. They charge for it, but it's a pretty slick product. When your client clicks on the log-in at your site (try mine if you like, www.hindsightinc.com) and watch the URL address at the top of the screen. It changes from www.hindsightinc.com to a secure server with a different name. But did you also notice that the look of the server has the feel and look of my company's homepage? Most of my clients never realize that they've been moved to another server.

Once the client has input a new applicant's data, we're notified immediately by e-mail, or if we're in the database, we'll see the new application come up in the Work Queue on the server. Either way we can start working the application right way.

Who are these guys that provide this service? Well again, I suggest using your favorite search engine and search "employment screening software," but two websites of reputable companies are www.tcicredit.com and www.tazworks.net. Do your research and figure out what works best for you.

Working the Application

With either of the above servers working for you, much of the application process can be handled automatically. These servers interface with the credit bureaus, driving record suppliers, Social Security traces, and criminal-record retrievers. Your website can be configured so that when a client inputs the application data, a Social Security trace is automatically pulled. We'll talk about why we do this in a minute. But also we can configure the program to automatically pull a credit report, a driving history, and a criminal history. The staff can be drinking piña coladas by the pool and let the computer do the work. Of course, if I catch them they're out of a job.

There are a number of different aspects to working an employment background. We'll only talk about five major parts. If you're going to specialize in certain niches like, airline pilots, for instance, you'll need to do your own homework.

The Criminal Record Search

The general idea in searching for criminal records is to search the best available data. The norm is a county level criminal search in the counties where the applicant has resided within the last 7 to 20 years. The records searched should be current to within 30 days. Some states only allow you, the consumer-reporting agency, to search back 7 years. Some states allow you to search back forever. You need to know the laws of the state where your client and the applicant are located. You can go to www.hrliability. com and click the link on the right side that reads "State law and public records" and see the applicable laws for some of the more-restrictive states. Take note, laws and regulations change, so use more than one resource when checking the laws.

So your client needs a criminal-record search conducted in Bibb County, Georgia. How do you get it done? There are several companies that have put together nation-wide networks of local county courthouse researchers. Four that I recommend are:

> Phoenix Research (www.hrliability.com)
>
> National Background Data (www.nationalbackgrounddata.com)
>
> Omni Data Retrieval (www.omindataretrieval.com)
>
> G.A. Public Record Services (www.gaprs.biz)

There are others that specialize in one portion of the country or in one state. The first two companies do not compete with you. They only sell wholesale and will not sell directly to your client. But the other two do a very good job and you might want to take a look at them.

There is a big misconception about national criminal checks and we need to expose it here. There is one, and only one, possible way to do a national criminal-history search. That is by searching the FBI's Criminal Justice Information Services Division records. The records at the division can be searched by fingerprints, or you can initiate a search of the Computerized Criminal History section of the Bureau's NCIC computer, which can be searched by name and date of birth. Anybody in the employment-screening or background-investigation business, who is honest, will admit that there is no other national criminal-history check. Period. A search through the FBI's records and the NCIC computer is only available to law enforcement and a few other federally mandated organizations.

The Division of Licensing

Some "search firms" sell what they call a "national criminal check," including NDB (on preceding page), which sells a COPs report. NDB's website tells you exactly which records in which states are being searched and how often these records are updated. These "national criminal searches" usually include department of corrections and sex offender records and many county court records. But not all records in all jurisdictions. If you decide to use one of these searches, make sure the county you need to search is covered by this search.

The Credit Report

Pulling credit reports on job applicants is becoming less common than previously. Still, there are clients who want that service, so you'll need to provide it. There are three major bureaus we've talked about in other chapters, but in case you turned to this chapter first, here they are:

Equifax (www.equifax.com)

Transunion (www.transunion.com)

Experian (www.experian.com)

Driving Records

Many employers could care less about a person's driving history. Others have their employees making deliveries and look for clear driving records. There are multiple choices for providers of driving records. You'll find it easier to sign on with these providers if your company is not a PI firm. One good company is American Driving Records (www.mvrs.com). If you are a PI firm, you can still get access. Try MVRS Inc. at www.mvrsinc.com. Both companies are owned by First Advantage, but cater to the two different segments of the industry. By the way, First Advantage also owns a whole host of background-screening companies and other diverse companies in the background-screening arena, including NDB, mentioned above.

The Social Security Trace

This is a cheap tool for finding where your applicant has resided in the past. It also will verify that the applicant's Social Security number has been issued and is not made up. It is largely based on credit-header information and lists addresses that have been reported by your applicant in the past, usually with the dates that the applicant is supposed to have resided there. It is a good tool, but since it is derived from credit data, it is very inaccurate. NDB sells one called "AIM," which is better than some, and the cost to their affiliates is less than a dollar.

Educational Verification

Some universities will verify dates of enrollment and/or degrees given to their students if you call the registrar's office at the school. More now than ever, universities are farming this task out to independent companies. Two companies that have a number of universities enrolled in their systems are National Student Clearing House at www.studentclearinghouse.org and Credentials Inc. at www.degreechk.com. These services are not free, but you're stuck with them.

Education verification is the one employment search where applicants lie the most. It's incredible. They'll claim to have degrees from universities when they don't. They'll indicate three years attendance when they only attended one semester. It goes on and on.

Think about this. If applicants misrepresent facts or lie on their employment application, what does that make them? If you hire them anyway, don't be surprised when you catch them in a lie later on.

The other checks that employers should consider include previous employment (especially salary information), references, medical databases required for hospital personnel, credential and special licenses, checks, Patriot Act-compliant search, federal criminal (remember PACER?), and some other specialized searches for special fields like the National Drivers Register and FAA Accidents and Incident for airline pilots.

And as food for thought, if you are going to begin an employment-screening company, you might as well include tenant screening also. But that's another book.

The Least You Need to Know

- ◆ A basic background check usually includes a criminal history, civil-record search, previous employers, and personal reference contacts.

- ◆ Before driving to the courthouse, check to see if they are online.

- ◆ You must have at least the name and date of birth to conduct a background search, and preferably a Social Security number as well. There are some tricks to obtaining this information.

- ◆ There is no "national criminal" search other than the NCIC, which is run by the FBI. Don't be fooled.

- ◆ Civil suits, particularly divorce files, contain many allegations between suing parties and provide good leads for additional witnesses.

- ◆ Applicants routinely lie about their educational credits. Many universities use outside agencies to report enrollment and verify degrees.

- ◆ There are a number of specialized searches for niche background fields like airline pilots and hospital health-care workers.

Chapter 22

The Diligent Search: Adoption and Estates

In This Chapter

- ◆ Increase your billing rate to $200 per hour
- ◆ The legal steps of a diligent search
- ◆ Extracting information from the post office
- ◆ Fourteen steps to complete the investigation

This chapter is for professional investigators who'd like to increase their billing rate. An increased billing rate means generating more income per hour. The Diligent Adoption or Estate Search is one of these cases that allows an investigator to earn $200 plus per hour instead of his usual $85 per hour.

Why is an investigator worth more on one type of case than on another? Why does someone with an MBA earn more than a fellow with a GED? More advanced techniques require a higher skill level and demand more in fees.

The Diligent Adoption Search is a search required by many states before parental rights can be terminated and a child can be adopted without the consent of one or both of his parents. This search is also used in estate cases where you need to find a missing heir or show that a diligent search was conducted and the heir cannot be located.

The quickest method for an attorney to be sued for malpractice is to have an adoption "go bad." This usually happens when one of the child's parents cannot be located and the attorney serves the missing parent by publication. The child is adopted and later the delinquent parent comes knocking, claiming that he would have been easy to locate if only somebody had taken the time to search for him. The missing father now wants custody of his child who has brand new parents. The attorney is sued by his clients. It's a big mess. Attorneys don't want that.

Who Are Your Clients?

This search is designed to meet the state requirements of a Diligent Adoption Search that is required before a missing parent can be *served by publication* or an estate can be settled.

def•i•ni•tion

Service by publication or notification is a method whereby an individual is served with process without physically laying papers in his hand. If one party can not be located, a notice may be published in a newspaper in the county where the court action is to take place over a period of several weeks. Once this is accomplished, the individual is considered to be served.

So who is our client? Our client is usually an attorney that specializes in adoption matters. Often your fee is paid directly by the "to be" adoptive parents.

What Is the Law?

Different state laws vary. The Florida statute can be found under Title VI, Civil Practice and Procedure, Chapter 63, Adoption, 63.088 Proceeding to terminate parental rights pending adoption; notice and service, diligent search.

We'll use the Florida statute as our guideline, but many states have similar statutes. Some are less-stringent than Florida, which is why we're using Florida. Some states like South Carolina specify that a search for the missing parent must be conducted, but don't specify exactly what the steps must be.

The following set of steps results in a very thorough search that should satisfy most state laws. You'll actually locate your subject about seventy percent of the time in these cases. Some attorneys are not happy when you locate the subject. That's because it's easier to serve someone by publication. But the really good attorneys will recognize that once the subject is located and served, then there's no way they're going to be sued for having an inadequate diligent search.

When we locate the subject, we find many of them were afraid they were being sued for child support and were delighted to be told they're actually being relieved of their parental obligations. The jerks. (Just my thoughts on deadbeat parents, in case you couldn't tell.)

The Division of Licensing

Before offering your services, check your state law requirements. Remember, this is a highly specialized area. If you don't know the specifics of your state, the attorneys who specialize in this field will write you off as incompetent.

A common statute will read something to the effect that if the location of the missing parent is unknown, but the identity of that parent is known, then the parent has not executed a consent to the adoption, the people in charge of the adoption process must conduct a diligent search for that parent, and the search must include the following steps.

The Current Address

The first step in any diligent search, whether for an adoption or an estate is to determine the last known "current address."

The Law Requires ...

The person's current address, or any previous address, through an inquiry of the United States Postal Service through the Freedom of Information Act (FOIA).

The Reality

The law wants you, the investigator, to send a letter to the Postal Service and request the current address or any previous address of your subject. Right. That's really going to work. Try that and the postal FOIA officer for your district will respond with

"Sorry, the post office has no information concerning the individual in question." Think about it. The post office doesn't have a master list of everybody in their town by name. The post office data is *address*-specific. You have to search by address to get information from the post office.

So how do you satisfy this requirement? Postal Regulation 39 DVR 265.6 (6)(ii) provides for the post office to relinquish a forwarding address if you have a subpoena for that subject. The information can be disseminated as long as it is for the purpose of "service of legal process in connection with actual or prospective litigation."

In these cases, if we locate the subject, he will be served; so our request clearly falls within the scope of the postal regulations.

The Form

Now, how do you get the information?. Their regulations state that you should deliver the appropriate form to the postmaster at the post office that covers the address in question.

The post office has a form for change of address and box holder information which you can find at www.usps.com/foia/_rtf/39CFR265-266.rtf. Copy it and print it on your letterhead.

But if you live in Phoenix and the address of your subject is in Okalahoma, go to www.usps.com and click on the top red bar—"Locate a Post Office." Input the last known address and you'll get the address and the fax number for the post office that covers your subject's address. Fax the form to the postmaster.

He eventually will fax the form back to you. I follow up with the postmaster every other day until I've bugged him enough to get it done. Rude but effective.

The post office forwards first class mail for 12 months. During months 13 through 18 the mail is returned to the sender with the new address. After 18 months all address data is purged from their computers and first class mail is returned to the sender endorsed "Forwarding Order Expired."

So far, your cost in requesting the information from the post office has been exactly zilch.

Alternate Light Source _____

We professionals don't give up easily. Check off these three additional steps and you've graduated from a journeymen investigator to a true craftsman.

- ◆ Send a letter to the subject but mark it "Return Service Requested."
- ◆ Address a letter to the subject and put on the envelope, "Please Forward." Send it to his last known address asking him to call you. He might actually call you. If it's returned, then document your efforts.
- ◆ I look up the owner for the property of my subject's last known address (see Chapter 5). I address a letter to the property owner asking them to call me. If they don't call, then I try and locate a phone number for them and call them. Often they'll have some idea where your subject moved to.

The Last Known Employer

These searches are usually out of state so pick up the telephone and call the employer.

The Law Requires ...

The last known employment of the person, including the name and address of the person's employer.

The Reality

Talk to the relatives. The ex-wife, the grandparent that is going to adopt the child. If you can't find any information on the last known employer, then in your affidavit you'll just have to state that you checked all logical leads and no previous employment could be developed.

The Division of Licensing _____

Trying to secure current employment information from the Social Security Administration or your state board of wages and employment is probably illegal. In the early 1990s, half a dozen private investigators paid a Social Security Administration employee to obtain employment reported data. Then they resold it to other private investigators and their own clients. They went to jail. Don't do it.

The Regulatory Agencies

Regulatory agencies would generally be considered government agencies within the state and local jurisdictions wherein your subject was last known to reside, or in the area where you have an indication that she might have moved.

The Law Requires ...

Regulatory agencies, including those regulating licensing in the area where the person last resided.

The Reality

Your subject's line of work might require state licensing. If your missing parent is a nurse, medical doctor, chiropractor, lawyer, massage therapist, surveyor, landscape architect, accountant, body wrapper, or nuclear medicine technologist, well, you get the idea. Many occupations require state licensing and most states will confirm if your subject is licensed.

To complete this portion of your diligent search, you must also check for a business license. Most cities require a business license, even if your subject is just operating a hot dog stand. Oh, right, hot dogs; don't forget to check for food and beverage licenses and health certificates. Generally, the city will only have the business license filed under the business name and not by the name of the owner. You do the best you can.

Alternate Light Source _____

Also check the state's secretary of state to see if your subject is an officer or director, or a registered agent for a corporation. The secretary of state's records might not strictly fall under the guise of a regulatory agency, but don't tell them that. Usually it's a free search and can be done online while you're watching the football game on Sunday afternoon.

The Families and the Relatives

If it's a family member that is adopting the child, sometimes they don't want the subject located for fear the missing parent will object to the adoption. Nevertheless, the law requires that you address this issue.

The Law Requires ...

Names and addresses of relatives to the extent such can be reasonably obtained from the petitioner or other sources, contacts with those relatives, and inquiry as to the person's last known address. The petitioner shall pursue any leads of any addresses to which the person might have moved.

The Reality

The single best source for locating a subject is the relatives. Your client is most likely some sort of relative to the subject and the child. A grandparent or an uncle or aunt. They'll tell you they don't know where your subject is. Note that in your file. But also ask them for names of other relatives of your subject. Track those relatives down and question them.

When I was looking for Jack Reading, his parents told me he worked on offshore oil rigs. They thought he was in Louisiana or Texas, but they hadn't heard from him in over three years. When I completed the searches, my affidavit read that his parents hadn't heard from him in over three years. It was good enough for me and the judge.

But when I was looking for Mary Chambers, I talked to her aunt. She gave me Mary's cell number. I left her a message. Mary called me back, gave me her address in Ohio. She asked for the phone number of the people who had custody of her four-year-old son whom she hadn't seen in three years. I'd have liked to accommodate her, but thought better of it and gave her the phone number of the attorney. We had her served three days later.

Dead or Alive

Your affidavit will have to include a statement as to whether you've checked sources to determine if your subject has died. After all, you don't want to serve a dead person by publication.

The Law Requires ...

Information as to whether or not the person might have died and, if so, the date and location.

The Reality

In the matter of diligent adoption searches, this is probably your easiest step. In Chapter 5, I gave you the website for the best search of the Social Security Death Master File. Here it is again, www.rootsweb.com. The best part is it's free and current.

I filed an affidavit in an estate matter for Roger Ball. Roger was from New Jersey and he disappeared 20 years ago in Oregon at the age of 23 and was never heard from since.

In 2006, both of his parents died and left a valuable estate. I completed all of these 14 steps. I even ran his New Jersey driver's license, which showed no activity for the last 20 years. He's either deceased as a John Doe, or he's out of the country. I provided the affidavit and the court decided that for the purpose of the estate he would be considered deceased. If the court had ruled otherwise, his share of the estate would have gone to the State's Unclaimed Monies Fund. With the court accepting our affidavit, the estate was split four ways instead of five. A considerable bonus to the remaining children.

Telephones

Directory information is easily come by, but not all telephone directories are equal. See Chapter 6 for the scoop.

The Law Requires ...

Telephone listings in the area where the person last resided.

The Reality

Not every step in these diligent searches is difficult. You'll end up searching directory information in a number of different locations. Each time you get a new lead as to your subject's whereabouts, the first thing you'll do is check one of your pay directory sites. Make a note in your file of each city that you check so that you can include them all in your affidavit.

Alternate Light Source _____

For you guys out there that want to save a nickel, this is the place to do it. Because the free white-page listings have old data, you might find your subject listed even though your up-to-date pay site shows no listing. He's moved, but he used to live there. The old data might provide an address with the listing. Sometimes old data can provide good leads. If you find him in the old listings but not the current, then use the pay sites to get the listing of whoever is living at that address now and call them. They might know where the previous occupant moved to.

Local Law Enforcement Agencies

Generally, searches can be conducted at the local level of law enforcement.

The Law Requires ...

Inquiries of law enforcement agencies where the person last resided.

The Reality

Local law enforcement agencies will often respond to phone calls. Ask for the record section and if they won't check your subject's name on the phone, see if you can fax or mail a request. There might be a charge for this search, usually less than $15. If they won't do a search, then document it.

State Law Enforcement Records

Some state law enforcement records are easily searched and others allow no access.

The Law Requires ...

Searching highway patrol records in the state where the person last resided.

The Reality

Whoever wrote the bill and included this requirement had no clue as to what records a state "Highway Patrol" would have. So what to do? We put on our gypsy fortune teller robe, turn the lights down low, and figure out what the bill's author had in mind.

In some states the highway patrol maintains the state's criminal record database. Most highway patrols investigate traffic accidents on the state's highways. You'll probably need accident report numbers to search for accidents, but you might find a state that allows searches by name or driver. The important item here is to make sure that this area is covered in your affidavit. If you can't search the highway patrol office records, then search the state criminal record database.

Our Prison System

The prison system in the United States is basically divided into three systems. The federal prisons, the state prisons, and the county and/or city jails. As a general rule, prisoners are held in county and city jails for six months or less, or while awaiting trials. Federal prisoners are also held in county jails while awaiting trial.

Elementary, My Dear Watson
There are approximately 300,000,000 persons residing in the United States. According to the U.S. Department of Justice, Bureau of Justice Statistics, in the year 2004, about 7 million people, or about 2.4 percent of the population of the United States, was either in prison, jail, or under some type of active "correctional supervision."

The Law Requires ...

Searching Department of Corrections records in the state where the person last resided.

The Reality

Most state correction facilities have websites where you can search. Use your favorite search engine and search by state name and "Department of Corrections."

As for the federal penitentiaries, you can search the entire federal system at www.bop.gov.

In a recent diligent search, I found that my subject had been released on parole. I noticed that the correctional website provided current addresses for their parolees. Guess where mine was. Yep, he was back in the county jail. I called the jail and verified he was there. This search was so easy that I felt compelled to return a large portion of the retainer I'd received. The subject couldn't really avoid service and was served within a couple of days. I now receive adoption diligent searches from this attorney on a regular basis.

Hospitals

You'd think with *HIPAA* and all of the privacy surrounding medical care that getting information out of hospitals would be difficult. Well, let's see.

The Law Requires ...

A search of hospitals in the area where the person last resided.

The Reality

The hardest part of this search is determining which hospitals are in the surrounding area of your subject's last known address. As strange as that sounds, it's true.

def•i•ni•tion

HIPAA is an acronym for Health Insurance Portability and Accountability Act. It was passed in Congress in 1996. A minor part of the act, but the part most quoted by medical providers so they don't have to release any information to you, is a section that deals with the security and privacy of health data.

Use an Internet mapping service like www.mapquest.com to locate the city where your subject last resided and find the surrounding cities. Go to one of your free yellow-page searches, or use one of your pay white-page searches and search using a keyword of "hospital." Print off all of the returns.

Now you start calling. Ask for patient information. The purpose of this search is to prove that your subject is not incapacitated by an accident and lying in a hospital bed.

Alternate Light Source

If you're in a really large city, you'll want to narrow your hospital search by zip code. Most of your telephone directory searches will allow for searches within a certain zip code.

Ask patient information if your subject is a patient in the hospital. They'll politely tell you no and you go on to the next one, right? Wrong. They'll politely tell you no and then you ask for hospital records. You ask the person in records if she has any record of your subject having been there, ever. Eight times out of ten they'll check and tell you yes or no. Amazing, but true. In fairness, they're not releasing any information that they shouldn't. It's basically the same information as patient information gives you, only it's back-dated.

Your affidavit will be more complete if you can say that he has never been a patient in those hospitals.

Why Are the Lights Cut Off?

Searching utility company records is sort of a crap shoot. Sometimes you make your point, sometimes you seven out.

The Law Requires ...

Records of utility companies, including water, sewer, cable television, and electric companies in the area where the person last resided.

The Reality

In some municipalities the utility companies are open to the public. More often the records are not releasable.

Call the city hall and ask the name of the major utility carrier in the area, both electric and water. Call the utilities' customer service numbers and ask if they have any subscriber by your subject's name. They'll want the Social Security number. Often you'll get a customer service rep that will decline to give you any information. But sometimes you'll get someone who will say, "Yes, but we can't give you the address or any information." Or they might indicate that they used to have service but no longer do. They might give you the date the service was terminated, but usually won't give you the address.

I was searching for the mother of a child in Colorado. I called the publicly owned water company in a city where I thought she might be. The customer service rep referred me to her supervisor where I left a voice mail. Three times I called him and he never returned my call. The information should have been public, but he didn't want to divulge it so he just ignored me. The customer service rep did say that they refer people to the city police department for background checks.

Right, I thought. I'm going to call the city police and they're going to run a record search for me over the phone. Now in Colorado, you can run the entire state over the website www.cocourt.com for about eight bucks. I'd done that and found a few old cases, but none of them helped.

Finally I thought, what the heck, and I called the records department of this small Denver suburb police department. The fellow checked his computer. They had my subject listed as a complainant on a malicious mischief case. Someone had keyed her car. This gave me a recent address.

Excited, I checked the address. No luck. My subject had moved out a few months earlier. I checked the free white-page listings (remember free = old data) and found the name the phone at that address had been listed under. Then I did a search in the pay white-page database (pay = current data) and found a listing for the same fellow in a nearby city. I called that number and guess who answered the phone. Bingo! My subject, the mother of the child up for adoption. We had a nice chat and she was served within a couple of days.

In this same case, I found the father of the child living in a tack shed on a horse ranch in Colorado. He came to the phone at the ranch house. He agreed he wanted to do whatever was best for his son. He gave me the street address where the process server could find him. When you find the subject, you don't have to complete the affidavit, but you've still earned your fee.

The Military: Where in the World Is He?

Finding one particular military person can be challenging. And service of process to military people, especially in a war theater, is a whole chapter by itself.

The Law Requires ...

A search of records of the armed services of the United States as to whether there is any information as to the subject currently serving in the armed services.

The Reality

Search the Defense Manpower Data Center site set up for compliance with the Service Members Civil Relief Act (www.dmdc.osd.mil/scra/owa/scra.home).

You input your subject's name, Social Security number, and date of birth and it'll let you know if your subject is on active duty or not. If he is, well, you just found him.

Getting him served is a whole different problem, and in some venues you can't serve an active duty military person. In some you can.

The Taxman Cometh

Above we dealt with business licenses and state required licenses. Here we'll deal with taxable obligations on the state and local levels.

The Law Requires ...

Records of the tax assessor and tax collector in the area where the person last resided.

The Reality

Start with the county of last known residence and check the property tax records. I've found sometimes my subject still owns property in the county even though he's not there. Sometimes the tax bill might even go to his new address.

Also, some states have their counties collect personal property taxes and intangible property taxes. (Intangible property always seemed like a contradiction in terms to me, but it's one of those things that if the government can find a way to tax it they will.) Ask the tax collector what other taxes your subject might be liable for in the jurisdiction you're searching.

Databases

We talked a lot about databases in Chapter 8. Isn't it interesting that even the government recognizes that private investigators have data resources that are not affiliated with the government?

The Law Requires ...

Search of one Internet databank locator service.

The Reality

You probably have searched your favorite database several dozen times by now. I always search each of the three that I have ready access to. So in the affidavit, you relate what your database told you: which address it showed as most recent and how you took that address and pursued all logical leads.

The Affidavit

Here is the culmination of all of your effort. Win, lose, or draw, you've completed a thorough search for your subject. A diligent search. Upon conclusion you will have successfully ended a complex investigation. You can be proud of your work, and if you've carefully documented each step, your affidavit will stand the test of any court, the probing of any attorney, the hindsight of any person who might come along later.

Don't skimp on any of the preceding steps. Sometimes it might be tempting. Don't do it. That would be dishonest, cheating, and in the end, you have to sign a notarized affidavit that you performed dutifully every required search in the process.

Now that you've done the work, it's important that the finished product appear professional. Your client and the judge will not see all of your notes in your file. They won't examine your telephone bill. So prepare an affidavit that lists each step we've outlined above, and the results you obtained.

A professional investigator wants his product to look professional. Satisfied clients generate more business without any additional marketing. Check the example in Appendix D.

How Much to Charge?

Don't bill this by the hour, but as a flat rate case. However, the minimum I'd charge for this type of case anywhere in the United States is $750. How long will the case take? Figure on two weeks, mainly because of slow responses from the post office. Actual time spent on the phone, at the computer, etc., is about 3 hours or a bit more. You do the math on the hourly rate.

The Least You Need to Know

- Many states require a diligent search in adoption and estate matters.

- Diligent searches are detailed investigations that command higher fees.

- Fourteen separate investigative steps make up a diligent search, including public, postal, governmental, utility, and hospital records.

- Upon conclusion of the search, if the subject is not located, a notarized affidavit detailing each step of the search is completed and presented to the court.

Chapter 23

Slaying the Paper Tiger

In This Chapter

◆ Using the evidence to make a case

◆ Understanding recorded and signed statements

◆ Handling the evidence

◆ The FBI FD 302

◆ Feeding the secretary

Reporting the results of your investigation to your client is in some sense just as important, if not more so, than the investigation itself. After all, no matter how well executed the investigation, no matter how valuable the information is to the client, and how sure the victory in court looks, it won't mean squat if the PI fails to submit a report detailing his findings, or if his reporting skills are inadequate, or the report is so faulty that it's unusable.

I've known investigative firms that sent investigators into the field. The investigators shot good video on workmen's compensation claims and verbally reported the results to their clients. The firm sends the tape and a bill to the client, but no detailed report, no documentation of their investigation. Three years later, the case goes to court. The attorney for the insurance company wants to use the tape to prove that the claimant wasn't really hurt, and needs the investigator to testify. Nobody in the firm can remember who shot the tape. Do you think they have a little problem?

In almost every investigation, there comes a juncture when the investigator has to step back and analyze the direction of the case and how the investigator's efforts are directed. We deal with that in this chapter. Then we take a look at how to wrap up the case and present it to the client in a professionally formatted report.

Sifting Through the Evidence

The general rule of evidence is, naturally, that somebody collected it and, logically, that same somebody needs to be present to introduce it into court. Below we'll discuss the need to maintain the chain of custody on the evidence. That is true not only for evidence collected at the crime scene, but also for anything of evidentiary value, including videotapes.

In surveillance matters, the videotape is really not the primary piece of evidence. Actually, the investigator's testimony is what counts. Videotape just corroborates what the investigator saw, and can do it in a very dramatic way. Remember, we've relied on eyewitness testimony long before videotape was ever invented.

I can testify that I saw a workmen's compensation claimant with an alleged neck injury standing on his head on a surfboard while surfing. That's good testimony. But let me play the tape, and the jury is totally convinced. You can tell when they laugh at the claimant that you've made your case.

Workmen's compensation evidence is fairly straightforward. Either you catch the claimant engaged in activities he says he can't perform, or you don't. In other types of cases, the evidence is not so clear, and we have to sift through it to see what we've got.

An 18-year-old boy, Darby, is employed at a restaurant as a server. The drinking age in the state is 21. One July evening after his shift is over, Darby leaves the restaurant in his pickup truck and prevails upon his older buddy to buy some beer. They start club hopping, drinking the beers in his pickup truck on the drives between clubs. Darby claims he only had two beers. Later, near closing time, Darby returns to the restaurant where he works, enters through the back door to the kitchen, and proceeds to the bar area. At the bar, the bartender, according to Darby, gives him three free drinks made with an expensive brand of whiskey. Darby leaves the restaurant and, while driving home, drives off the road, hits a tree, and is now paralyzed from the neck down for the rest of his life.

Darby and his parents sue the restaurant/bar for serving Darby because he is underage and then allowing him to leave the bar and drive while under the influence. It's a terrible tragedy. Now you be the judge and tell me who's at fault.

Two years later, the attorney representing Darby asks us to investigate the circumstances of that night in July. He wants a blow-by-blow account of what transpired in the restaurant and the bar. And, oh yeah, the restaurant/bar went out of business over a year before he decided to take the case.

We have to track down the former employees and interview them, then sift through and evaluate what they can remember about that night. While that night was momentous in Darby's life, to everyone else it was just another night. Can you remember where you were on July 23, two years ago? Neither can I.

We obtained the police reports and rescue reports detailing the accident investigation. No question about it. Eighteen-year-old, underage Darby was drunk. His blood alcohol level was more than twice the legal limit.

The bar records from that night were examined. There is a log of the drinks served and at about the time, 11 P.M., when Darby says he was served, the log shows three double drinks of that same expensive liquor being rung up as complimentary drinks.

A pattern emerged from the interviews of the former employees: the young owners of the restaurant allowed their underage employees to drink alcohol on the premises. They were "cool." They sponsored several employee parties after work and provided the booze, allowing everyone there, regardless of age, to imbibe. They even had an employee meeting to discuss the subject of underage employees drinking, and the owners seemed to think that, even though 21 was the statutory drinking age, their employees could pretty well do whatever they wanted, as long as "it didn't get out of hand."

Not everybody that we talked to was so forthcoming. Some, in an effort to protect the owners, said they never saw anybody underage drinking. Others maybe did. They came to work, did their job, and went home. Some seemed to hang around after hours until the lights were turned off.

As for the bartender who'd actually served Darby the drinks, all we had was a fairly common first name. No last name, no Social Security number, nothing we could use to help us locate him. Since we represented the plaintiff, we didn't have access to all of the employee records.

We also had not talked to any employee who could say definitively that Darby had been drinking at the bar. We had employees who saw Darby return to the restaurant. One of the cooks in the kitchen said when Darby came in he was carrying a beer can, and the cook told him he couldn't bring outside beer into the restaurant.

Everyone in my office worked the case pretty hard for two weeks, locating and interviewing the former employees. Some only worked at the restaurant for a month, others worked the entire two years it was open. Some of the former employees were never found. But let's sift through what we've got.

Positive for the plaintiff Darby:

◆ Darby worked at the restaurant.

◆ Testimony as to a clear pattern of underage employees being allowed to drink inside the restaurant.

◆ Testimony that the owners knew underage employees were drinking and almost implicitly encouraged it.

◆ The bar tab shows three doubles of the same liquor being served as complimentary beverages at about the time Darby says he was served.

◆ Darby was drunk when he hit the tree, and he'd just left the restaurant.

◆ While there were beer cans in the bed of the pickup truck, nobody could say how long they'd been there.

Positive for the defendants (the restaurant):

◆ At the accident scene, there were numerous beer cans in the back of Darby's pickup truck.

◆ Some employees never saw any underage drinking.

◆ Darby left the restaurant sober after his shift was over.

◆ Darby returned to the restaurant with a beer can in his hand.

◆ No one witnessed Darby drinking at the bar the night of the accident.

Does Darby have a case? We don't want to get into a discussion here about personal responsibility, and a good PI must learn to compartmentalize such things from the hard-core legal issues of any case he's working. Legally, the bar will have liability if Darby was served alcohol and had a traffic accident afterward. True, nobody poured the liquor down his throat, but it shouldn't have been offered to him. Even though the bar was now out of business, the bar owners and their insurance company would still be on the hook if the case went to trial and Darby prevailed.

Our client, Darby's attorney, called and informed us that the next day they were to have a pretrial settlement hearing. What have we got? I synopsized for him all of the statements we've taken and couriered them over to his office. We'll talk later in this chapter about how to do recorded statements. The attorney wanted to know where the bartender was and why hadn't we found him. We were looking for him as hard as we could.

Periodically, while working a case, a good investigator will take a step back and evaluate the evidence he's collected so far. He'll know what the attorney needs to make the case, and so he'll adjust his investigative efforts, shift the focus or the direction he's going to meet those needs.

Late that afternoon, I contacted another employee who used to room with the bartender. We got lucky. He gave me the bartender's complete name. He'd moved to another state, but we tracked him down on the west coast, and the time there is three hours earlier. The bartender finally arrived home after midnight our time. I got a recorded statement from him saying yes, he did serve Darby three drinks and his recollection was that the liquor was that particular brand which Darby said it was. His memory was pretty clear about it because the next day at work all the buzz was about Darby's wreck and he knew he'd served him some drinks.

I called the attorney at home and woke him up. After I related what I'd just gotten, he was elated and said we'd just found the Holy Grail. The next morning, I faxed the attorney's office a synopsis of the bartender's statement. During the pretrial settlement hearing, he read the synopsis to a representative of the insurance company and the attorney representing the restaurant. After a few minutes of private consultation, the company agreed to settle for the policy limit, which was $1 million. Our client agreed to the settlement and, right or wrong, it was done.

Taking Recorded and Signed Statements

Private investigators need to know how to take *recorded* and *signed statements*. A written statement, signed and sworn to by the person signing it, is a very good piece of testimonial evidence. Recorded interviews are very beneficial as well.

def•i•ni•tion

A **recorded statement** is a voice tape recording made by a witness concerning facts and/or the witness's recollection of the pertinent incident. A recorded statement can be taken either over the telephone or in person. A **signed statement** is a written declaration made by a witness concerning facts and/or the witness's recollection of the pertinent incident that is signed by the witness.

You might recollect the law concerning the recording of communications from Chapter 19. In that case, we talked about one-party and all-party states. There is a list in Appendix B of which states are one-party consent states and which states require all parties to consent to being recorded. Those rules apply to the interception of telephone calls. There are separate rules that apply to the interception of oral communications not conducted over a wire.

When a telephone call crosses state boundaries … beware. The recording of the telephone conversation might be legal in one of those states but not in the other.

Many states make it illegal to record a conversation, other than telephonic, between two or more people, unless all parties agree to the recording. Therefore, if you're going to take a recorded statement from a witness to an accident, be sure the witness affirms verbally on the tape recording that he is aware he is being recorded and you, the private investigator, have his permission to do so.

Why would you want to record a witness? Remember, sometimes a case might not go to trial for three or more years after an accident. Witnesses might forget what they saw, or at least what they told you they saw. There is nothing better to help refresh a witness's recollection of the incident than to let him listen to his own voice telling you what he witnessed.

As a PI, it's important to understand that the witness's sympathy might really be with the plaintiff. If your client is the defendant, that means you're asking for a statement from "the opposition." By getting the witness's statement on tape, you're protected, so that when the witness's wife berates him for "helping" the wrong side, and all of a sudden he can't remember exactly what he saw, it won't matter. It's on the tape. This happens all the time.

As I've noted over and over again, a good investigator just gathers the facts and lets the evidence chips fall where they may, but witnesses often have their own agenda and flexible standards to suit it. A recording of the witness's statement, therefore, can be used to *impeach* her testimony in court if she has a sudden change of heart and testifies to something other than what she originally said.

When a witness changes his testimony, the courtroom dialogue would go something like this …

def•i•ni•tion

> **Impeaching** a witness's testimony means to call into question the reliability or truthfulness of the testimony being given.

> Attorney: Mr. Witness, didn't you tell our investigator that you witnessed the blue car run the red light and strike the white car?
>
> Witness: No, I don't believe so. The light was green when the blue car entered the intersection. I have a very good recollection of that.
>
> The attorney plays the tape with the witness telling the PI that the light was definitely red and the blue car ran the red light.
>
> Witness (looking at his wife and shrugging): I guess it must have been red. It's been so long, I got confused.

That's how impeachment works in a courtroom. You want the tape so the egg ends up on the witness's face and not yours.

Raymond was in a custody battle with his wife, my client, Sheila. Part of the court order was that Raymond, an alcoholic, would not drink. Raymond was about 28 years old, a tall, lanky, good-looking fellow who happened to own a very popular restaurant. Our client needed to prove that Raymond was still drinking and carousing.

I followed Raymond on numerous occasions. I photographed him using the drive-through window of a liquor store. There was an exchange of funds and the clerk passed a brown paper bag with his purchases to him.

Raymond also frequented topless bars. While in the bars, he drank a lot of beer. I documented how many beers he drank and what brand they were. When the case was ready to go to court, I interviewed the waitresses at these topless bars. (I know, you're thinking I probably interviewed more than I needed to, huh?) I found one good witness who remembered Raymond and what she served him. The waitress remembered the brand of beer he preferred, how he tipped, and how many beers he usually drank while he was there. He was a regular and would come in about three times a week.

We subpoenaed her the next day for the trial. In court, she testified that she never told me Raymond drank beers, that when he came in, he always ordered a soft drink. She didn't ever serve him beer or any other alcohol, always a cola drink. Do you think Raymond got to her? You can bet on it. I wished I'd had a recorded statement from her, but I didn't get one. What I did get was egg in my face in front of the jury. Took me a couple of hours to wash it all off.

People lie in court. It always amazes me that they will perjure themselves, but it happens every day. Oh, and what did Raymond say about the drive-through liquor store? He claimed he bought a two-liter bottle of cola. Right.

The Format for the Recorded Statement

A recorded statement should begin like this: "This is investigator [enter your name] and today's date is [enter the date]. I am speaking with [enter the witness's name]. Mr. [witness], you are aware that I am recording this conversation, is that correct?"

Make sure the witness says yes. A nod of the head can't be heard later.

"And I have your permission to record this, is that also correct?" Again, make sure you get a verbal yes.

"Now, Mr. [witness], for the record, please state your name and your address." Then make sure you get his telephone number, his date of birth, and his Social Security number.

Next, ask where he is employed and what hours he works. Why? You want all that detail, because if it takes a couple of years for the case to go to court, that might be the only way you can track him down.

After the introduction, ask him to tell you what he witnessed. Let him talk. In addition to the recording, take good notes. I try not to interrupt the witness. When he has finished I go back, using my notes, and ask appropriate questions for clarification purposes, or to elicit more details or facts that the witness didn't give the first time through.

If there is something you want to ask the witness, you need a potty break, or you need to talk about something that is not relevant to the case, it is permissible to turn off the tape recorder and deal with whatever it is. Before turning the recorder off, state what time it is and that you are turning the recorder off. When you go back on the record, be sure to state the current time and get the witness's permission again to record the conversation.

You'll know you've exhausted the interview when you can't get another fact out of the witness. To officially conclude the recording, state the time, that the interview is finished, and that you're turning the recorder off.

It never fails. After we've recorded the interview, as I'm walking out the door, the witness remembers something very important and just blurts it out. You should stop and discuss it in detail. Then sit back down, turn the recorder back on, reconfirm the person's identity and permission to record the conversation, and have the witness repeat that last tidbit of detail for the recording.

Do all recorded statements have to be done in person? No. Most of the recorded statements my firm takes are done over the telephone. We use the same Radio Shack device mentioned in Chapter 19. We follow the same rules as laid out here in the preceding paragraphs. The format is the same; you just don't have the eye contact with the witness. Remember the bartender from Darby's case? He was in California, I was in Florida. The settlement hearing was to begin in less than 12 hours. There wasn't even time to have a local investigator go to his house and take a statement. A telephonic recorded statement is just as valid as one done face–to–face.

To be successful at interviewing, you have to build a relationship with the interviewee. That's harder to do over the telephone, but it can be done. I prefer all interviews be performed face-to-face, but that's not always possible. Frequently, budget and time don't allow it, so you have to settle for a telephonic interview. If you utilize the techniques in Chapter 10, you can accomplish a successful telephonic interview and obtain a recorded statement that will hold up in court all the same.

Formatting the Signed Statement

Signed statements are a pain to do. The reason is the private investigator usually has to sit and handwrite the statement for the witness. And the statement might be several pages of handwritten material. I usually try to get a recorded statement. Then, if necessary, I type up what we need in the signed statement, go back to the witness, and have her sign it. If your client is an attorney, she'll want to have some input into what's included in a signed statement, and she may draft it herself.

Why take a signed statement instead of, or in addition to, a recorded statement? An attorney can take the signed statement into court and present it as evidence. It's easily readable, is concise and, if it is properly notarized, the person who signed it probably won't have to appear in court.

def•i•ni•tion

SSAN is the standard abbreviation in most federal law enforcement circles for Social Security Account Number.

A signed statement should begin with:

> I, [name of witness], reside at [insert residence address]. My date of birth is [insert DOB] and my Social Security number is [insert *SSAN*]. I am making the following voluntary signed statement: … Then proceed with the statement.

At the end of the statement, the following sentence should appear:

> I swear that the above statement consisting of this and [insert the number of other pages in the statement] is true to the best of my recollection. (If the statement is a total of three pages long, that sentence would read, "consisting of this and two additional pages.")

Then have it signed by the witness. If you are not a notary, take one with you and have her notarize the statement. You'll have to pay the notary for her time, but you can charge that to the client anyway and add a markup on it to increase your bottom line at the end of the month. PIs notarize lots of odd things at odd hours in odd places, so find yourself an adventurous one or become one yourself. In my firm, one of my investigators or secretaries always keeps her notary status current. When she goes with us into the field we charge her time to the client at our investigative rate.

The requirements to become a notary are different in the different states. The National Notary Association's website (www.nationalnotary.org) lists all 50 states and the District of Columbia and each state's respective requirements.

Originals and Duplicates

As a private investigator, you're maintaining evidence in your office. You've shot some videotape. You have recorded interviews and you have signed statements. What do you do with all of that evidence? How do you store it?

An investigator needs to "maintain chain of custody on the evidence." This means that any evidence collected by you, videotape, beer cans from a crime scene, recorded statements, and any thing else that might be introduced into court as evidence should be:

1. Initialed and dated by the investigator.

2. Kept in a locked cabinet or room with limited access.

When the case goes to trial, the investigator that gathered the evidence can testify that this evidence has been under his care, control, and custody (or in the custody of the agency) and has not been tampered with.

Most importantly, when you send your report and your bill to your insurance client, you also want them to see the videotape you're so proud of. Send them only a duplicate of the videotape and not the original. The last thing you want to do is mix up the original with a copy.

It took my firm a long time to educate the insurance companies not to ask for the original videotape. Insurance adjusters come and go. Companies merge, reorganize, and close offices. If the original tape is in their possession, it will most likely get lost or misplaced. In addition, the investigator who shot the video is going to have to testify in court and introduce the video into evidence, not the insurance adjuster.

As to maintaining chain of custody on the evidence, here's the first thing one of the attorneys will ask you: "Is this tape you're introducing an original?" The second question will be: "Has the tape been in your care, custody, and control since it was made, and has it been tampered with in any way?" If the tape has not been in your control the entire time, then you can't answer yes. You don't know if it's been tampered with or not, do you?

We had an insurance company client for which we worked a lot of liability cases, such as slip and falls in grocery stores. We took a lot of recorded statements. The insurance company representatives insisted that we provide them the original of the recorded statement. We refused, to a point, but they were paying the bills, so finally we agreed. We did make them sign a release saying that they had the original tape and would not hold us responsible in the future for the safety of the tape. I can't tell you how many times they would call us a year or two down the road, asking us where the tape was. We'd fax them a copy of the release and tell them happy hunting.

Alternate Light Source

If you're the PI, charge the dictation and the time spent writing the report at the same rate as your normal hourly rate. If you don't, you'll be losing money.

As far as recorded statements are concerned, we rarely transcribe them. If the client wants it done, we quote him our secretarial rate for the service. If I'm paying a secretary $12.50 an hour, we charge the client at least $18 an hour for tape transcription. If they want a transcription, it's usually so one attorney can send it to the other, hopefully encouraging him to settle the case.

What usually satisfies the client is a synopsis of the witness's recorded statement that the investigator dictates into a handheld recorder. Our secretary types the synopsis, which is included in the full report to the client, and that way, the report of the interview is full and complete.

Superior Reports Are the Mark of the Professional PI

A competent private investigator should produce a clear and concise report, written in good, grammatical English. If the report has a lot of misspellings and grammatical errors in it, do you think the clients will be excited about you representing them on the witness stand? Or will they be embarrassed that they hired you?

If spelling is not your bag and you don't know the difference between *your* and *you're*, or *billed* and *build*, then hire somebody who has mastered proper English to do your paperwork. A talented secretary can make even a bozo look good.

Police departments are notorious for producing poorly written reports. They don't get much in the way of report-writing instruction in the police academies. Having had several years to cement some bad writing habits, an officer retires or leaves the force and starts his own private investigative agency. How is the quality of the reports he writes then? About the same as what he did on the force. The same mistakes and the same poor formatting, because that's what he's done for 20 years.

A proper PI report should look very much like an FBI report. Why? What's the big deal? Because most law school graduates are familiar with *FD 302s*. An FD 302 is basically a blank sheet of paper. The format of the words on the FD 302 is what is important.

One way or another, the whole purpose of most private investigations is to win a case in a court of law. Certainly, not every case you work will go to court, but the PI should prepare each and every one of his cases as if it will. The bureau's been writing reports for a long time, and its reports are clear and unambiguous.

The following is a typical example of the wording at the beginning of an FD 302, or, in your case, a good investigative report …

> The following investigation was conducted by Steven K. Brown, of Millennial Investigative Services, on April 15, 2007, at Jacksonville, Florida:
>
> On this date Mary Jane Doe, date of birth 10/20/1947, SSAN 261-00-0000, was interviewed at her residence of 1234 Any Street, Jacksonville, Florida, and provided the following information:
>
> Doe advised that she witnessed an accident between ….

Alternate Light Source _____

An FD 302 is a federal form number used by the FBI for part of its report. Specifically, it reports the results of interviews conducted by FBI agents. All interviews are reported in a standard format and are typed or printed onto FD 302s. Law school students learn this early in their schooling, and the forms are referred to throughout judicial opinions.

In the reporting of this type of interview, the investigator's name, agency, and date the interview took place are laid out at the beginning. Once that's done, the reader knows who did the interview, as well as when and where it was conducted. The investigator's name doesn't have to be repeated again anywhere else on the page, nor does the investigator refer to himself as "the writer," which is so often the case in police reports. By following this format, your reports will be plain, clear, easily read, straightforward, and done in a style that all attorneys are familiar with. If you tell your client up front that your reports are similar to FD 302s, they'll make you for a professional from the beginning.

If you produce good reports, you will earn your client's respect and, most importantly, his repeat business. Remember, you can be the best investigator in the world, but your client only sees two things from you: the quality of your report and the quality of the evidence you collect, be it videotape or photographs. You can have a lousy car and a rotten pair of binoculars, and duct tape patches on your pants, but your client will never see those. If your reports and tapes are superior, then he'll figure you for a superior investigator. This is the best way to produce a professional image. Talk is cheap. What's left on your client's desk when you leave his office is what counts.

Show Me the Money

In the business of running a private investigative firm, there are a couple of cardinal rules you must follow for the business to thrive:

1. You have to get paid.

2. You have to get paid soon.

The best way to get paid is to collect a retainer before beginning a case. Always do this, without exception, in domestic cases, or when your client is an individual as opposed to a corporation. View this as the acid test. If she can't scrape the money together to pay you the retainer, what makes you think she'll have any more money when you hand her the final bill?

Work the case up to the amount of the retainer you have, and then inform her that you'll need more money if she wants more work. Don't let her get into your pockets, and don't be shy about asking for money. If you don't ask, you won't get it.

If there is any piece of advice I can give you that will help you succeed in the PI business, this is it. Always present a bill with the report. We always put the bill on top so the client sees it first thing. And try to collect the money due right then. If you hide the bill on the bottom of the report, it'll get overlooked, and you'll be begging for your money six months after the case is completed.

Alternate Light Source

I'm about to share a company secret with you that we've never shared with any other PI, ever. It's something I came up with after a few years in business and several different attempts at weaving our secretary's time into our investigative invoice. She has to be paid. She told me so. That means I have to charge for it, and so do you. Just ask your secretary, I'll bet she says the same thing. The problem is, if you bump up your hourly rate to include her time, then you might price yourself right out of the market. Your competition's rate will look much lower.

I came up with a solution that has worked for 22 years. In all that time, I've never had a complaint or even a question about it from a client.

On the invoice, under Expenses, we include a charge for Secretarial and Administrative Charges. We look at the total fees billed on a case and multiply that amount by 8.25 percent. That is our secretarial charge. This spreads our administrative costs over all of our cases and doesn't increase our quoted hourly rate. Other PIs have adopted this practice, but as far as I know, I originated it.

It's best to keep the client apprised of the tab he's incurring as the case progresses. Nobody wants any surprises at the end of a case. He might be thinking he's only spending a few hundred dollars. Imagine his surprise when he receives a bill for a few thousand. And, likewise, you're not going to be happy when he refuses to pay. It's best to keep a running tally and give him the current total periodically.

Being a professional investigator requires performing superior investigations, properly maintaining the evidence, and reporting the results of your investigative efforts in such a manner as to distinguish your firm apart from the competition.

In the over 20 years I've been running a PI business, I can count on one hand the number of times I've been "stiffed" by a client. Two were attorneys, one of whom was out of state. One was a client whose retainer check bounced, but we didn't know it until the work was completed. She filed for bankruptcy. The other was a large out-of-state corporation that left me on the hook for over $50,000. They filed for bankruptcy right after we completed the work. That's why a retainer is so important. I should have gotten one from that corporation, but they had several thousand employees and I figured they were good for it. I haven't made that mistake again.

The Least You Need to Know

- During the middle of a complex case, a good investigator will step back, look at the direction of the case, and shift the focus, if need be, to obtain what will be important in making the case in court.

- Recorded and signed statements are valuable items of evidence and can be used to impeach a witness's testimony should the witness change her story during a trial. There are specific formats and certain verbiage that should be used in recorded and signed statements.

- Original videotapes and recorded tapes should always be held in the investigator's control until needed for trial. Each tape should be labeled, initialed by the investigator who took the tape, and dated as soon as the tape comes out of the recorder.

- A superior method of report formatting is to follow the FBI's use of FD 302s. This is a clear, concise method of reporting, and is a standard that all attorneys learn in law school. It will set your firm apart from the competition.

- Always submit a bill with each report. Getting paid is necessary to running a successful PI business. Always charge for report writing and secretarial time.

Chapter 24

The Judges' Chambers

In This Chapter

- ◆ Ghostwriting from jail
- ◆ Time to testify
- ◆ Swearing under oath
- ◆ Understanding the privileges
- ◆ The secrets to the secret grand jury
- ◆ Putting your best foot forward
- ◆ Directing and redirecting in the courtroom

As private investigators, we deal with facts. I use the term "we" because if you've read this entire book, then you're pretty close to being an investigator, and "we" means you and me.

All of an investigator's effort comes to fruition when the case goes to court. In this chapter, we'll talk about how to accept a subpoena. Once the investigator has been subpoenaed she has to be ready to testify. Her testimony may come in the form of a deposition, or even an appearance before a grand jury.

You'll learn first about legal privileges, such as work product rules. Also, how to charge your client different rates for testifying and waiting to testify. And finally, how to testify in court and maintain your professional "cool" while under cross-examination. Going to court is the "final exam." You should be ready for it.

Just the Facts, Ma'am

Most of the cases that a PI works will have something to do with the law. Divorces, traffic accidents, nursing home abuse, child custody, asset location, slip and falls, criminal defense, and witness locating all start out headed toward court. Few of those cases actually end up in court. Ninety out of one hundred will settle before reaching the trial date. The private investigator must prepare his case in such a manner that the evidence is admissible in a court of law. The investigator must present his findings in such a manner that the judge, jury, and opposing attorney will be able to recognize him as a impartial professional investigator.

If you learn nothing else by reading this book, learn that you must not only *appear* to be impartial in your investigation, but also, in fact, you must *be* impartial. You should have this next statement memorized by now, since I've repeated it and similar statements throughout this book. It is the cardinal rule of private investigation. Say it out loud with me:

> *The professional private investigator searches for all the facts.*

There. You got it. The best PI in the business seeks the truth and reports his findings to his client accurately and uncolored by the position his client has taken.

def•i•ni•tion

Ghostwriting, in PI terms, refers to an investigator who makes up reports or details of reports. Often it is practiced by a dishonest investigator, who rather than do the work, just writes a report indicating he performed the investigation, but actually spent the day at the beach.

Unfortunately, there are many PIs who don't follow that standard. They report only the facts their clients want to hear. Some even deliberately misstate witnesses' statements in order to please their client. Others even practice what is labeled in the industry as *ghostwriting*.

Thomas, an investigator I subcontracted with, worked in the Orlando, Florida, area. When Thomas began working for me, he usually shot some pretty decent video on the insurance claimant cases. After a few months, I noticed that he no longer seemed to shoot any videotape whatsoever.

On one particular case, Thomas had been out on surveillance on a lady named Sarah. He submitted his report and, again, there was no accompanying videotape. The report showed absolutely no activity on Sarah's part on one particular day, June 22. I thought this highly unusual and, noting Thomas's lack of productivity, I reassigned the case to another investigator, Camille.

Camille went to check out Sarah's residence and discovered that Sarah no longer lived where we thought she had. I called Sarah on a pretext and chatted with her. In the conversation, I verified her new address and asked her when she'd moved. "Oh, it was June 22 I moved. I had my two nephews there and the three of us spent all day moving my stuff down those stairs and into that pickup truck. We must have filled that pickup truck at least a dozen times, making runs back and forth to the new place, before we emptied everything out of that apartment. Why, I never knew I had so much stuff."

Amazed, I asked Camille to go to the apartment manager and verify the move-out date. She did. June 22. Do you think I ever subcontracted with Thomas again? Now think how embarrassed Thomas would have been if he'd gone to court to testify to the "facts" in his report. Sarah would have stood up and said, "That's not true. I was moving on June 22." And my firm's credibility would have suffered more than just embarrassment. It would have cost us some business and some bad word of mouth.

I know of another investigative firm that actually was criminally prosecuted for ghost-writing reports. The principals of the firm apparently just made up reports, like Thomas did, and went ahead and billed the insurance company for work that was totally fictional. Eventually, the Florida Department of Insurance found out about it and prosecuted the owners of the company for insurance fraud. They were fined and spent time in jail.

Do your job. Do it professionally. Gather all the facts, good or bad, for your client. Present them to your client in a professional manner. Then let the chips fall where they may.

Accepting the Subpoena

As an investigator, you will be receiving *subpoenas* for court appearances or depositions. We'll cover depositions in the next section. Sometimes, even your own client will send you a subpoena. Attorneys are strange that way. Even though they hire you, they still feel the need to subpoena you. I recommend telling your client there is no need to subpoena you, just let you know when and where they need you, and you'll be there. Save the client the $50 it will cost them to have you subpoenaed.

def•i•ni•tion

A **subpoena** is a command from the judge of a court requiring that the person or representative of an institution named in the subpoena appear in court or at another specified location on a specific day at a certain time.

Don't play hide-and-seek with the subpoena service agent. Be professional about it. If your client doesn't want you to be served, then don't call up the opposing counsel and give him your schedule, but don't hide or try to evade the service, either. As much as you'd like to accommodate your client's desires, you are a professional, and you should conduct yourself as such. If you are served, the subpoena is an order from the court, or an attorney acting as an officer of the court, for you to appear. If you don't appear, then you're in contempt of that court. Better to have your client mad at you than to be held in contempt.

If you don't respond to the subpoena and you're held in contempt, you could be fined and will be required to testify anyway. The reality of the business is such that if you fail to respond to the subpoena and your client wanted you there, you'd lose a client. If the stakes are high and the opposing counsel issued the subpoena, you might find the sheriff on your doorstep with his handcuffs out.

If you are subpoenaed as a witness for trial, you're eligible for a witness fee. The witness fee, big deal that it is, usually amounts to about $20 or less.

Getting paid for your time is another good reason to have a contract with your client. I always bill my own client, even if I am subpoenaed by the opposing counsel. I am there because of my client's needs, and I expect her to pay for my time and mileage. You'll note that the contract specifies a minimum amount that will be paid for courtroom appearances. The contract can, of course, be modified any way you desire. Change it to suit your own needs. There is a sample contract in Appendix C.

The Division of Licensing

Don't take the report you sent to your client with you to court or to a deposition. If you need notes to refresh your memory, then take notes. There could be facts in your report that your client doesn't want the other side to know. If you refer to your report during your testimony, then the other side has a right to a copy of it. And you certainly don't want them seeing your bill. The last thing your client, the insurance company, wants is the claimant's attorney announcing to the jury that the company paid you $8,000 to sneak around and spy on that little old lady claimant, instead of paying her doctor's bills with that money.

Usually, the subpoena you receive will be for you to appear at the trial at the courthouse. Other times, you'll get subpoenaed for depositions, which usually take place at one of the attorneys' offices or at the office of the court reporter.

Most of your testimony will be given in your county, but not always. We routinely get subpoenaed for areas all around our state, and sometimes across the country. If your client is an insurance company, a large business, or an attorney, they know the standard is for you to be paid for your time, including travel, and to reimburse your travel expenses.

If your client is an individual, get your travel expenses and anticipated hourly rate up front in the form of an additional retainer. It's always easier to get money from your client before you perform the service than it is afterward.

Some investigators bill their clients a lower rate for waiting time in the courthouse and at their usual rate for time spent testifying. I don't. I bill it all at our usual rate. Time spent waiting to testify at trial might go as long as several days. The attorney will usually have a good idea on what day she'll need you, but sometimes she will guess wrong. You've set everything in your schedule aside for this trial when you could be out working other cases. The attorney's office owes you for that time.

In order to speed the legal process along, I tell my secretaries that they have my authority to accept a subpoena on my behalf, as long as I am in town. If I am out of town on an extended trip, then they ought not to accept the subpoena. Why? I might not be back in time to testify on the date desired, and I don't want to be held in contempt of court. Normally you'll be given several weeks notice, but I've been subpoenaed one day for testimony the next.

Everything You Wanted to Know About Depositions

A *deposition* is the meat between the bread in the legal sandwich of our jurisprudence system.

def•i•ni•tion

A **deposition** is a statement made under oath by a witness, usually written or recorded, that may be used in court at a later time. If there is the likelihood that the deponent will not be available later—for instance, due to illness—it is not uncommon for the deposition to be videotaped. The deponent is the witness being deposed.

Private investigators are deposed by the opposing counsel all the time. There would be no need for your own client to depose you. Since you are working for him, he already has your reports.

Alternate Light Source

A PI should give his client a progress report every few days. It can be as simple as a phone call or an e-mail. This regular updating has two very beneficial purposes. First, your client will appreciate knowing how the case is moving along. Second, it's not unusual for your client to assign you additional work, either on the current case or on a new assignment. Just talking to your client makes him think about other cases he has where your services could be useful. And more work means more billable hours and a better bottom line for your business.

Typically, a court reporter is present and makes an official record of the deposition. Your client, or your client's attorney, will be there, as well as the opposing attorney. The court reporter will have you raise your right hand and swear under oath what you are about to say is true.

With all that high-priced talent in one place, you can just hear the cash-register cha-chinging, can't you? There's the court reporter, both attorneys billing their clients for their time, and you, the PI, billing your client for your time. Conducting a deposition can be expensive. And that is the precise reason why private investigators are in business.

By having the private investigator first go out and interview potential witnesses, attorneys can make a decision as to which witnesses to depose. There is no need to go to the expense of deposing someone if they have no recollection of the incident or matter at hand, or never even saw, for instance, the traffic accident you're investigating. It's a lot cheaper to pay the PI his hourly rate than to orchestrate a deposition that will be totally nonproductive.

def•i•ni•tion

A **reluctant witness** is an individual who might have considerable knowledge of the incident that is in question, but will not discuss her knowledge of this incident unless she is forced to by a court.

Another reason for deposing someone is if they are a *reluctant witness*.

Leslie was an emergency room nurse working in a local hospital. Our client, Hugh, had been a resident in a nursing home. The rules of common care in nursing homes require that patients be bathed daily. In addition, any sores or open wounds should be noted on their files, and a nurse specializing in wound care is supposed to tend to these sores.

The attendants, or certified nursing assistants, at these nursing homes are also supposed to make notes as to whether or not the residents are eating their meals. If the residents don't eat, their health can quickly fail. Nursing homes have nutritionists on staff who can help residents with eating disorders.

Hugh was already in delicate health due to his age and some other exacerbating physical conditions. He apparently hadn't been eating any of his meals, but it was not noted in his file.

Finally, one day, a nurse noticed that Hugh was having difficulty breathing. She called for an ambulance, and Hugh was transported to the emergency room where Leslie was on duty.

In making a preliminary examination of Hugh, Leslie discovered many open sores and wounds on the lower portion of his body, including not only his legs, but also his groin and genitals.

Leslie made note that the wounds were infected. She saw maggots crawling throughout the open sores. She cleaned the wounds and admitted Hugh to the hospital because he was severely malnourished.

One of the witnesses that Hugh's attorney wanted me to interview was Leslie. I tracked Leslie down and one day dropped by her house unannounced. Leslie was cordial, but insisted on calling the legal department of her hospital before talking to me. Note that the hospital was not being sued. In this case, the nursing home, a totally different institution altogether, was the defendant.

I had several discussions with the legal department at that hospital before they finally agreed to let Leslie talk to me—if she wanted to. The discussion had to be limited to Leslie's original observations when Hugh was admitted. We could not discuss his treatment while at the hospital. That was fine, because all we wanted was her testimony as to the neglectful physical condition Hugh was in when he arrived at the hospital.

Leslie still refused to be interviewed. She wouldn't tell me why she wouldn't talk to me. Consequently, my client, the attorney for Hugh, set her deposition. Once she was under oath and compelled to talk, she testified to what she'd seen that day when Hugh was admitted. Leslie was a reluctant witness. A witness will have her own reasons for not wanting to testify. It might be inconvenient for them. It might be company policy that employees don't testify unless compelled to, or she might harbor fears that her own actions, and in this case, the quality of the way she treated this particular patient, might come into question.

Alternate Light Source

Generally speaking, it's better to talk to witnesses without first making an appointment to see them. If the witness knows you're coming and he really doesn't want to talk to you, he won't be there when you arrive at the appointed time. Also, the witness's sympathies might lie with the other party, and if he knows you're coming, he'll call the other party, who probably will tell him not to talk to you. Then, when you arrive for your appointment, you will have wasted your driving time because the guy's not going to give you a statement.

True, an investigator can waste a lot of driving time making repeated trips to the witness's home, trying to catch him there without an appointment. An investigator has to weigh the time involved with the lost opportunity of surprise.

Overall, a private investigator will get better witness statements if he just shows up unannounced, but that's not always possible.

Work Product from the Attorney's Office

There is a general rule of law that says that work performed or originated by one attorney is not discoverable by the opposing attorney, unless it is violated by the attorney and given to other parties. This is called the *work product* rule.

In a case headed for trial, each attorney is under the obligation to present, to the opposing side, a list of the witnesses he intends to use during the trial. The opposing counsel can then interview or depose these witnesses and discover what the nature of their testimony is going to be or what evidence the witness will introduce. This is called "discovery."

If the attorney voluntarily gives a particular piece of work product to the opposing counsel, then he has violated the work product privilege for that item and that work product no longer enjoys the privilege. It can be used by the opposing counsel, even if the attorney who originated the material has changed his mind and does not want it to appear in the court record.

For instance, if your client, the attorney, shares a copy of your report with the opposing attorney, your report will no longer enjoy the work product privilege.

As most of us know, anything you discuss with your attorney is confidential and cannot be disclosed to another attorney, law enforcement officer, or the court without your permission. This is called the attorney-client *privilege*.

def•i•ni•tion

Work product is described as the attorney's notes and research materials and other documents or matters that the attorney makes, prepares, or uses as he works up the case. The reports of a private investigator, hired directly by the attorney or working out of the attorney's office, are also considered work product. A **privilege,** under law, is a special right that someone enjoys that the public at large does not enjoy. For instance, the marital privilege asserts that a wife cannot be forced to testify against her husband, or vice versa. The clergy privilege declares that communications between a clergyman and his parishioner are considered privileged.

Why do private investigators care about work product and privileges? Many private investigators are "in-house" investigators and work directly for attorneys.

Most private investigators hopefully have a broad range of clients, including attorneys. If a PI is contacted directly by an attorney to perform an investigation, then the results of that investigation are usually considered work product from the attorney's office, and are not discoverable.

Mary Ellen was 69 years old. For her birthday, she took a week-long cruise, departing from Fort Lauderdale and touring islands in the Caribbean. The cruise ship had an elevator to carry passengers between decks. Mary Ellen had the misfortune to be on the elevator when it broke down. She was trapped inside that small cubicle for about three hours.

Eventually, a mechanic managed to free the elevator, but couldn't get it to stop exactly on the next floor. The elevator stopped about two-and-one-half feet above the landing. To get out of the elevator, Mary Ellen was forced to jump down to the deck. In doing so, she fell and fractured her hip. She sued the cruise ship line and the manufacturer of the elevator.

Our assignment was to put Mary Ellen under surveillance to determine her lifestyle and range of motion. We videotaped Mary Ellen over several successive days as she drove to the grocery store and ran other normal errands.

> **Elementary, My Dear Watson**
>
> In some states, investigators who work solely for one law firm do not have to meet the licensing requirements of the state and do not have to have a private investigator's license.

She definitely walked with a limp and used her cane occasionally. The evidence we collected basically was noncommittal. It pretty much showed a 69-year-old woman who'd undergone hip surgery.

Alternate Light Source

When an individual, not an attorney, first calls to discuss a new matter, the PI should ask if the client is represented by an attorney. In order to protect the work product rule, the case needs to come from an attorney. It is also suggested that the report and invoice be directed to the attorney and the attorney should pay the invoice out of his own firm's funds. In this manner, the investigator can answer truthfully that his client is the attorney and not the individual.

If the caller has no attorney, don't refuse the case. Just be aware that later, your reports will be discoverable by the opposing side, and the individual who called you will be your client, not his attorney.

Our client, the attorney for the cruise line, did not want to use the videotape or any of our reports in the trial, not because there was anything damaging to his case, but because he was afraid that the jury would be incensed that the insurance company had hired private investigators to snoop on this nice little old lady.

The other attorney figured that there was probably a video of his client and he wanted to play the "big bad insurance company" card at trial with the jury. He subpoenaed me for deposition. At the deposition, I refused to testify on the grounds that my work was work product from an attorney's office.

This case went to trial and the attorneys argued before the judge, out of the presence of the jury, about the admissibility of the videotapes. My client, who'd paid for the tapes, didn't want them admitted. Mary Ellen's attorney did.

Finally, again, out of the presence of the jury, I was called in and I showed the video-tapes to the judge. He agreed that there was nothing significant on the tapes that would help either case and declined to let the jury know that the tapes or the investigation even existed.

If the insurance company had hired me directly, then there would have been no work product privilege, and the tapes and my testimony would have been admitted. Mary Ellen's attorney would have made a big deal about the insurance company stooping so low as to spy on this nice little old lady, and the jury's sympathy might have been swayed toward Mary Ellen more than it otherwise had been.

In this case, Mary Ellen was awarded several hundred thousand dollars for her injury. At least her award was not prejudiced by the fact that the insurance company hired a PI to check her out. Right or wrong? You be the judge.

Elementary, My Dear Watson

The rules covering privileged communications are usually found in the state statutes concerning the rules of civil evidence or the rules of criminal evidence. Some states vary in what privileges they allow.

There is a general misconception that there is a privilege between a doctor and his patient in criminal matters. Most states recognize no privilege in that relationship with reference to a criminal matter.

However, in civil matters, there is a doctor-patient privilege that applies to the doctor's treatment or diagnosis of any condition of the patient. But, if the patient confides a matter to the doctor that is not related to the patient's medical condition, there is no privilege.

The Cross-Examination

On the witness stand, you'll be sworn to tell the truth. The attorney for your client will ask you the questions that she's prepared you for, and you'll give truthful answers.

Next, the opposing counsel will ask you questions. Answer his questions straightforwardly and truthfully, even if you think the answers will hurt your client's case. The judge and/or the jury are not stupid. You are only one part of the case. Be professional and answer assuredly. Don't hesitate while trying to phrase your answer in the best light possible. Just answer it.

After the opposing counsel asks you his questions, your client's attorney will have another chance to redirect questions to you. It's her job to clear up any doubts that the questions from the other attorney may have raised, not yours.

The job of a private investigator is the search for truth, the facts that surround every accident and every lawsuit. Let the attorneys present only the evidence that is beneficial to their cases.

Their job is to take all of the facts that the investigator gathers, sift through them, and present the evidence in an order that will substantiate their case. The attorneys may omit facts. That's okay. There is no law or rule that says they have to present all of the facts. There is a rule that says the PI must present all of the evidence to his client or his client's attorney. After that, the job of the private investigator is done, and it's on to the next case.

The Least You Need to Know

- ◆ Some investigators are guilty of ghostwriting reports. This is illegal and is a prosecutable offense.

- ◆ Subpoenas command the investigator to appear for trial or depositions. Not responding places the investigator in jeopardy of being held in contempt of court.

- ◆ Privileged communications exist between attorneys and their clients. Also, if the circumstances are right, an investigator's work may be considered work product of an attorney's office, making it not discoverable by the opposing counsel.

- ◆ Testimony in court by the private investigator should be straightforward and honest. It is the attorney's job to rectify any misleading impressions caused by the opposing counsel's questions.

- ◆ The job of the private investigator is the search for truth. He must present to his client all of the evidence that he gathered.

Glossary

ANAC   Automatic Number Announcement Circuit is a telephone number that, when dialed, will announce back to you the number you are calling from. These numbers vary within area codes and sometimes within switches in the same city.

arbitration   Arbitration refers to a process where the plaintiff and the defendant in a civil lawsuit meet with a third party, known as a professional arbitrator. This arbitrator is skilled in negotiating, and it is his or her responsibility to help the two different sides come to an agreement. This process reduces the number of cases going to trial and helps clear the court calendar for cases that cannot be settled.

bandwidth   For our purposes, bandwidth means the amount of data that can be moved along a line of transmission at a certain time. The wider the bandwidth, the more data is moved.

being made   Being made means that a covert operation like a surveillance has been exposed and its presence made known to the subject of the operation. It's a clue you've been made when the person you're following gives you the finger.

binding arbitration   Binding arbitration means that a settlement must be reached during arbitration. If the parties cannot decide upon a settlement considered fair by all, then the arbitrator, after being fully informed of the facts, will reach what he considers a fair conclusion. His determination is binding on both parties.

breaking squelch   The squelch is the point where a radio receiver is tuned to its most-sensitive setting. If tuned beyond this point, the squelch is "broken" and the radio makes a loud, piercing sound similar to a screeching parrot.

burglary   The FBI's Uniform Crime Report defines burglary as the unlawful entry of a structure to commit a felony or a theft. The use of force to gain entry is not required to classify an offense as a burglary.

burned   Getting burned has the same meaning as *being made*. The subject has become aware of the surveillance.

butt set   A butt set is a handheld device that looks like a cordless phone, has a touch-tone keypad, and is used by telephone and electronic service people to identify telephone lines. It will have a set of wires with alligator clips at the end. You can buy butt sets for less than $100 over the Internet or at Radio Shack.

center-weighted average   Many single-lens reflex cameras have a built-in light-metering capability that automatically adjusts the f-stop and the shutter speed. A good photographer will know if his or her light meter averages the measurement of the light over the entire surface of the lens or center-weights the average, giving more importance to the amount of light coming through the center of the lens, where presumably the important image is located.

city directories   Sometimes called *reverse directories* or *criss-cross directories*, these books are privately published, frequently by Cole, Polk, Donnelly, and other publishers. These directories sort their listings by name, address, and telephone number. You can take a telephone number, check it in the "reverse" listing, and find the subscriber information. Likewise, you can take an address within the city, search the directory by address, and it will give you the person living there and his or her phone number.

countermeasure sweep   A countermeasure sweep is an active measure by an individual with the goal of finding or countering an aggressive action taken against him or her. Typically, the term is used in the sense of actively searching for and eliminating any electronic transmitters (bugs) or wiretaps that are directed toward locations or facilities where the target of the measure would likely be heard. A variation of the term is also used with respect to surveillance.

countersurveillance   This is a surveillance initiated by an individual to determine if he or she is under surveillance by an outside group. If properly conducted, a counter-surveillance will identify the entity conducting the surveillance. So you'll know who at the diner counter is watching you.

courtesy officer   A courtesy officer is usually a local police patrol person or sheriff's deputy who is given some sort of discount in his rent at an apartment complex in exchange for parking a marked patrol unit on the grounds and handling disturbance complaints at the complex when he is present. This is usually considered a good deal for the apartment management and the law enforcement department, as it reduces crime and does not increase law enforcement costs.

credit scores   A credit score refers to one of several types of numerical rating systems devised by credit companies to give a credit grantor an instant evaluation of a person's risk as a credit applicant.

crime scene investigation   Conducting a crime scene investigation entails the collection of evidence or possible evidence toward the goal of placing suspects at the scene of the crime. The evidence must be collected according to the rules of evidence, which have been established by law and judicial precedence.

criss-cross directories   *See* city directories.

data brokers   Also known as *information brokers*, these are individuals or companies that have access to specialized sources of information or use advanced techniques to gather information and then resell it to the private investigator. An example of this would be asking an information broker to obtain a nonpublished telephone number, or a list of credit-card charges that the PI couldn't get himself.

defendant   Legal actions require a minimum of two parties. The plaintiff is the party who initiates the action or lawsuit. The defendant is the person on the receiving end of the action.

deponent   The deponent is the witness being deposed.

deposition   A deposition is a statement under oath, usually written or recorded, that may be used in court at a later time. If there is the likelihood that the deponent will not be available later—for instance, due to illness—it is not uncommon for the deposition to be videotaped.

depth of field   Depth of field refers to the apparent range of focus in a photograph. In portrait photography, the background and the foreground may be intentionally blurred and out of focus while the subject, in the center of the photograph, is in focus.

diligent search   A diligent search refers to specific steps, often specified by state statutes, undertaken to locate an individual. Usually, diligent searches are required in locating parents of children who are about to be adopted or for heirs to estates that are needed to settle the estate.

drive-by   A drive-by is performed by private investigators to make a casual check of a subject's residence to see if he or she is home, or to observe what activities are taking place at a particular location during a specific time.

dropped   When a cell or telephone bill has dropped, it means that the billing cycle has ended, and the charges are en route to the consumer. Usually, even the customer cannot access the list of phone charges until the bill has entered the billing system's computer. With enough pressure, in exigent circumstances like tracing a runaway, you might get the cellular company to give you the calls daily as they're made.

due diligence   A due diligence search can be a check of an individual, but more often of a company's reputation, ability to perform under contract, and verification that there are no liens or judgments filed against the company. A good due diligence search will also encompass any lawsuits, pending or potential, or other current or potential areas of liability, such as a pending bankruptcy.

ESN   An Electronic Serial Number is the unique number that identifies a single particular cell phone. It is this number that is continuously broadcast to the cellular network from the phone which lets the network know where you are when your cell phone is turned on and through which cell towers to transmit your calls.

f-stop   F-stop refers to the setting on an adjustable single-lens reflex camera. F-stops are numbers and indicate to what degree the iris of the lens is opened or closed. The f-stop setting is one factor in determining the amount of light that passes through the lens and exposes the film. As the f-stop number increases, the iris is then "stopped down" to a smaller aperture and less light is allowed through the lens. Larger numbers equal less light, all other factors remaining the same.

FD 302   The FD 302 is a federal form used by the FBI that reports the results of interviews conducted by FBI agents. All interviews are reported in a standard format and are typed or printed onto FD 302s. Law school students learn this early in their schooling, and the forms are referred to throughout judicial opinions.

felonies   Criminal offenses are categorized according to the severity of the offense. Crimes that are punishable by one year of jail time or longer are called "felonies."

Field Identification card   A Field Identification card is a card used by patrol officers when questioning persons who might have been acting suspiciously. It will contain the subject's identifying data, the date and location of the incident, and a short synopsis of why the subject was questioned.

GPS   GPS stands for Global Positioning System. It is a system of about 24 satellites that orbit the earth and send out very closely timed signals. The GPS receivers on the earth receive the timed signals from multiple satellites and can calculate the receivers' latitude, longitude, and altitude.

grand jury   A group of men and women, usually culled from the voter's registration rolls, that hears evidence and determines if there is probable cause to believe a crime has been committed and that a particular person committed that crime is called a grand jury.

HIPAA   HIPAA is an acronym for Health Insurance Portability and Accountability Act. It was passed in Congress in 1996. A minor part of the act, but the part most quoted by medical providers so they don't have to release any information to you, is a section that deals with the security and privacy of health data.

hot sheet   A hot sheet is a current list of recently stolen vehicles. Police departments, of course, sometimes have hundreds of patrol cars driving around their jurisdiction all day long. Patrolmen are on the lookout for any car that is on the hot sheet. Many police department patrol cars are now in communication with their headquarters by computer, and they access the hot sheet list on the computer rather than a physical printed list, as in smaller departments.

hyperlink   A hyperlink is an area, picture, word, or phrase on a web page that you can select with your cursor in order for your browser to take you to another page or website whose content is linked in some manner.

image stabilization   Image stabilization is a function available with almost all digital video cameras and incorporated into many newer SLR camera lenses. The camera or lens digitally stabilizes the image to reduce blurring from a not-so-firmly-held camera. An image-stabilized lens on an SLR camera means you can open the iris as much as four extra stops (good for low-light photography) when the image stabilization is turned on.

impeaching   Impeaching a witness's testimony means to call into question the reliability or truthfulness of the testimony being given.

informant   An informant is an individual who cooperates, usually without the knowledge of others involved in the case, by providing information during an investigation. He or she might or might not be a witness or a participant in the particular case under investigation. Frequently, an informant may receive compensation, or other benefit, for this information, whereas a witness never should.

information brokers   Also known as data brokers, information brokers are individuals or companies that have access to specialized sources of information or use advanced techniques to gather information and then resell it to the private investigator. An example of this would be asking an information broker to obtain a nonpublished telephone number or a list of credit-card charges that the PI couldn't get himself.

jog and shuttle   Jog and shuttle are two functions of a videocassette recorder that allow an operator to play the tape backward and forward, one frame at a time, or in multiple-frame increments that are determined by the user. Generally, the jog-shuttle control is a wheel device on the VCR that the operator rotates forward or backward, causing the VCR motors to rotate in sync with it forward and reverse, faster and slower.

judgment   Judgment refers to a final determination by a court of competent jurisdiction setting forth the rights and liabilities of the parties in a lawsuit. Usually, the term "judgment" refers to a money judgment where the court may decide that a plaintiff is owed money by a defendant in a case. These judgments are recorded in the official records at the clerk of the courts office and are generally public records. Credit bureaus review these records on a regular basis and include them as part of their credit report.

junction box   A junction box is a piece of telephone company equipment where several customers' telephone lines are housed and connected to a phone company cable. Typically, these junction boxes house from two to two dozen connections. There is normally one on every block, or one for every 10 to 12 subscribers.

landline telephone line   This refers to a normal telephone line that has a physical demarcation point at a residence, business, or pay telephone. The phone call at least begins and ends its transmission along a pair of wires, regardless of whether transmission of the call includes microwave or satellite in between both ends. This is in contrast to a cellular phone, or any type of radio communication, which is considered wireless communication—literally, not connected to the ground at some point with wires.

latent fingerprint   A latent fingerprint is a print that is not immediately apparent to the naked eye, but can be made visible by dusting, or fuming with chemicals. Latent prints can then be compared to inked prints of suspects. An inked print is a fingerprint taken in a controlled environment where the pads of a suspect's fingers are covered with ink and rolled onto a fingerprint card.

light-meter averages   Many single-lens reflex cameras have a built-in light-metering capability that automatically adjusts the f-stop and the shutter speed. A good photographer will know if his light meter averages the measurement of the light over the entire surfaces of the lens or center-weights the average, giving more importance to the amount of light coming through the center of the lens, where presumably the important image is located.

lines of resolution   This will tell you how fine an image you'll get from the camera under optimal conditions. The higher the number, the better the resolution, and the better the picture.

lux   This refers to the camera's video board's or video chip's sensitivity to light. Some cameras use charged coupled devices (CCD). For our purposes, consider them chips. Whatever they use, the lower the lux, the more sensitive the camera is to light, which is very helpful in indoor applications.

misdemeanors   Criminal offenses are categorized according to the severity of the offense. Less serious crimes, those typically involving a potential penalty of less than one year, are called "misdemeanors."

motor vehicle theft   For the purposes of the FBI's Uniform Crime Report, motor vehicle theft is defined as the theft of automobiles, trucks, buses, motorcycles, motor scooters, snowmobiles, etc. This does not include the taking of a vehicle for temporary purposes by those having lawful access.

NCIC   This stands for the National Crime Information Center. Among other things, the NCIC maintains a huge database, run by the FBI, where subjects with outstanding arrest warrants are listed. Also listed are stolen properties and missing persons.

no bill   The grand jury will return a "no bill" if it finds there is not sufficient evidence of probable cause that a crime has been committed or that a particular person committed that crime.

optical zoom   On camera lenses, optical zoom refers to the focal length achieved by physically moving the lenses further apart from each other, thereby achieving a greater focal length (hence the term "zooming out" with a zoom lens) and increasing the relative size of the image as it appears on the film or recording media.

PACER   An acronym for Public Access to Court Electronic Records.

parole   Parole means an individual was sentenced to and actually spent time in jail, but was released earlier than the original sentence called for. He also must behave himself for a specified period of time.

permissible purpose   Permissible purpose refers to one of eleven (depending upon how you count) legal purposes for pulling a credit report as defined by the Fair Credit Reporting Act, last updated by Congress in 2004.

pinhole lens   A pinhole lens is literally a lens for a camera that is about the size of the tip of a ballpoint pen. It's not literally "pin" size, but close. It can be concealed quite easily, particularly in dropped ceilings, where the ceiling tiles have a rough texture. This size lens is also popular in Nanny Cams, where the hole for the lens can be concealed behind a small piece of plastic, such as you might find on radios or many other appliances. They are frequently used when installing a camera in an air-conditioning vent.

plaintiff   Legal actions require a minimum of two parties. The plaintiff is the party that initiates the action or lawsuit. The defendant is the person on the receiving end of the action.

plead down   This means that the prosecuting attorney's office, in order to expedite the flow of cases and reduce his or her load and the burden on the court, reduces charges from higher offenses to lesser offenses. He or she does this if the defendant agrees to plead guilty to the lesser offenses.

point man   A point man on a surveillance is the investigator who actually has "the eyeball" or has physical sight of the subject.

premise liability   A premise liability case involves the allegation that a property owner was negligent by not curing some default in the premise or real property owned or managed by the defendant, and this negligence led to the harm of the plaintiff. An example of this could be the plaintiff alleging that the defendant failed to provide adequate exterior lighting, and the ensuing darkness was responsible for the rape or assault inflicted upon the plaintiff.

pretext   A pretext is a subterfuge or ploy used by private investigators to encourage an individual to reveal information about himself or herself or another party, without being aware of the true reason for the conversation. In the course of responding to what appears to be a normal everyday query, the individual unsuspectingly releases the information the investigator actually is seeking.

privilege   A privilege, under law, is a special right which someone enjoys that the public at large does not enjoy. For instance, the marital privilege states that a wife cannot be forced to testify against her husband, or vice versa. According to the clergy privilege, communications between a clergyman and his parishioner are considered privileged.

probation   Probation indicates that a person was convicted of a crime, but rather than receiving a jail term, he is given probation to see if he can behave himself over a specified time period.

pro bono   Pro bono derives from the Latin, *Pro Bono Publico*, "for the public good." Usually it's shortened to just pro bono and means legal work undertaken without expectation of payment.

random access memory   RAM is an acronym for random access memory. It is the memory that the computer accesses when it processes information and runs computer programs. If there is not enough RAM in a computer, then the information being processed is swapped back and forth to the hard drive, which slows down the processing speed and leads to more rapid hard-drive failure and computer program lockups and crashes.

RBOC   RBOC stands for Regional Bell Operating Company. That is the generic term we'll use for all of the standard landline telephone companies, even though there are a number of independent companies and major carriers not associated with the Bell Companies. Corporations change, names change, one company gobbles up another, but we'll just call the land line carriers the RBOC.

real property   Real property is described as anything that is not personal property. Real property is anything that is a part of the earth or attached thereto which cannot be easily moved. Think dirt.

recorded statement   A recorded statement is a voice tape recording made by a witness concerning facts and/or the witness's recollection of the pertinent incident.

registered agent   An individual who agrees to be available to accept service, subpoenas, or other legal documents for a corporation is its registered agent. In the event you need to sue a corporation, your attorney will need to have it served with the lawsuit. The registered agent is the person who will accept notice of the suit on behalf of the corporation.

reluctant witness   An individual may have considerable knowledge of the pertinent incident relevant to the matter under suit, but will not discuss his or her knowledge of this incident unless compelled to by a court.

repeater   A radio tower that receives the signal from a mobile radio, such as a walkie-talkie, and repeats the broadcast signal over a larger area than a five-watt walkie-talkie could cover. The signal may bounce from one repeater to another to another, and possibly could be received over an entire state. This is common with the FBI radios. An agent in the field should be able to reach his division headquarters from almost anyplace within the geographical boundaries of his division's area. Most commercial repeaters, set up for business purposes, do not have such a broad area of coverage.

results billing Results billing is the practice of charging more than a standard hourly rate if the results achieved justify a higher bill or a higher hourly rate.

retainer Money paid by the client at the beginning of an investigation. Frequently a small portion of the retainer is nonrefundable if the case is canceled. Typically, the investigator bills his time against the retainer on hand. Once the retainer is used up, the investigator will ask for additional funds before proceeding any further on the case.

reverse directories *See* city directories.

safe phone A safe phone is a telephone that is not traceable back to the user. It does not reveal its number to the caller ID services on outgoing calls, but it has caller ID service for incoming calls. It is set up in such a way that it can be answered in any manner necessary and is used for only one case at a time. As a good PI, you should have one of these phone lines available in your office at all times.

search engines Internet sites that allow a user to input a search criteria. The engine then searches its own database of researched Internet sites and provides you a list of sites that most closely meet your criteria.

service by publication or notification This is a method whereby an individual is served with process without physically laying papers in his hand. If one party cannot be located, a notice may be published in a newspaper in the county where the court action is to take place over a period of several weeks. Once this is accomplished, the individual is considered to be served.

signed statement A signed statement is a written declaration made by a witness concerning facts and/or the witness's recollection of the pertinent incident, and is signed by the witness.

single-lens reflex A single-lens reflex (SLR) camera is a camera where the light (the image) passes through the lens and is reflected by a mirror to the viewfinder, where it is viewed by the photographer. When the shutter button is depressed, the mirror flips out of the way and the image passes directly to the film. The advantage of SLR cameras over other cameras is that the photographer sees the exact image that will appear on the film. Also, with most SLR cameras, the photographer has a wide range of lenses from which he or she can choose.

skip tracing   Originally referring to collection agencies' attempts to locate a debtor who'd "skipped out" on his obligation, skip tracing generally now refers to anyone that a private investigator is trying to find. Perhaps this person is intentionally eluding creditors or is merely a witness whose address is not currently known, but is sought by attorneys for an interview or a deposition. Universally, however, a person who is eluding his creditors is referred to in the business as "a skip."

Social Security trace   A Social Security trace is the searching of a database by Social Security number. The search normally returns residence addresses connected to your subject.

spoofing   Spoofing a caller ID is a technique where numbers are substituted in the caller ID data stream so that the "real" originating number is not shown, but "fake" numbers appear, or seem to appear, on the caller ID screen.

SSAN   The standard abbreviation in most federal law enforcement circles for Social Security Account Number.

subpoena   In a subpoena, the judge of a court requires that a specific person or representative of an institution appear in court or at another specified location on a specific day at a certain time.

subpoena deuces tecum   A subpoena deuces tecum is a subpoena that requires the individual or institution to provide documents to the clerk of the court as outlined in the subpoena. Or a subpoena could require both an appearance and the retrieval of documents.

suspect   An individual who might have committed or aided the commission of a crime that is under investigation is a suspect.

telephone break   A telephone break is the process of taking a telephone number, with no other identifying information, and obtaining the subscriber information, including the subscriber's name, the service address if it's a landline, or the mailing address if the number rings to a cellular telephone or a pager.

true bill   The grand jury will return a "true bill" if there is sufficient evidence to find probable cause that a crime has been committed and that a particular person committed that crime.

voice over IP   Voice over IP (VOIP) is a popular and cost-effective method of making telephone calls. IP stands for Internet Protocol, and VOIP utilizes your broadband Internet connection to transmit your voice and make your phone calls rather than normal RBOC telephone wires.

web browser A web browser is the software program you use to "surf" on the Internet. Most likely it is Microsoft Internet Explorer, Netscape, AOL's browser, or Firefox. Apple uses Safari as their default browser.

wild card A wild card allows the use of only partial names in searches. This is accomplished by inserting an asterisk after the beginning of a name. For instance, if you're not sure if a person's name is Rick or really Richard, you can input "Ric*" (without the quotation marks) and the search will return Rick, Richard, Ricky, and Ricardo.

witness A witness is an individual who might have testimony pertinent to an investigation.

work product Work product is described as the attorney's notes and research materials and other documents or matters that he or she makes or uses while working up the case. The reports of a private investigator hired directly by the attorney or working out of the attorney's office are also considered work product.

writ of execution A writ of execution is an order from a judge of competent jurisdiction commanding that certain actions be taken or cease to occur. A custodial writ would command the person having custody to relinquish custody to the person named in the writ.

Appendix B

State Requirements for Telephonic Recording

Federal law allows any party to a telephonic conversation to tape record the conversation without notifying other parties participating in the conversation that the recording is taking place. Violators of the federal statute can be imprisoned up to five years and fined $10,000 (Title 18, Sec. 2511 (4)).

Thirty-eight states and the District of Columbia follow the federal precedent. Twelve states insist that all parties to the conversation should be notified and be made aware that the conversation is being recorded.

Also, different states have some peculiarities that don't apply to all states. Arizona, for example, may allow the subscriber to the telephone line (the person who pays the bill) to record conversations on that line with no party consent. Some states require tones or beeps be placed on the line every 15 seconds during recording. If you have questions, check the statutes in your state. Don't rely solely upon this list, as the state laws change. Michigan just switched from being an all-party state to a one-party state.

Search the list to determine what the law allows in your state.

All-Party States

California	All Party
Connecticut	All Party
Delaware	All Party
Florida	All Party
Illinois	All Party
Maryland	All Party
Massachusetts	All Party
Montana	All Party
Nevada	All Party
New Hampshire	All Party
Pennsylvania	All Party
Washington	All Party

All others not on this list are one-party states.

Sample Client Retainer Contract

The following is a sample contract between a client and an investigative agency. It was provided by and is used with permission of Vicki Childs of Blazer Investigative in Charleston, S.C. It is also used by the author's agency. It is strongly suggested that before using any contract, you have your company attorney review it. They'll make some changes to justify their fees.

INVESTIGATIVE AGREEMENT

This hourly rate investigator-client fee agreement is between ABC INVESTIGATIVE AGENCY, a licensed Florida investigative agency and _____ client. The general nature of the case is _____ _____ _____

This case will begin on or about the date below and continue for 90 days or until Client withdraws.

Client employs and ABC INVESTIGATIVE AGENCY will accept employment to perform investigative services in connection with Client's case regardless of the disposition of this case. The Client agrees to fully cooperate with ABC INVESTIGATIVE AGENCY and provide accurate information as a basis for this investigation.

ABC INVESTIGATIVE AGENCY is not responsible for results of inaccurate information or leads provided by Client. Client understands that ABC INVESTIGATIVE may withdraw from this contact if Client should fail to pay all fees and costs set forth below.

Reports, video/photos will be provided within 10 days of a request by the Client, but may be withheld until payment is received.

FEES AND RETAINER

ABC INVESTIGATIVE AGENCY shall be compensated for all services rendered Client at the hourly rate of $ _____ per hour and $ _____ per mile. Client agrees to pay the sum of $ _____ as a retainer fee. ABC INVESTIGATIVE will bill hourly against the retainer fee. Client further agrees to pay for any other expenses incurred during the investigation, including but not limited to hotel bills, videotapes, photos, etc. If travel is anticipated, a fee of $ _____ will be applied toward costs and expenses incurred in the pursuit of this matter. Once any investigative effort is initiated in this case, a minimum of $250.00 of the retainer will be withheld should Client decide to end the investigation. Any other balance will be refunded to the Client upon request.

COURT APPEARANCES

If any agent of ABC INVESTIGATIVE AGENCY is called as a witness for deposition or Court, the cost will be a minimum of $250.00. If the Court appearance or deposition requires more than 4 hour's time, the Client will be charged the hourly and mileage rate set forth above.

CLIENT AGREES THAT NO AGENT OF ABC INVESTIGATIVE AGENCY, INC. HAS MADE ANY PROMISE OR GUARANTEE REGARDING THE OUTCOME OF THEIR CASE OR FACTS GATHERED DURING THE INVESTIGATION PERFORMED BY ABC INVESTIGATIVE AGENCY, INC.

Client does hereby bind his/her heirs, executors, and legal representatives to the terms of this contract as set forth herein.

I HAVE READ THIS CONTRACT AND AGREE TO ITS TERMS AND CONDITIONS.

_____   _____

CLIENT   ABC INVESTIGATIVE AGENCY

Date: _____

Affidavit of Diligent Search

Steven Kerry Brown, licensed private investigator in the State of Florida, has performed a diligent search for Jane Doe as required by Florida Statute Chapter 63.088 in an adoption matter with the following results:

Jane Doe's personal identifying information was discovered through investigation in this matter and determined to be the following:

Name:	Jane Doe
Date of Birth:	06/13/1985
SSN:	xxx-xx-xxxx

Last known address: An aunt, Martha Smith, provided a last known address of 6001 River Rd., Apt 240 Elyria, OH 44000, indicating Doe lived there in 2006. Property records for this address show it is owned by Richard and Carol Brown. Efforts were made to locate the Browns and they were successfully located. Carol Brown advised on 7/6/06 that Jane Doe had occupied apartment 107 but had vacated the apartment near the first of the year. She had left owing the Browns rent money and had left no forwarding address.

Last known employment: No employment has been established for Doe.

Regulatory Agencies: Patrick Jones (440-329-5207) of the Lorain County Ohio Auditor's office, which regulates occupational and business licenses, advised on 07/12/06 that their office had no record of any license in the name of Jane Doe.

Relatives: The following individuals have been identified as relatives of Valene Ranney:

> **Grandmother:** Shirley Doe, DOB 08/08/1934, SSN#: xxx-xx-xxxx, last known address of 123 Robin Rd., North Ridgeville, OH 44039. A letter has been directed to that address for Shirley Doe, but no response has been received.

> **Cousins:** Patricia and Ricky Holt, 123 Robin Rd., North Ridgeville, OH 44039. The Holts are tenants at this property. The telephone number at this address is nonpublished. The landlord is Steven L. Duke, 1234 George Washington Ave., Lakewood, OH 44107. Duke was contacted and advised that the Holts currently reside at the Robin Rd. address. He agreed to contact the Holts and ask them to contact the investigator in this matter. The Holts have not contacted the investigator and presumably either do not know where Jane Doe is currently, or have passed the information to her and she refuses to be contacted. A letter was directed to the Holts, but no reply either in writing or by telephone has been received.

Death Records: A search of the Social Security Master Death Index revealed no listing for Jane Doe and the Social Security number of xxx-xx-xxxx was negative.

Telephone Records: A current search of telephone listings in the state of Ohio showed one listing in area code 440, which includes Loraine County. That listing was for a Michael and Janet Doe. A telephonic contact was made with Michael Doe and he denied having any knowledge of Jane Doe or being related to her in any way.

Law Enforcement Records: Records from the Court of Common Pleas for Loraine County, Ohio, were searched from 1989 to the present, both criminal and civil records, and there was no record for Jane Doe.

Highway Patrol Records: Records of the Ohio Highway Patrol were searched with negative results.

Ohio Department of Corrections: A current search was performed of the inmates of the correction department for Jane Doe with negative results.

Hospitals: The following hospitals in Loraine County were checked for current patients and former patient information:

> **EMH Regional Medical Center,** 630 East River St., Elyria, OH 44035. She was not a current patient and the medical record department refused to disclose if she had ever been a patient.

> **Allen Medical Center,** 200 West Loraine St., Oberlin, OH 44074. This institution indicated that she was not currently a patient there and they had no record of her ever having been a patient there.

Proceed with each required step and the results of those searches. End with a statement like the following:

I understand that I am swearing or affirming under oath to the truthfulness of the claims made in this affidavit and that the punishment for knowingly making a false statement includes fines and/or imprisonment.

_____   _____

Signature   Date

_____

Printed Name

_____

Address

_____

Telephone

State of Florida

County of St. Johns

Sworn to or affirmed and signed before me on _____ by _____

_____

Notary Public-State of Florida

_____

Print, type, or stamp commissioned name of notary

Index

X–Y–Z

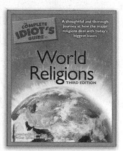

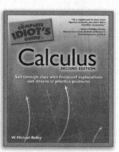

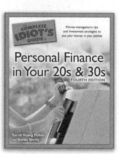

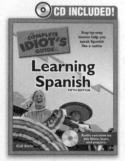